VOICES INTERNATIONAL PUBLICATIONS

PRESENTS

M000272169

She's All Caught Up!

A MEMOIR
BASED ON THE REAL-LIFE STORY OF
JAMILA T. DAVIS

WRITTEN BY:
JAMILA T. DAVIS

VOICES
INTERNATIONAL PUBLICATIONS

She's All Caught Up!

This book is written as a cautionary tale based on the real-life experiences of author Jamila T. Davis. All characters in this book are real, and all the events portrayed are true-to-life. Some details in the story line have been embellished to illuminate the author's message: Every negative choice we make in life comes with a consequence, whether immediate or futuristic.

She's All Caught Up was not created to defame any person or to shift the blame for the author's own actions. This book is designed as a tool to enlighten readers to the detriment of bad choices, and to illuminate key age points and influences that shaped the author's negative thinking patterns, which ultimately led to her imprisonment.

Printed in the United States of America
Second Printing, 2015

Library of Congress Control Number: 2012951659
ISBN: 978-09855807-3-5

Voices International Publications
196-03 Linden Blvd.
St. Albans, NY 11412
"Changing Lives One Page at a Time."
www.voicesbooks.com

Cover Design by: Keith Saunders, www.mariondesigns.com
Typesetting by: Jana Rade, www.impactstudioonline.com
Edited by: Dr. Maxine Thompson

*T*his book is dedicated to my beautiful parents, Liddie and Hosea Davis. Through it all, you both have held me down and showered me with your unconditional love. I couldn't ask for greater parents than the two of you! From the bottom of my heart, I love you both so much! This one is for you.

Dedication

Jamila T. Davis in 2008, featured in a photo shoot
for her clothing line Pink Passion Couture.

Acknowledgments

First off, I'd like to thank God for opening my eyes and allowing me to see the purpose in my pain. Knowing my purpose during this journey has made this difficult season bearable. Thank You, Lord, for Your grace, patience, and mercy. Yeah, I know, I was a hot mess, but thank You for loving me despite my faults. This journey has taught me: There is no way I can live without You. You are my EVERYTHING! I love You.

Thank you, Mom and Dad, for your continuous support. I can't believe after I caused you to lose your entire retirement fund to pay Lehman Brothers Bank, you *still* stood behind me! When the smoke cleared and everyone abandoned me, you were still there. How can I ever repay you? You both are my heroes! I love you.

Thank you, Kywuan and Diamond, my two wonderful children. You are the reason that I earnestly push forward each day. Sorry for not being there for you guys when you needed me the most. I miss you so much!

To my three lifelong girlfriends, Talia Johnson, Tracey Smith, and Hadmira Leacock, I love you all for life. Thanks for weathering the storm!

To Jeremiah Sills, Rasheene "Cat" Craig, Craig Pittman, Willie "Bobo" Thomas, Jules Bartholomew, and Quadree Smith, I love you all for life. Thanks for holding me down.

To my prison sisters Loretta Fields, Ivy Woolf-Tuck, Virginia Douglas, Shakila Wallace, Roxanne Troy, Rhonda Turpin, Edwina Bigesby, Rose Caban, Theresa Marchese, Nicole Pfund, Darly Estinval, Latanya Jones, Angie Rogers, Stephanie Davis, Miquel Nolan, Michelle West, Sakora Varone, Rochina Brown, Dianne Wilkerson, Yajaira Navarro, Theresa Squilacote, Anne Lockwood, Renese Flowers, Denise Dixon, Wynter Rose, Shaunice Fischer, Shalyce Davis, Carmen Wilkes, Jasmine Clarke, Tawana Logan, and Keiha Laviscount, you all will forever hold a special place in my heart. Thanks for helping me get through this bid.

A very special thank you to Dr. Maxine Thompson for editing this book. You have inspired me to produce my best!

Thank you Lauryn Hill for being my medicine and reviving me. During some of my darkest hours you have been my light. Thank you for imparting your wisdom and sharing your perspective about life's obstacles. In a short period of time, I have learned a lot from you, which I will forever treasure!

June 10, 2012

"Every negative choice we make in life comes with a consequence. Sometimes the costs we are forced to pay are severe!"
—Jamila T. Davis

I'm writing this introduction sitting on the top of my bunk bed in a 5½-by-9-foot cubicle at the Danbury Federal Prison Camp in Danbury, Connecticut. I never thought in a million years, that at the age of thirty-four, this would be the residence I would call my new home. I always viewed prison as a place for bad people, like murderers, robbers, and rapists. I never thought I'd fit into the category of a prisoner. I guess I thought I was above the law or that the law would never catch up to me. Boy, was I wrong!

During my four years of incarceration, I've had nothing but time to think, reflect, and explore. The question that has constantly repeated in my mind is: How did I get here? The judge that sentenced me also questioned how a young girl with my background got caught up in a lifestyle of criminal behavior resulting in several run-ins with the law.

As I analyzed myself and watched firsthand the vicious cycle of women who come in and out of prison, I discovered, for the most part, we all share common denominators. Sad to say, most of us haven't taken the opportunity to identify the root of our dilemmas, accept responsibility for our actions, and most importantly, experience inner healing. Therefore, the cycle continues.

Caught up in the chase to find fulfillment, many of us sought after people, places, and things, believing they would fill our inner void. Even worse, we based our success and self-worth on obtaining material possessions. As a result, imprisonment for many of us took place way before we experienced actual physical imprisonment. We became slaves to people, places, and things, and they became our idols.

At all cost, we were willing to do whatever it took to maintain our status and gain the esteem of our peers. In hot pursuit of what we perceived to be fulfillment, we were all caught up in the chase. Many of us simply desired to be loved; yet, we sought the wrong channels to obtain true love.

Influenced by lovers, peers and so-called friends, we committed crimes without contemplating the consequences or the cost our loved ones would have to suffer because of our actions. We selfishly only sought the reward we stood to gain.

Whether it was chasing money, notoriety, acceptance, or love, we honestly believed external factors would provide the means to cope with life, so we passionately pursued the bait. In the end, we got caught up—entrapped in a tight web that wasn't easy to escape.

To most, we are now labeled as "the bottom of the barrel," "convicts," and "culprits." Many falsely believe we all are ignorant people who possess no morals, compassion, or education. That is far from the truth!

We are women who possess beauty, tenacity, street smarts, and courage. We are skillful and talented, yet we misused our gifts. We are women who could have become whatever we desired in life. Women who once had great dreams, hopes, and aspirations. We differ very little from many of the women in today's society; we just got caught in the act. We are women who made poor choices that have now drastically altered our lives.

I am one of these women. This is my story!

On July 16, 2008, I was sentenced to twelve-and-a-half years in federal prison for my role in a multimillion dollar bank fraud scheme. And unfortunately, this wasn't my first run-in with the law, but it was the first time I was sent away to prison. Once the prison doors shut behind me, life for me, as I knew it, would never be the same!

From living as a multimillionaire surrounded by rappers, entertainers, and professional sports figures, who I once called my clients and friends, I became federal prisoner #59253-053. My new home was a tiny prison cell which I had to share. Stripped of all my worldly possessions and my dignity, I felt worthless and hopeless. I had no clue how I would overcome what appeared to be my worst nightmare.

One day while lying in despair on my bunk, I received a revelation. Either I'd make the best out of this experience and discover the purpose behind it, or I'd spend the rest of my time in prison in a miserable state. I opted to make the best out of my situation.

Through reading the Bible and every self-help book I could get my hands on, I began a journey to inner healing and restoration. As I awakened to the truth of my dilemma, I was able to go back and pin-point the exact places and influences in my life that helped mold me into the person who I had become. Through my reflections, I realized what I had experienced was similar to the pitfalls of the other women whom I encountered during my journey. I hate to admit it, but I discovered I was plagued with low self-esteem, severe codependency issues, and I didn't love myself enough. I was tremendously dependent on receiving the acceptance of my peers, and often, I was willing to go to any length to receive the esteem of others.

As I began to shed away layers of fear, anger, unforgiveness, shame, and guilt, and I rid myself of the poisonous thorns of materialism, I began to revive. In a lonely dark place in my life, as I discovered my divine purpose, true joy and happiness emerged within me. It is this discovery that empowered me with the strength I needed to sustain my faith and inspired me to share my findings with others.

While imprisoned, with the help of family and friends, I was able to create a self-help book series detailing the road map I used to find inner restoration, titled the *Voices of Consequences Enrichment Series*. This series is geared to help incarcerated women heal, recognize their potential, and recapture their dreams. In the place I perceived as my greatest nightmare, I birthed my greatest professional accomplishment! It's been my deepest pleasure to see others empowered by utilizing the techniques and strategies I utilized along this journey.

I thought this message I had burning inside of me was simply for prisoners, but as I shared my story with at-risk youth through a prison community outreach program, I discovered the lessons I learned could help women and people universally. From the responses I got from teens, many, of whom others were not able to reach, I recognized the power of my story and its ability to save lives. I also realized today's youth are experiencing the same dilemmas I experienced as a youth. If I had someone who I could have identified with, who would have warned me of the pitfalls I was to encounter, I probably wouldn't be sitting in prison today!

Therefore, this book was written as a cautionary tale to warn others about the detriments of poor choices and negative associations. I don't claim to be an expert writer. But, I do claim to be a living example that illustrates the severity of poor choices. Therefore, I decided to put my "pen-to-paper." I share the experiences that influenced my thinking patterns and the pitfalls that forged my current circumstance—imprisonment.

She's All Caught Up was created as a tool to help readers reflect and explore their own lives or the lives of their loved ones. It is my goal to inform readers of the pitfalls I fell prey to, so they will be empowered to avert adverse behavior. Most importantly, this book is a precautionary measure to warn others of severe consequences of negative choices.

Every bad choice we make in life comes with a consequence. Sometimes the costs we are forced to pay are severe! Prison life is not fun. I've lost my freedom, and I'm forced to abide by the rules and regulations of others. Many of my hopes, dreams, and aspirations have been put on hold. I've been abandoned by many I trusted and thought were my friends. I have been humiliated, ridiculed, and stripped of my dignity. And, I have left outside these walls two beautiful children who are forced to figure out life without me. This reality has awakened me to the fact that nothing was ever worth risking my freedom for! I can't change my past, but you can control your future. Take heed!

My message to you is *all crime comes with negative consequences*. Some consequences are immediate, others are futuristic. Regardless, in the end, the past will catch up to you! Therefore, do not attempt to live life in the fast lane. The consequences are too steep to bear! What you actually perceived to be a shortcut will turn out to be the long, wrong route!

I urge every teenager or young adult who reads this book to slow down and get your education. Build your life on a strong foundation, and you'll never have to worry about your success being taken away. Be smart, and never ever forget—crime just doesn't pay!

—Jamila T. Davis

January 29, 1995

"Pull the car over now!" I heard blaring from a bullhorn as I was suddenly awakened from a deep sleep.

"Oh my goodness, Jamila, wake up!" Theresa shouted as she fiercely nudged me from the driver's seat of her gray Mitsubishi Mirage.

"What in the world!" I shouted as we pulled over on Capital Boulevard and close to a dozen cop cars surrounded us.

"Oh, God, girl. We are in trouble. I'm so nervous," Theresa whimpered in a panic as sweat began to pour down her jet-black petite face.

"Calm down, girl. Just act normal," I instructed, trying hard to gather my composure. My heart pounded intensely as I watched the police gather through the rearview mirror. Two cops exited their vehicle.

"You don't understand! I've got a ton of drugs in the trunk. Oh, man, Jamila, I think we are in big trouble," Theresa ranted as the cops quickly approached us.

"Young ladies, step out of the car and show me some identification," the tall, white cop said in a strong Southern drawl as he approached the driver's door of the vehicle, with his hand tightly gripped on the gun in his holster.

We stepped out of the small, two-door car and fear engulfed me as I watched several other officers swarm our vehicle. It became apparent this was not a routine traffic stop.

"You can make this difficult, or it can be easy. Do you give us permission to search this vehicle, gal?" the officer asked Theresa sharply in his strong Southern accent.

"Well, um," Theresa mumbled, clearly confused and frightened. "I don't . . . um. Well, I guess so."

That's all the officers needed to hear. They had Theresa's consent and began to ransack the car. After a brief search, the drugs that were hidden in the luggage in the trunk of the car were quickly apprehended.

Tears rolled down my eyes as Theresa and I were read our rights, handcuffed, and placed in the back of the police car. I was seventeen years old and under arrest!

My life flashed in front of me. What was I going to tell my parents? How could I ever explain this? I was supposed to be enjoying my freshman year at St. Augustine's University. Instead, I sat in a tiny holding cell at the Wake County Jail in Raleigh, North Carolina.

I nervously stood silent as I was finally taken before a magistrate judge, who formally announced my charges and determined my bail.

"Jamila Davis," the old white judge announced as he banged his gavel, "I hereby set your bail at two million dollars."

Two million dollars! I thought in rage and disbelief.

I was escorted out of the small courtroom by the bailiff and sent back to the dark holding cell. I cried uncontrollably as the reality of the consequences of my lifestyle had suddenly crept up on me. I had no clue the power a few bad decisions could have. My life didn't have to turn out this way. It was one poor choice that ultimately altered my entire destiny!

"Hosea, Hosea! I think it's time! This pain is killing me!"

It was a humid night on July 11, 1977. The tall grandfather clock in the hallway of the Davis residence had just struck 7 o'clock and began to chime.

"Pumpkin, are you sure?" my dad, Hosea, asked my mother, Liddie, who he nicknamed Pumpkin. His brow furrowed in concern. "I'm not trying to sit around the hospital all damn night like we did with Kee. Woman, I got to go to work in the morning." He paused for a moment, trying to soften his tone.

"You know what? Just give me the keys to the car. I'ma drive myself. I know what I feel. I'm not trying to have this baby on the kitchen floor. Just give me the keys!" Liddie demanded reaching for the car keys, which were in my dad's hand.

My dad pulled his arm back and put the keys in his pocket. "Okay, okay. If you're sure this is it, I'll take you. Where's your overnight bag at?"

"Oh . . . um, I didn't pack it yet," Liddie mumbled in a disgruntled tone being caught off guard by his response.

"This is just what I'm talking about!" Hosea scolded. "Why don't you have your stuff in order? This is not the first time we've done this. Then you gonna wanna rush me."

"Nelson, please. It's gonna take me a couple minutes to get my things in order. Go start the car. I'll be right out." My mother addressed my dad by his middle name, Nelson.

Pushing her hands into her back to balance herself, Liddie wobbled her petite frame with her huge pregnant stomach to the bedroom. She held her abdomen as she quickly packed her gowns into an overnight bag for the hospital. As she was getting her toiletries ready, she began to cry out again in pain. Her labor pains began to come closer and closer together.

"Nelson, Nelson! Aw, this pain is killing me." She doubled over in pain.

At that point, Hosea knew it wasn't an over exaggeration; it was actually time. He hoped he was getting ready to have the little girl he'd always wanted. They already had one son together, and he had another son from a previous relationship.

"Pumpkin, Pumpkin, I'm right here, baby! I got you, love. Just breathe and take it easy. I'm going to get you ready to go. Sit down, baby." He quickly changed his attitude as he thought about the excitement of possibly having his own baby girl.

Hosea quickly assembled the rest of Liddie's belongings. He put the bag on his shoulders and swept Liddie off her feet into his strong muscular arms. He carried her to the door of their two-seater Camaro. He opened the car door, pushed the passenger seat all the way back, and gently placed Liddie in the car.

Quickly, he shut her door and sprinted around to the driver's side and jumped in. Then he sped through the streets of their suburban neighborhood and jumped on the highway. It was unusual traffic for a weekday night. He began to get impatient as Liddie started to cry, "Nelson, Nelson, I don't think I'm going to make it to the hospital. I'm hurting so bad. Help me!"

Hosea pushed down on the gas pedal, speeding up. Feeling a rising sense of anxiety, he beeped his horn loudly several times.

"Get out of my way. My wife's having a baby!" He jumped on the shoulder lane and began to go around the traffic. Bobbing and weaving through traffic, he finally landed at his destination. He pulled up to the emergency room entrance, jumped out of the car, and raced up to the nurse at the desk.

"Help me, miss. Please, please, my wife is in the car. She's about to have our baby."

The nurse recognized the panic in his eyes, and she immediately paged for help. Then, she gathered the wheelchair, raced out to the car to get Liddie, and pushed her to the delivery room.

"Ohhhhhh. This pain is killing me," Liddie screeched.

"It's okay, Pumpkin. I'm right here." Hosea ran behind the staff and gently rubbed her hand.

"Don't touccccch me!" she screamed at him. "This is all your faulllllltt. Get away from meeee!" Liddie was becoming hysterical as the pains tore through her body.

"Now, woman, get a hold of yourself," and he started to fuss, but he caught himself. This was his night, and he wasn't gonna let anything snatch his joy. Keeping his composure, Hosea made sure she got to the delivery room safely, then he went back to move his car which was illegally parked out in front of the emergency room.

Liddie just made it in time. Within minutes after she arrived at the hospital, she gave birth to a healthy baby girl with big bright eyes who was 7 pounds and 11 ounces—yours truly, Jamila Takiyah Davis had entered the world.

Hosea rushed into the hospital room. "Nelson, Nelson, it's a little girl. Look, ain't she beautiful?" my mom asked as she glowed with joy. She held me up for my father to see.

Hosea quickly grabbed me and held me in his arms. Tears of joy streamed down his face. "Oh, yes, baby, she's beautiful. We picked the perfect name for her."

You see, my name in Arabic means "Beautiful."

During the '70s, my parents both wore Afros and were into the Black Power Movement. They wanted their children to have African names to represent their heritage. My name was picked out of the *African Names* book they received from a friend a few weeks earlier.

My father grabbed my mother's head slowly, and he gently reached down and kissed her cheeks as he held me in his arms. This was a special moment for them both.

"Honey, she is 7 pounds and 11 ounces. Today is July the 11th—July 11th—ain't that something?" my mother cooed.

"Yes, Pumpkin, she's sure going to be special. Matter fact, I'm going to go play the number when I get out of here. I got me a baby girl, and she's special. This is it, Pumpkin, I'm telling you, that's a sign from God." They both laughed.

My father was so proud, he went around the whole hospital telling everybody, "I'm a dad. I got me a new baby girl, and she's special. She's 7-11. I got me a miracle baby."

He had no clue at that moment exactly what he was in for. He was certainly in for a treat. He got that baby girl that he so desperately wanted after he had two other sons already. He was right, this baby girl was special—she was sure going to rock his world!

My mother and father, in the early 70s, before I was born.

Chapter Two

"Mommy, mommy, I want my mommy!" my brother Kee yelled loudly as if he was losing his mind. "Let me go, I want my mommy!"

It was a nice, hot summer day in July of 1977. Straight from the hospital we pulled up to my new home, a cozy two-level brick Cape Cod house in a quiet suburban section of Queens. The house had a beautiful white awning fence that was accented with brick trimmings. Before we could approach the door, my aunt Shortie, who is my father's youngest sister, opened it to greet us. She had my big brother, Kitwana "Kee" Davis, in her arms who was two-and-a-half years old at the time. He kicked and screamed, reaching for my mother who had me in her arms, and he demanded that Aunt Shortie put him down.

"Oh, baby, why you crying, little man?" my mother said as she approached the door. "Look, I got your new little sister with me."

Those words didn't faze him at all. He was a feisty little thing! He yelled louder, "Mommy, mommy, I want my mommy!"

She opened the door and walked into the kitchen and set my car seat down on the floor and placed my brother, Kee, on her lap. He clamped his arms around her and hugged her hard, refusing to let go. She was in the hospital for three whole days, and this was the first time he was ever away from her.

"Look, Kee. See what I have for you? Do you see your new baby sister?" She gently tried to put him down so she could pick me up, but he kicked and hollered in protest. I should have known at that moment things weren't gonna be easy for me in this new environment. This little boy didn't want any part of me. In his eyes, this family wasn't big enough for the two of us!

* * *

My mother's instinct saved me a many day, even as an infant. One morning, my mother was suddenly awakened, and something told her to go to the room I shared with my brother on the second floor. His crib was in the front of the room by the closet door, and mine was by the window. I was sound asleep, but my brother was up. He was three years old, and he was able to climb in and out of his crib. I was just a little baby, only a couple months old. As my mother peered into the room, she noticed that my brother had climbed into my crib, and he was trying to drag me out of the crib by my arms. Just in time, my mother entered the room and screamed, "Kee, what are you doing?" She said his eyes looked like they would pop out of his head. He was caught in the act! My mom rescued me out of my brother's arms and beat him.

It was on and popping from that day forth. My brother made his position clear: He didn't like me. He would often say, "Why don't you go back to where you came from? Life was just fine without you."

I would cry and tell my mother. She, in turn, would fuss at him. "Kee, leave Jamie alone! I'm so sick of y'all fighting!" Jamie was the nickname my parents called me.

We were complete opposites. I basked off the love and attention I got from my mother and father. I quickly noticed getting good grades is what appeased them, so I did my best to get straight *A*s throughout my childhood. On the other hand, my brother was a poor student who barely got *C*s. He was often on punishment because of his bad grades. I guess it didn't help that I would race home when we got our report cards to proudly show my parents my grades. He was trying to hide his to avoid punishment, and I let the cat out of the bag.

"It's report card time," I would say.

He'd just suck his teeth and roll his eyes at me.

"I can't stand you, for real."

"Oh, well," I would say and stick out my tongue at him. "I can't help that you're just stupid."

I always managed to get his blood boiling, and boy, did he get me back. He would pull my hair and act as if he never touched me. He'd pour water on my homework so I'd have to do it again. He would even hide my things and, at times, throw my stuff in the garbage. It was always war. He couldn't stand me, and I couldn't stand him. We might play together for a couple of minutes, but things always led back to the starting point—war!

*M*y parents are really good, loving people, who came from humble beginnings. Born and raised in a small town called Kinston in North Carolina, during the era of segregation, they were high school sweethearts who were a year apart in age. My father, the eldest, grew up in the country. He would often tell us stories about how he had to milk the cows and care for the chickens on the farm. He was born to Retha Mae Blackwell and Hosea Nelson Davis, Sr. My grandfather worked on a farm, and my grandma did odd jobs for "white folks" to care for the family. They didn't have television back then, so their recreation was making babies. My grandmother had seven children, four boys and three girls. My dad was their middle child.

My father grew up on a small family farm. The family struggled to make ends meet. My grandparents were grandchildren of slaves. Back then, the South wasn't nothing nice. Black people were "them coloreds" or "them niggas," and it was clear what their standings were.

Granddad was a fine, handsome young thing. He was often sought after by the ladies. Grandma had a mean fight game. She was known to have knocked a couple women out over her man. Grandma held on, determined to keep her family structure together, but my grandfather couldn't take the pressure of poverty and racism in the segregated South, so one day, he got up and left for the Big Apple—New York City—in hopes of achieving success.

My grandmother was devastated. She couldn't believe he left her to raise seven children on her own. The youngest one, my uncle Clarence, was also mentally disabled.

This was a lot for my grandma to manage on her own with her low income, so she packed the kids up, and they moved to a small house in the city limits of Kinston.

My grandma Retha was a "fox" back in her day. Even though she didn't have that much money, she knew what to do with the little she had. She cleaned up nicely, dressed impeccably, and kept her weight down. In fact, she had the eyes of everybody else's man. Grandma knew the bills had to get paid so she made it happen—by any means necessary!

Chapter Three

My daddy was a young boy who watched all types of men drop money off to pay the bills. Things quickly turned around for the poor family. They weren't poor no more! Grandma got a part-time gig, bootlegging liquor. Back then, selling alcohol in public establishments was illegal, so if you did it, you had to be discreet. Grandma rolled up her sleeves and got her hustle on! She sold liquor out of the basement of her house.

Throughout my dad's childhood, Grandma maintained her hustle. She was the talk of the town and envied by many women because of her independence. She was also sought after by men because of her looks and business savvy. She drove all the latest cars. Her favorite sedans were the Lincolns and the Cadillacs. Back then, black folks weren't doing it like that, but my grandma was! I loved to listen to my folks talk about her long white Cadillac sedan.

They would often laugh and say, "I don't know which was cleaner, your grandma or the car. Boy, your grandma was something else, baby."

Life remained good for the Davises until alcohol became legal. Shortly after, Grandma got heavily involved in the church, and she cleaned her life up.

On the other side of town, on N.E. Thompson Street, my mother, Liddie Mae Cobb, lived in a run-down shack. She was raised by her two twin aunts, Carrie and Katherine. Their brother, who was my mom's father, died of cancer when my mother was ten years old. My mother's mother was sort of on the wild side and didn't want to stay locked down with no child. So she left my mother with her aunts and moved to Durham, North Carolina, where she made a living as a hairdresser.

My mother was raised very well by her two aunts. Carrie worked in the local 5 &10 Cent store, selling hot dogs, and Katherine was a caretaker for the elderly. Neither one of them had any kids, so they delighted in taking care of my mom.

My mother did very well in school. She always maintained her status on the honor roll and participated in numerous school activities. One day she was walking to school, and she noticed my dad by his signature walk. You see, Daddy had a swagger!

My dad was a ladies' man; all the girls loved him. And he loved them back. He got a kick out of living the role of a "mack." He mastered the mack-daddy style, charisma, and charm of the town's most popular men that were my grandma's customers.

The girls in the town were very mad and jealous about my mom. My mother and father were together, but it was not official. Hosea wanted to do grown men things, and Liddie wasn't having that! Her aunt taught her, "Never do nothing with nobody, baby, 'til you got a ring on your finger. Tell them no ring, no sweet thing."

My mother always remembered that, and she stuck to her guns. My dad ended up getting another girl from his school pregnant. At seventeen years old, he had his first child, James Davis, my oldest brother.

My mother was devastated, but she got over it. She exchanged words with my stepbrother's mother a few times, but she accepted and loved James as if he were her own.

My mother and father got engaged and shortly after, my dad was drafted to go to the Vietnam War. He and my mother decided to hold off the wedding until he got back. My mother went away to college at North Carolina Central University, and my dad went away to the war. They wrote each other faithfully, and the absence actually made them grow closer in their relationship.

My dad went away as a boy, but he came back as a man. The military molded him and groomed him into a responsible, loving, caring individual. During the war, he was awakened to the importance of family and the things that mean most in life. In Vietnam, he had several near-death experiences, and his best friend died right in his arms. My dad promised God if He would let him return home safely, he would live his life to please God.

Vietnam served Dad straight! My dad hung his player coat up and became a responsible family man. His old friends would come over and joke about how my dad turned into a minister in Vietnam.

"Oh, yah, Daddy got a gift. That boy's a preacher, I tell you. He almost got my soul saved." His friends would laugh as they drank and reminisced old times.

As soon as my dad came home from Vietnam, he married my mother. The two of them decided to move to New York to provide a better life for themselves. My father got reacquainted with his dad, who had moved to New York to make a better living. Both he and my mom moved in with my grandfather and saved their money up to buy a house. My mom got a job as a schoolteacher, and my father became an electrical worker for the New York City Transit Authority. They struggled at first, but they made it. They bought a nice house in Queens Village, New York, in 1972, and they overcame the stronghold of poverty.

My mother attempted to have children for several years after she was married. She had gone to a gynecologist, and the doctor said she was fine. She didn't understand why she still had no children, so she was deeply disappointed.

My mother prayed to God that He would open her womb, and one day, He answered her prayers. On November 26, 1974, she had my brother, then two-and-a-half years later, she had me. My parents were overjoyed. They made a vow that we would never have to struggle like they had to, and they lived up to their promise! My parents worked hard and utilized education as a weapon to overcome the barriers of poverty. Like the Jeffersons (a popular African American sitcom in the '70s), the Davises finally claimed their stake, and we were moving on up! My brother and I got whatever we wanted. All we had to do was ask. We became the new, improved Davis generation!

My brother Kee and me as toddlers.

*M*y mother kept my brother and me well-rounded. We had a schedule full of activities each week. Mom was determined her children would be talented and successful. She wanted us to learn how to swim, how to do judo (so we could protect ourselves), how to play tennis, how to sing, how to dance, and how to act. In her mind, we were gonna be smart, athletic, and artistically inclined.

My mother had been a drama major at North Carolina Central, and she played the leading role in several college plays. She would take pride in showing us her newspaper clippings of her play reviews. Because my mom grew up poor, she didn't have the money for any formal training, but she was passionate about providing us the opportunities she missed out on.

I followed in my mother's footsteps. As a little girl, I wanted to be just like her. I walked like she walked, and I talked like she talked. When she wasn't looking, I would even put on her high heels, take the cans out of the pantry, and teach the cans like I saw my mother teach her students at JHS 231 in Jamaica, Queens. I was always up under my mom. I went everywhere with her, even to the bathroom. I would wait outside the bathroom door for her to come out. I wanted to grow up and be just like my mom. She was my hero!

My mother was a schoolteacher who was serious about education. She taught me how to read when I was three years old. Ever since then, I loved to read, and I always liked school because it was the place where my mom taught at. I observed my mother well enough to learn her techniques of teaching. Little did I know learning this skill set would pay off in life. My mother enrolled me in the elementary school right behind the junior high school where she worked, PS 251. During the first week of school, I was so excited about finally being in a real school. It wasn't like nursery school. We didn't take naps in this school.

My kindergarten teacher's name was Ms. Nederwriter. She was a tall, slim, middle-aged white woman with short, black curly hair.

"Class, I'm passing out these books today. We are going to learn how to read. Are you all excited?" Ms. Nederwriter asked.

Chapter Four

"Yes," the whole class shouted with excitement. I stared and raised my hand.

"Yes, Jamila?"

"Ms. Nederwriter, I already know how to read. My mommy showed me that a long time ago."

"Did she really?" Ms. Nederwriter addressed me sarcastically in disbelief.

"Yes, she did!"

"Okay, well, read this book for me," she said and she passed me a higher grade level book to read. I stood up and began to fluently read, but before I could finish, she interrupted me. "Now, now, that's enough. You must give everyone a chance to learn."

From that point I knew Ms. Nederwriter was clearly not happy with me. As a result, I lost my zeal for attending school, and I became bored in her class and started acting out. I would often fake like I was sick so my mother could come and get me and take me next door to her school. I loved going to work with my mother. She was so theatrical. She always made her students laugh. Her students dare not get smart with her! In a matter of seconds, she could rip you a whole new frame in a real comical manner and have everyone laughing. It was fun being around my mother's students. They would baby me and show me attention, treating me like I was their favorite little sister.

I noticed after spending time in Ms. Nederwriter's class that many of the children weren't picking up how to read. One day when she walked out of the classroom during playtime, I grabbed a little boy named Antuan, who was having trouble reading.

"Antuan, do you want to read?"

At first he thought I was being funny so he responded, "You're such a show-off, get away from me."

"No, Antuan, come here; let me teach you how to read. You see this letter?"

"Yes," he responded.

"What is it?"

"T," he said.

"Okay. *T* sounds like this, 'Ta.' Say it with me."

"T-tah."

"Okay, *A* is ahh. Say Ahh."

"Ahh."

I showed Antuan just what my mother showed me, and he caught on.

Suddenly the teacher came back in the room and snuck up on us. She had been watching me from afar as I taught Antuan the basics in reading.

"What are you doing, Jamila?" she said abruptly.

"Oh, oh, um, I'm showing Antuan what my mother showed me," I responded.

"Antuan, do you understand what she showed you?"

"Yes, Ms. Nederwriter." Antuan opened the book and slowly began to sound out the words and read. After that day, Ms. Nederwriter had faith in me. She let me teach all the kids who had trouble reading the techniques my mother taught me. I was excited, because I was finally doing something fun. I taught every student who would listen.

Shortly after that, all of the kids in the class knew how to read. I thought I had done a good thing until one day my mother asked me what I was learning in school, and I told her how I was teaching the other kids how to read. She became furious! The very next day when she dropped me off at school, she came upstairs to have a talk with Ms. Nederwriter and the principal. She wanted me out of Ms. Nederwriter's class. She didn't feel as though it was my job to teach others how to read. Ms. Nederwriter put up a big fight and protested about letting me out of her class. It was crazy! She didn't want me to go to the gifted class, where my mother felt I belonged.

That was my first encounter with a person who intentionally tried to hold me back. I realized at that point I would have to fight for what I wanted in life, and my fights would not be easy!

After several months of fighting with the principal and the district office, my mother finally prevailed. It was ordered that I be moved to the gifted class, but ironically, the class was full. Therefore, I had to remain in Ms. Nederwriter's class, and she practically hated me at that point. Kindergarten ended rocky.

* * *

At the end of the school year, my mother ended up pulling me out of the school, and she bused my brother and me to Floral Park, NY, to PS 191. This was a preppy school in a predominately white area. I managed to fit in, and I quickly began to flourish in my studies. By the time I reached second grade, I was testing in our statewide test on a fifth-grade level. That was because my mother taught the seventh grade, and I would sneak and study the test and work she gave her students. The more success in school I achieved, the more my parents praised me. I became their rising star!

Me, at age four, posing in my tap dance outfit for dance recital photos.

M y favorite activity growing up was going to dance school. Every Saturday morning, I would get up early, be dressed, and ready to go. I went to Bernice Johnson's Dance School in Jamaica, Queens, NY. It was a prestigious African American dance school that produced some very talented, well-known dancers. Back then, Ben Vereen and Michael Peters were our two most recognized alumni. Ben Vereen was the famous dancer-actor from the movie *Roots*.

Michael Peters was the choreographer for many of Michael Jackson's videos, including *Beat It* and *Thriller*.

I studied tap, ballet, jazz, modern, and African dance. I loved African dance class. *Funga alifi yah, ashay, ashay. Funga alifi yah, ashay, ashay*." I sang as I vigorously danced across the floor to the fast-paced drumbeat.

"Oh, no, girls. I need to see more energy! Get them knees up!" I would get lost in the beat of the drums. It was like my whole soul would be in a trance.

"Arch your backs. I need to feel your energy!"

"Miss Thing, that is not it! You look like a broken-down record, now get on beat," Mrs. Johnson, the owner of the dance school, further belted as she walked through our African class, criticizing the girls harshly.

Mrs. Johnson was a dark brown-skinned, short lady in her late sixties with pepper-gray, beautiful, silky short hair. She was the widow of a famous jazz player, Budd Johnson. For an older lady, she had it going on. She was very well groomed. She wore a beautiful red velour jog suit with crisp Reebok classics, straight out of the box. "Stop the drums."

"Miss Thing, Miss Thing," she said to me in a sassy, aggressive tone.

"Are you talking to me, Mrs. Johnson?" I asked nervously.

"Yes, baby," she replied. "Listen up. I want y'all to come over here and watch this girl."

I stood proudly as the whole class came over to watch me. I was four years old, and I had a made-up mind that I wanted to be

Chapter Five

a star. I had already successfully completed my first dance recital, and I was drawn to the energy and the excitement of the spotlight. This was my time to shine. I was center stage, ready to accept my calling.

"Five, six, seven, eight, and knee, knee, clap, clap, push, push, push, push, and knee, knee, clap, clap, push, push, push, push," she instructed as I danced my little heart out. I felt the strong tone of the African drums hit. I forgot about my audience, and I got lost in the strong beat of the drums. "Yes, baby, yes, that's how you do that thing," Mrs. Johnson was motioning for me to stop, but I was oblivious to her instructions.

I performed so well, she stopped and talked to my class instructor as I was dancing.

"This little girl here, she's got it! We've gotta put her into our pro class," Mrs. Johnson whispered to the teacher. The drummers started egging me on with a drum ovation. Finally the music stopped, and I stopped. The whole class began to clap. The feeling I felt was unexplainable. From the bottom pit of my soul, I knew I had found my passion. I wanted to be a dancer!

After the class that day, Mrs. Johnson told me to get my mother. I ran and grabbed my mom who sat patiently waiting for me in the waiting area of the dance school, reading her newspaper.

"Mommy, mommy, Mrs. Johnson wants to see you," I said as I tugged on her hands with excitement. My mom looked bewildered, but she came. I guess she was wondering why Mrs. Johnson wanted to see her. My mom quickly gathered her items and went to see the honorable Mrs. Johnson, the dance instructor, extraordinaire!

"Hello, Mrs. Johnson, I'm Jamila's mom."

"Why, you should be proud of yourself. You have a fine daughter here. She's very talented."

"Oh, why, thank you, ma'am," my mother said proudly.

"I want her in my pro class. Now this is going to require more of a commitment. She will not only have to come to dance school on Saturdays, but also on Tuesday nights. I'm going to count on you to make sure she practices. She's gonna need special colored leotards and tights and special shoes for her Modern classes. I want her to start next Saturday. Is that okay with you?"

"Yes, ma'am, yes, ma'am. Oh, I'm so excited for her," my mother responded.

I was blown away! You couldn't tell me I wasn't going to be a star. I felt it in my soul; it was written.

The whole ride home I sang away in the car, *"Fame, I'm gonna live forever. I'm going learn how to fly high."*

During that time, *Fame* was a hot series on television and several of our junior dance instructors went to the *Fame* High School of Performing Arts in Manhattan. I felt like making it to the *Fame* School was the highest achievement on the planet! I was just a little girl, but I had my mind set on *Fame,* and I was determined to make it!

* * *

In my dance school class, I had two really close friends. They were twin sisters by the name of Renée and Michelle. They were racially mixed, half white and half black, Jamaican American girls with beautiful curly hair down to their waist. I was like their third wheel. We did everything together. My mother would pick them up and take them to dance school with me and their mom would drop us off. For many years we were inseparable.

All the guys at the dance studio liked the twins. Everybody talked about how pretty they were. Mrs. Johnson had a grandson by the name of T'chaka Johnson, better known to many as rap star "Prodigy" from the group Mobb Deep. He was a real cute short boy, with caramel skin and silky Indian-textured hair. T'chaka was fine, and he knew it. People often told him he was cute and showered him with attention because of his prestigious background. He had a best friend named Chris whose grandmother, Ms. Barbara, was like Mrs. Johnson's right-hand lady. She helped run the dance school and collected the tuition payments.

T'chaka and Chris were both spoiled, but T'chaka put the cake on spoiled! He lived a double life. He spent half his time with his mother in the ghetto and the other half of his time with Mrs. Johnson, in her mansion. T'chaka was Mrs. Johnson's son's child. His father was never around, and he split on T'chaka's mom.

T'chaka's mom, Ms. Fatima, was a light-skinned, pretty young lady with beautiful curly hair and bright eyes. She struggled bringing T'chaka up in a run-down housing development in Lefrak, Queens, after the fall of her career as a member of the once popular singing group, The Crystals.

Mrs. Johnson, on the other hand, lived in a plush mansion in Hempstead, Long Island. We went to a birthday party she had for T'chaka there, and we were blown away. This kid lived like Richie Rich! He had all types of gadgets in his house, including his own arcade-style games. Back then that was huge! He lived among the thugs during the week and like a rich boy on the weekend. He got whatever he asked for. Mrs. Johnson spoiled T'chaka!

T'chaka was in love with my best friend, Renée, one of the twins. Every Saturday when we had our hour lunch break, he would take us to McDonald's and pay for every-thing. We loved this kid! We would run wild up and down Jamaica Avenue for our break. Jamaica Avenue was the busy downtown district of Jamaica, Queens, New York. They had tons of stores in a row. All the latest fashions hit Jamaica Avenue first. We had a ball going in and out of the stores. T'chaka always had a wad of cash, and he would often buy us stuff.

From a young child, as early as I could remember, I loved to shop. I loved clothes, accessories, and shoes. Whatever I saw that was hot, I wanted it. The twins and I were seven years old and T'chaka was ten. He was my first encounter with a "get-money" dude. I quickly learned money equated to power and freedom. It was the main ingredient I needed to make me successful and independent. It was my goal to make money my friend!

*A*s a child, my mother always wanted to learn how to swim, but her aunts couldn't afford to send her to swimming lessons. As an adult, my mother hated the fact that she never learned how to swim. To make up for her childhood mishaps, from an early age, my mother enrolled my brother and me into swimming lessons at the YMCA in Bellerose, New York.

We went to the YMCA at least two nights a week after school. We took up swimming, judo, tennis, and gymnastics. We even went to the YMCA summer camps and took classes in the summer. It was important to my parents that we were well-rounded children that knew how to defend ourselves.

The YMCA we attended was in a predominantly white neighborhood. My brother and I were oftentimes the only blacks in their classes. We were used to intermixing with white people because our elementary school was predominately white, so we didn't mind. But we quickly found out the feelings weren't always mutual.

It was a Thursday afternoon in the summer of 1984. I had just recovered from my episode with chicken pox. My entire body was covered with chicken pox bumps. The bumps had dried up, but my skin still itched. My mother constantly poured Calamine lotion on my itchy skin, to soothe me.

"Jamie, you're okay now, so I'm going to take you to your swimming lessons at the YMCA. Today is the last day so you have to attend to take the test to see if you'll make it to the next level of your swim class."

"Mommy, I don't like the way my skin looks. I got all these dark marks all over my body."

"Baby, those are going to take time to heal. You can't just stay in the house. Come on, we are going to go outside, and you'll feel much better."

I stared in front of the mirror at my marked up body. I had spots on my face, all over my back, on my legs, on my arms, even in my hair and on my ears. The chicken pox really took a toll on me. Tears ran down my eyes as I examined the damage in the mirror. I felt ugly inside and out.

Chapter Six

"C'mon, Jamie and Kee, let's go! You're going to be late," my mother said. I grabbed my bag and threw in my swimming suit, my towel, my goggles, and my swim cap. We loaded in the car and went to the YMCA.

My mother came with me to the locker room and helped me change. As I walked through the door I noticed the stares and the pointing of the white children who saw me. I was so embarrassed.

"Jamie, you are going to be all right," my mother said as she tucked my coarse hair under my red rubber swim cap and kissed my forehead. I entered the pool area where I met my brother who came out of the boys' locker room. We were both beginner swimmers in the Pollywog class. I was still scared of the water, so I used the orange floats that the teacher helped me tie on my arms along with a life vest over my chest.

My brother started with the life vest, but he had gotten the courage to take his off. My worst fear was jumping into the water and not coming back up to the top. I would even test out the jumping with my dolls in the bathtub. I would make them fall off the ledge of the tub and wait for them to rise to the top of the water, with one eye open and the other closed.

I grabbed my orange floats and my life vest and waited for my instructor when I saw three white little girls pointing and whispering about me. One of them, who had long blond hair and blue eyes, approached me.

"Hey, what's all those spots all over your body?" she said.

"Oh, I had the chicken pox."

"The chicken pox? That is contagious. You're going to give us your dirty germs!"

"No, no. I went to the doctor; it's gone now!" I said in a defensive voice.

"Then why are all those marks on you still?"

"They take time to go away!" I responded sharply.

The girl's friend approached me. She was skinny with two black long braids. "Why do you wear that swim cap on your head?" she asked.

"Oh, because I don't have the same type of hair as you. My hair will get damaged in the water."

"You people are strange!" she said as she looked at me as if I were a disease.

"*You people?* What people?" I asked.

"Black people," she said without hesitation.

"Where do you black people live?" the girl with the blond hair questioned.

"They live in the huts in the jungle like on TV," the black-haired girl responded.

"You girls are ignorant. You don't even know what you are talking about. Your mama lives in a hut!" I said. I balled up my fist ready to defend myself physically.

My brother walked over as he saw me put my hands up. "What's going on?" he asked.

"They said black people live in huts," I yelled.

The girls stared at my brother in awe.

"Don't worry about them, Jamie; let's go," he said as he grabbed my arm and pulled me away.

"He's kind of cute," the blond-haired girl whispered to her friends.

"Okay, children, we are going to go over all the techniques I taught you in this class, and then each of you will perform, which will determine whether you graduate to the Minnow class in our next set of sessions. If you want to graduate out of this class, you must be able to swim without your life vest and floats. I repeat, you cannot go to the next level still wearing a life vest or floats," the instructor said loudly after she blew her whistle that was tied around her neck. She was a tall white woman with curly blond hair and blue eyes in her midthirties.

The instructor had us all get into the water and practice the techniques she had shown us throughout our classes. I actually began to like the water. I could swim very well with my life vest, but I was scared to death to take it off.

"Okay, kids. It's time for testing. I'll call your names one by one and instruct you on what to do," the instructor yelled from the sidelines of the large Olympic-sized pool. The pool went up to twelve feet of water. There was a large diving board at the foot of the pool in the deep end. The pool was roped off into four sections. Our class performed on the right side while the Minnow class, the class above us, swam on the left side.

My brother was one of the first to be called up.

"I want to see you do the breaststroke straight down to the end of the pool, and then turn on your back and do the backstroke all the way back down to the beginning of the pool," the instructor said to my brother.

"Yes, ma'am," he replied as he got in the water.

"Ready, set, go," the instructor shouted as she started her timer. Kee swiftly swam doing the breast stroke to the end of the pool. Then he turned on his back and did the backstroke all the way back.

"Good job, young man," the instructor said giving my brother the thumbs-up, and the class applauded.

I was so nervous. I wanted to go to the next class. Kee was going to leave me behind and I couldn't stand the thought of that! I watched several children pass and others cry because they didn't want to take off their life vest. I said a short prayer to myself and unhooked my life vest.

"Jamila, are you ready?" the instructor asked.

"Yes, ma'am," I said as tears rolled down my face. I jumped in the water and to my surprise, I rose to the top without my life vest.

"Ready, set, go," the instructor prompted, and I took off. At first I was doing okay until it sunk in that I didn't have my life vest on. Then, I began to sink. The instructor jumped in the water and came and got me.

"Are you okay?" she yelled as she grabbed me.

"Yes, I'm all right."

"You don't have to finish this test if you don't want to. This is the first time you've swum without a life vest."

I thought to myself how my brother would excel over me and I would be left behind in her class.

"No, I can do it. Give me another chance," I quickly responded. The teacher honored my request and led me back to the beginning of the pool and set me in position.

"Are you sure, Jamila?" the instructor asked once again.

"Yes, ma'am, I can do it!" I responded.

"Okay. Ready, set, go!" she shouted, and I began to swim.

This time I had it! I told myself I could pass this test, and I was determined to do so! I remembered the story they taught in school about the little train that could. *I think I can, I think I can, I know I can, I know I can,* I said to myself as I reached the end of the pool. I quickly flipped on my back and did the backstroke back to the beginning of the pool. As I made it to the finish line, my instructor began to applaud. *I did it!* I thought to myself.

"In the history of me teaching this class, I have never seen anyone take off their life vest on the day of the test and swim like you did, young lady," the instructor said to me as I came up out of the water. "I'm very proud of you, but I want you to repeat the Pollywog class. Your timing is still off, and I want to make sure you are ready for the Minnow drills before you move ahead."

I was proud of myself and upset all at the same time! Kee left me and went ahead to be a Minnow, but I learned from that day I would never be afraid of anything ever again! I became very competitive. I played to win. Everything I did had to be done exceptionally well. I was very hard on myself, and I never settled for less. I always remembered the feeling of being left behind in the Pollywog class, and I was determined I would never be left behind again!

*M*y mom raised me and my brother in the church. We had to go to church every Sunday, like it or not. I liked it; my brother did not! My mother wasn't no super-spiritual woman. She'd cuss you out at the drop of a dime, but she revered God. She desperately wanted my brother and me to serve Him! At a very young age, she made us join the Sunbeam Choir. We went to choir rehearsal every Thursday night, and my mother became the parent chaperone.

I loved to sing, so the Sunbeam Choir was right up my alley! Lounging around the house I would take my mother's brush and use the handle as my mic and get in front of the long, tall mirror that covered the entire wall in our living room, and I would sing the songs I heard in church. I would stand in front of the mirror and imitate Sister George, a heavyset, middle-aged, dark-skinned lady with a very deep voice. She was the choir director of the adult choir. When Sister George sang, she had the whole church catching the spirit. Her deep soulful voice would echo into the pews and just jump into your spirit. You couldn't stay still listening to Sister George. She'd have everybody in the church up on their feet praising God, both young and old.

"I'm running, I'm running, running for my life. If anybody asks you what's the matter with me, you can tell them I saved, sanctified, and I'm running for my life," I sang my heart out imitating Sister George in the mirror. I even hit the low notes with the riffs, like Sister George did.

"Can I get a witness? Do you love Him? Yeahhhh! Yeahhhhh! Can I get an amen? Tell me do you love Himmmm? Ain't nobody do me like Jesus!"

I paced back and forth in front of the mirror, imitating how Sister George would preach in the middle of her songs. I threw my hands in the air and shouted, "Can I get a witness? Ain't He all right? Yeah, yeahhhhh, yeahhhhh. Yes, Lord."

Then I started shouting and catching the Holy Ghost like Sister George did after she sang. "Jesus, Jesus, I love You, Lord. Yeah, yeah!!!"

Chapter Seven

I was getting into my imitation when my mother snuck up behind me. "Jamie, what the hell you doing?"

Frightened by her sudden appearance, I said, "Oh, oh, ah . . . was just doing like they did in church," I responded reluctantly.

"Now, girl, you better not be playing with the Holy Ghost. That ain't nothin' to play with, girl! You hear me, child?"

"Yes, Ma."

"Now give me that damn brush and go to your room."

I quickly handed her the brush and went to my room. I didn't understand why she just didn't let me have my fun. To me, adults always had to ruin everything!

* * *

It was a beautiful Thursday night in 1987, right after my tenth birthday. "Come on, Jamie and Kee," my mother called. "It's time for choir rehearsal. Put your shoes and your jackets on and let's go."

"Yes, Mommy," my brother and I replied in unison. I loved choir rehearsal. I hurried and got my things together so I could get there early and get a seat in the front of the choir stand. My brother and I charged out the door. We left my mother behind to race to the car. You see, whoever got to the car door first got to sit in the front seat of the car.

"I'ma get to sit in the front. I bet you!" Kee challenged as he ran ahead of me and beat me to the door.

"It's not fair! You always get to sit in the front." I was livid. "Mommy, mommy, why he always get to sit in the front, and I never do? It's not fair, Mommy."

"Look, I'm so sick of you two fighting like cats and dogs. Y'all supposed to love each other. Now, Kee, that's your little sister and the only sister you got. You suppose to love her, protect her, and take care of her. Share, for God's sake. Y'all both get on my nerves!" my mother said in a frustrated tone.

"Okay, okay, man. You can sit in the front, but I'm sitting in the front on the way home," Kee said as he rubbed against me, slightly shoving me to get to the back door.

"You're such a brat," he mumbled so my mother couldn't hear.

"Whatever," I said back to him. We loaded in the car and rode four blocks down the street to the church. The church was walking distance, but my mother didn't believe in walking nowhere.

We pulled up at the church, and I quickly hopped out and ran in. There were at least twenty kids running around the church, hitting each other, playing, and talking loud.

My mother was the parent chaperone. She walked in the church yelling ferociously,

"Get down from there right now. Stop it!"

You could see the terror in the children's faces when they saw my mother walk in. She knew just how to discipline children. She learned all the tricks from her seventh-grade students.

"Jamaal, get your behind off the pulpit. Don't make me call your grandmother, boy."

Jamaal quickly jumped off the pulpit, where he was imitating Pastor Mixon. "Yes, ma'am," he said as he got down.

By then, all the children had run to their seats. The choir director, Marvetta Edwards, sashayed through the doors with her husband Lawrence, the organist. "Hello, everybody. Y'all ready to get started."

"Yes," we all said.

Lawrence walked up to the organ and opened the cover and sat down. He began to play a few chords.

"Okay, guys, the Sunbeam Choir Anniversary is approaching, and I want to teach you two new songs tonight. The first song is called 'This Little Light of Mine.' The words are on these sheets I'm going to pass out. Ms. Davis, would you pass these out to the children for me please."

"Yes, Marvetta, hand them here, baby," my mother said. Marvetta was a tall, slim lady in her midtwenties who had smooth black skin. She and her husband, Lawrence, had recently married. She was a good singer, and she loved children.

My mother passed out the music sheets, and we got up and sang following Marvetta's instructions. *"This little light of mine, oh, I'm gonna let it shine. Oh, oh, oh. This little light of mine, I'm gonna let it shine. Let it shine. Let it shine. Let it shine!"* we began to sing.

"Okay, now y'all got to get on key. Let me hear the sopranos first."

The sopranos began to sing. When they were done, she moved over to my section. "Okay, now, altos, don't let the sopranos show y'all up."

We looked at the sopranos, giving them a competitive stare. We sang in our best voices to show them up.

"Yeah, that's what I like to hear."

Then she moved onto the boys.

"Now let me hear my tenors. I know y'all not gonna let the girls outshine you."

"This litt-le light of mi-ne, I'm gon-na let it shi-ne," the little boys sang passionately, letting us know they weren't taking any shorts.

"Okay, let me hear everybody together now."

We all sang together and tore the house down! We sure were some singing little kids. There were about fifty of us all together. We traveled all throughout New York singing at different churches. Our group became popular, and everybody wanted us to sing for their church. Marvetta knew just how to bring the best out of us.

"Okay, y'all got that song, now I want to teach you the next song, but this song I'm going to need a lead vocalist for." She got out the tape recorder and placed in Albertina Walker's, "I Can Go To God In Prayer." I listened intensely to the woman who sounded very similar to Sister George.

After the song played, she stopped the recorder. "Does anyone want to try out for the lead?"

I quickly raised my hand among the others. My mother walked up to me and said, "Put yah hand down, little girl; now you know you can't sing! Don't be embarrassing me in here now. Put yah hand down!"

"No, Mommy, I can do this," I pleaded.

By that time Marvetta had already called me out. I was very nervous as my mother had shaken my confidence. I guess I couldn't sing since that's what she said. *I hope I don't make a fool of myself*, I thought silently to myself. There were five of us who tried out for the lead.

I got on the back of the try-out line and I prayed, "Dear God, I want more than anything to be able to sing for You like Sister George. I know I can't sing, but You can do anything, God. That's what Reverend Mixon tells us on Sunday. He said if we ask You, we shall receive, so I'm asking You, God. Please help me sing like Sister George." I quickly finished my prayer, and it was my turn. I grabbed the mic and turned my back to my mother, who had her head down with her hand on top of her forehead covering her face in shame.

Lawrence played the intro, and I missed the first cue to come in. "Baby, you got to listen for your cue," Marvetta said softly.

I nodded my head yes. Lawrence began to play again. I listened closely for my cue. I took a deep breath and sang, *"Makes no difference what the problem."* The choir backed me up singing, *"I can go to God in prayer, ooh, ooh, ooh. Church, I have this, this assurance. I can go to God in prayer, ooh, ooh, ooh."*

I sang the first part and realized that I sounded good. Marvetta had a smile on her face that was out of this world. I looked back at my mom who stood astonished with her hand over her mouth. I knew I had it then. I pretended I was Sister George on a Sunday morning and continued, *"He can work it out, and He can work it out."*

"Yes, He can, yes, He can, yes, He can, oh, yes, He can," the choir backed me with excitement. I finished the song, and the music stopped.

Marvetta came and hugged me and looked at my mother. "I didn't know she could sing like that! She sounds like a grown lady in this little girl's body," Marvetta said as she turned to Lawrence. "Lawrence, ain't she something?"

"She just blew me away for real," Lawrence commented.

We left choir rehearsal, and I climbed in the backseat of my mother's blue Mazda. My brother got in the front. I didn't even care about being in the back that night. I was in my own little world! I was astounded. I really could sing! I couldn't wait for the choir anniversary!

My brother Kee in his choir robe at the Sunbeam Choir Anniversary.

"Daddy, Daddy, I can sing," I shouted as I ran into my house, jumping straight into my father's arms.

"Yeah, baby, you can do anything. You're daddy's special little girl," he replied, hugging me tightly.

"Daddy, why don't you ever come to church with us?"

"Baby, Daddy is very busy, and on Sunday I'm so tired. I work at the Transit Authority, Monday to Friday, and on Saturday, you know, I spend all them hours down at the Military Reserve base. I pray though to God by myself. But, baby, look, do me a favor.

"Every time you got to church, pray for Daddy, then God will take care of me. If you don't pray I might be in trouble."

"Oh, no, Daddy, don't worry, I'ma pray for you every single time I go to church. Daddy, can I ask you another question?"

"Yes, baby."

"Daddy, why do you work so hard? I never get a chance to see you like I want. You always at work and on trips with the military. Don't them people know you got a family you need to spend time with?"

My dad laughed and held me in his arms. "Baby, I love you, your mom, and your brother very much. I'm a man. I have to take care of y'all. I also have to take care of my mother and sisters.

"I work hard to make sure y'all will never have to work hard like me. You going to college one day, and I have to make sure it's paid for. I want you to have all the things I didn't have as a little boy. I love you, baby, and Daddy gonna always make sure you okay. Now you understand?"

"Yes, Daddy, you are a good man. You doing all that hard work just for me?"

"Yes, baby, just for you," he said as he kissed me softly on my cheek. I felt so special.

"Daddy, one last thing."

"You sure?"

"Yes, just one last question, Daddy. It's okay that you don't go to church 'cause I'ma pray for you like you told me to, but my teacher in my class told us cigarettes kill you.

"Daddy, I don't want you to die. Please, please, Daddy, don't smoke no more cigarettes." I leaned into his chest and hugged him as hard as I could.

"You know what, baby?" he said as he reached in his back pocket and took out his cigarettes. "'Cause I love you sooo, sooo much, I ain't ever going to smoke another cigarette again."

My father threw his cigarettes away from that day on and he never, ever smoked another cigarette again!

I knew that day my daddy really loved me, more than anything in this world! I loved him back the same. He was hardly ever around, but he was my hero, and he always had my back.

My mother loved me, but she resented my relationship with my father at times. I could get him to do things that nobody else could convince him to do; not even my mother or his mother had the influence I had on him. I am his Jamie, and he is my heart. I love him with everything in me!

My dad was very serious about taking care of his family. He never wanted us to suffer like he did when his father left him, so he worked hard, and he provided well for his entire family. He even financially took care of his mother.

As a little boy, my father had promised his mother she would never have to rely on another man. He told her he was gonna make it out of Kinston, and when he did, he would take care of her. My father was a man of his word. He kept his promise. My parents moved to New York, worked hard, and made several smart investments with their money. They moved my grandmother to the ritzy, upper-middle-class section of Kinston, where the white folks lived. They bought my grandmother a beautiful brick house that wrapped around the block. It was three times as big as the house we lived in New York. He also helped my grandmother buy a brand-new brown Lincoln sedan. Honey, you couldn't tell my grandma nothing! Everything was about her Hosea; she loved my dad, but I believe I loved him more!

I loved going to Kinston, North Carolina, as a child. Going down South was like going to Disney World. We had so much fun! The night before, my mother would stay up all night and pack our bags. She would make fried chicken and deviled eggs. My mom's food was off the chain! She was a country girl that could cook her butt off! I loved Mommy's cookin'. My dad would wake us up at three in the morning, and we would get on the road.

My father had a van that he named "Brown Sugar." This is the vehicle we used to take on vacation. My father took a regular van and customized it. The van had a bed in the back, a toilet, a small bar, a sink, and even a refrigerator. The inside was lined with plush dark multicolor carpet. This van was the joint, especially for back then! It had chrome wheels and a special customized brown paint job that always seemed to sparkle. On the back of the van in script writing, by the part that carried the spare tire, it read, "Brown Sugar." I lived to go on vacation just to ride in the van.

Daddy had a walkie-talkie CB system in his van. "Breaka one, breaka one nine, what's the traffic lookin' like on southbound I-95?" he radioed in.

"All is clear ahead, partner," some strange person responded.

"I appreciate that, young man," my father responded back in his radio-friendly accent.

My father called everybody "young man," even the old men. He put in his '70s mix tape music, and we cruised. I can sing almost every song from the '70s, because the tapes repeated over and over for the whole eight-hour trip.

Daddy wasn't into stopping on the road. Once he took off, he was in a zone. We had the portable toilet in the back, and Mom brought the food. Dad was into breaking his record of time getting to North Carolina. He was focused and all about getting to his destination! The only time he stopped was for gas, and if we didn't need any gas, he wouldn't stop at all! We all knew the routine. You better not have to do the number 2. You would be clean cut out of luck, 'cause he wasn't stopping!

Chapter Nine

Most of the trip I slept away in the bed in the back of the van. While I was up I would observe the scenery. It was cool looking at the change of environments as we rode through different states and noticed the people traveling on the road.

I would watch the signs and often ask, "What state are we in? Did we get there yet?" I was always anxious to arrive. I couldn't wait to see my cousins. Oh, we cut up in Kinston. It wasn't like the city. Kinston was safe. It was a small town where everybody knew each other. Practically the whole town was related.

It was around eleven in the morning when we pulled up to my grandmother's house in Kinston, North Carolina. Wow! *We finally arrived,* I thought to myself. I raced out of the car and rang the doorbell. "Grandma, Grandma, it's me, open up," I said as I banged loudly on the door.

My grandmother opened the door and greeted me with her warm beautiful smile. "Hey, baby," she said grabbing me tightly in her arms. My grandmother was a tall, stocky woman. She stood 5 foot 9, and she had beautiful bronze skin. She wore her hair in tight curls, rolled to the back. I hugged her, then I quickly broke loose. I was anxious to see my cousins. My father's second-oldest sister, Connie, had five children. They were all older than me.

The two oldest daughters, Pee Wee and Yvonne, had kids my age, and her young-est son, Eric, was a year older than me. Everybody lived at Grandma's house. She had six bedrooms, and they were always filled up with family. My father's youngest sister, Shorty, had two kids, Donnell and Vickie. They were five years or so older than me.

Unlike my brother, Donnell was very loving and protective of me. He took care of me like I was his own little sister. He was my favorite boy cousin. I could count on him to beat my brother up for me when he treated me wrong. I loved Donnell for that. I looked up to him and admired him very much.

Donnell was a hustler who got big money selling crack cocaine. He spoke with a strong Southern accent, but he had a swagger that was out of this world! When you opened Donnell's room door, he had at least twenty pairs of tennis shoes lined up and down the wall, and all types of clothes in the closet. Donnell was 5 foot 11, with light brown skin. He had chinky eyes and a muscular-built shape. Donnell was fine! All the ladies in the town wanted my cousin.

"Donnell, Donnell, will you please take me to the store. Please!" I pleaded as I grabbed his hand.

"What, girl? Where yah mama at, girl?" Donnell abruptly responded.

"She ain't here. Come on, you know you my favorite cousin. I'm hungry," I said as I batted my eyes and played on his sympathy.

Donnell was a sucker for women, and I knew he had a soft spot for me.

"All right, girl, but give me a minute. Let me call Monique over to drive us."

My dad had moved my grandma out of the hood, so she stayed in a white section that was kind of remote from everything. You needed a car to get around. My cousin called his girlfriend, Monique, and she came to pick us up.

The little silver car approached the driveway and a pretty light-skinned, long-haired, petite girl rolled down the window.

"Hey, pretty little girl," she said in a high-pitch country accent.

I smiled and said, "Hey!"

My cousin Eric, my brother Kee, and I loaded in the back of her car. Donnell got in the front seat and reached over to kiss his girl. "Hey, baby, I missed you," he said to her, and he kissed her lips.

"I missed you too, baby," she gently replied.

We pulled off from the big brick house and drove down the street to go to the other side of town.

"Baby, I want to go to the skating rink on Saturday night with my cousins, but I don't got no outfit to wear," Monique said, not wasting any time.

"What you mean? What about all them clothes I just bought you?" Donnell asked.

"Come on, babe, I done wore all of them."

"What about the money I gave you two days ago?"

"I told you I had to get my hair and my nails done, then my mother asked me for money to pay the light bill."

"Hold up, I just gave your mother money for the lights last week."

"You know she be trying to get over. Let me know first before you give her anything. Anyway, Boo, I really want to go. Rocky done gave my cousin Tiny money for an outfit, and I don't want her looking better than me. Then he gonna try to be stuntin' on you. You know he already telling everybody he get more money than you."

"Who he telling that to?" Donnell quickly interjected.

"You know, he tell all his crew that and Tiny came back and tell me."

"That dude ain't getting money like me, babe!"

"I know that."

"All right, how much money you need?"

"I don't know, but I want to wear something nice."

"Okay, let's go to the block so I could pick up some money."

In the backseat I was listening hard to their conversation. I wanted an outfit too! This chick had my cousin wrapped around her finger. She knew just what to say to get what she wanted. I have to admit, I was jealous.

We approached the spot they called the Front, which was a minisupermarket in the heart of the hood. There was like twenty dudes standing outside with dirt bikes and posted on the wall of the store. My cousin hopped out of the car, and it was like Michael Jackson arrived.

"Solo, Solo, what's up, man?" they said as they slapped him five. Solo was his "street name."

All movement stopped in the block, and all eyes were on Donnell. "Nothin' much, what's up with my money? What's it looking like out here?" Donnell responded.

"Monique, take the kids in the store and get them what they want," he said as he pulled out a whole wad of cash and passed Monique the money.

Monique reached for the money, but I spoke up in a feisty tone, "Uh-uh, I want to hold my own money, Donnell." Donnell smiled and handed me a twenty-dollar bill.

Back then, that was like me hitting the lotto. His girlfriend tried to be nice to me, but I was rude back. I felt like my cousin was my man and she was taking my money. I ain't like that, so I didn't like her.

We walked in the store, and my cousin Eric saw his friend. "What's up, Dino? What's good?"

"Hey, Fishkell, where you been at?" the boy Dino replied. He was a cute chocolate brown boy, with a low Caesar haircut who quietly caught my attention.

Dino responded, "I be in the house, man. Since we moved, my grandmother don't let me come down here no more."

"Oh, for real. What's up with Retha Mae anyway?"

"Oh, she good."

"She still fishing?"

"Yeah, she still go faithfully every Friday. Man, what you doing out here so late?"

"Man, I'm getting money. You know my brother Billy and Solo got this spot on lock. Why don't you ask if Solo will let you come out here and rock? Boy, I done made four hundred dollars already today!"

I listened to the boy's talk, and I was blown away. This little boy couldn't have been more than ten years old, and he was making four hundred dollars in a day! This was amazing to me. In New York I was sheltered. I never saw any street transactions. Boy, in my eyes, Kinston had it going on!

"Fishkell, who that little girl with you?" Dino asked, pointing to me.

"Oh, that's my cousin Jamie. She from New York."

"All the way from the Big Apple? Wow! I want to holla at her. Introduce me to your cousin."

"I ain't. She ain't into no boys, fool! She too young!"

"Later for you. I'ma introduce myself." Dino muttered in his thick country accent.

"Ah, Jamie," he said to me.

"Hey," I responded, kind of taken back. Dino was cute, and I wasn't used to any boys trying to talk to me.

"How long you down here for?"

"Just for the Easter holiday."

"Oh, word? What you like to do in your free time?" he asked me as I placed the items I wanted on the counter.

"I like to dance and sing, and I guess, just play. What do you like to do?" I asked.

"I like to get money! Do you like money?"

"Yes," I smiled as I reached in my pocket to show off the twenty-dollar bill my cousin handed me to pay the cashier.

"Put that away, Lil Mamma," he said as he reached in his pocket and pulled out a knot full of cash, bigger than my cousin had in his pocket. He paid for my stuff with a fifty-dollar bill. "Here's your change, sir," the cashier responded.

"No, that's my lady's money. Hand that to her," Dino said smoothly and smiled at me.

I quickly took the money from the cashier and smiled back. *Man*, I was thinking to myself, *I done hit the jackpot!* Before I could say thank you, my cousin Donnell and Dino's brother Billy were on our heels. Kee stood behind them shooting Dino an evil stare.

"Ah, yo, little boy, don't make me kill you," Donnell screamed at Dino.

"What you talkin' about, man?"

"That's my little cousin. She only ten years old, fool."

"And I'm twelve, so what?"

"Don't play with me. I'll kick your butt, little boy."

Donnell grabbed the money Dino gave me and gave it back to him. "She with me. She got money. She don't need yours."

Donnell grabbed me by the hand and dragged me in the car. "I don't want you talking to no little boys. You hear me? You too young for this; besides, you got a good life for yourself in New York. Don't let nothing mess that up. You hear me, baby?"

"Yes, Donnell," I said, feeling embarrassed. I sank down in the seat of the car. Donnell had his own girl. I didn't understand why he was trying to stop my action. I had the money in my hands, and he gave it back. I couldn't believe it! I needed that money. I was gonna take it back with me to New York and go shopping on Jamaica Avenue.

We got back to the house and were greeted by my parents. "Where have you been?" my parents demanded. It was clear that they were both upset.

"Oh, Solo, I mean Donnell, took us to the store. We all right," Kee quickly rebutted.

Donnell cleared his throat and spoke up. "Yes, I just got them a few things. They said they was hungry, and y'all was gone. You know they were safe with me."

Kee interjected, "Yeah, we went to the store and some little boy paid for Jamie's food with a whole bunch a money, Mamma. He had a fist full of cash, and he gave Jamie his change, and she took it."

"What?" my mother screamed in outrage.

"Now, now, Aunt Liddie. That was Dino, you know, my best friend. Billy Blast's little brother. They like family, Auntie. I took the money and gave it back."

"You little fast-behind, girl! I can't leave you nowhere. You don't take no money from no men!" she said and slapped my face. Kee stood behind her smiling.

"Go get your stuff together and get ready to go to bed."

"Yes, Ma," I said with tears flowing down my eyes, I went to get my pajamas out of my suitcase. I was so mad at my brother, and so was Donnell. When Kee came upstairs, Donnell cursed him out and whopped his butt. That gave me some pleasure to know he was handled.

* * *

It was our last day in Kinston before we went back to New York. I didn't want to leave. I'd had such a good time there. It was Easter Sunday, and we all prepared to go to church. I was in the bathroom getting dressed. I put on a beautiful pink ruffled dress with matching lace stockings. I wore black patent leather shoes to match and pink gloves.

I came out of the bathroom and modeled for my grandmother. "Oh, look at my princess," she said as I spun around.

Grandma was sharp, too. She had a pretty lilac silk suit with flowers on it and a hat that was so huge that it was wrapped around her entire face covering the eyes. It had beautiful fake flowers on top of it. Her heels matched the outfit, and so did her bag.

Grandma was sharp, and she knew it! When she put on her Sunday clothes, even her walk switched up. Grandma strutted like she was worth a million bucks. She threw on her dark Jackie-O-style shades, then grabbed her car keys and her Bible. She was ready to go.

"Baby, do you wanna ride in the car with Grandma?"

"Yes, ma'am." I was excited to travel to church with her. Her presence alone made me feel like I was related to royalty.

We all exited the house. She locked the door behind us as I ran to her car. Not only was I gonna sit in the front seat, my grandma and I were gonna ride together. I had her all to myself. My brother, my mother, and my father followed behind us in Daddy's brown van.

I watched my grandmother intensely. She fixed her mirrors in the car, started her ignition, and took hold of her wheel like a pro. She drove her Lincoln like a female "mack." Her moves were discreet, and she looked so strong and sexy. You could tell others felt the same way as men stopped and waved and tooted their horn as we rode. Grandma had a natural flair and confidence about herself. I was mesmerized watching her.

We pulled up to a small underpass bridge that led us down a small dirt road. We traveled about a mile or so on the dirt road in the middle of the country. Finally we arrived at this big white church, the Sand Hill Baptist Church. As we walked in the door, the choir was marching in. All the little kids showed off their pretty Easter clothes. Everyone was dressed to impress!

"We're marching to Zion, beautiful, beautiful Zion. We're marching upward to Zion, the beautiful city of God," the choir sang as we walked through the doors. The church had beautiful wooden pews on both sides and a large blue altar with the choir stand behind it. The choir assembled in the stands as they marched into the building. The usher directed my grandma and me to sit in the second row. We had a good time singing songs together.

Midway through the service the pastor said, "Sister Retha, would you come up and lead us in a selection."

My grandmother stood up, acting surprised, yet honored. She left me in the pew and went up to the podium.

She paused before speaking. "I was glad when they said unto me let us come into the house of the Lord. Ain't God good! I'm so happy today. I got my favorite son here with me all the way up from New York City and his beautiful wife and kids. I'm blessed today, folks. I'm happy to praise the Lord. Will you praise Him with me?"

The crowd roared, "Amen, that's all right!"

My grandmother closed her eyes, lifted her hands, and sang, *"Amazing grace, how sweet the sound, that saved a wretch like me. I once was lost but now am found, was blind but now I see."*

My grandmother sounded like an angel to me. This was the first time I ever heard her sing, and I was proud. I looked back at my dad who had tears in his eyes. My grandmother moved him through the spirit. That's the day I gained a new hero. I wanted to be just like my grandma when I grew up.

After church, we went back to the house where Grandma had a feast ready that was sure to please a king. We had collard greens, yams, rice, turkey, fried chicken, neck bones, macaroni and cheese, and all types of cakes and pies. All of my aunts and cousins came over to eat. Even the preacher from the church came to the house to eat that day. We all had a good time. My mother could cook, but she had nothing on my grandma!

Afterward, I changed my clothes and sat out on the porch playing with my cousin Eric, when a blue car pulled up to the house. Dino, the boy I met at the store, jumped out with his brother Billy Blast.

My heart was racing as I recognized that it was him. "Fishkell, where Solo at?" Billy asked.

"He inside, man," Eric responded. Billy quickly ran up the steps of the porch and made his way inside. Dino sat next to me on the porch. My heart pounced.

"What's up, Jamie? You ain't think you'd see me again, huh?"

I laughed. "No," I answered.

"I had to come by and see you before you left. I'm coming to New York City."

"When?" I said bewildered.

"Not now, but I'm coming. I'm saving my money up, and I'm going shopping."

I smiled, thinking this boy was right up my alley. "I like to shop too," I said.

"For real? What's it like in New York?" he asked.

I told him all about the stores and my life in New York. He listened intensely. While we were talking, my mother came out on the porch. I could tell by the look on her face this was going to be ugly.

"What are you doing out here, Jamie? Take your fast behind in the house."

I quickly got up and left.

"Listen, you black ugly billy goat gruff, crusty-eyed boy. My daughter don't want nothing to do with you. You stay the hell away from her, you hear?" she said, pointing her finger in Dino's face.

"Uh-uh," Dino responded nervously.

"Uh-uh hell. You hear me? I am gonna tell your parents you out here messin' with a little-bitty girl."

"Yes, ma'am," Dino said, and he walked away.

I went in the house mad and so embarrassed, knowing this was the last time I would see Dino. We were scheduled to leave in the morning. I closed the door to the guest room I was staying in and I cried.

About a half hour later, my cousin, Eric, peeped in. "What you crying for, Jamie? You really like that boy, huh?"

I didn't respond.

"Oh, you don't want to talk to me. Well, I guess you don't want to know what he left you."

My eyes opened wide, and I immediately stopped crying. "What did he leave for me, Eric? Boy, you better not be playing with me. Come over here."

He approached me and reached in his pocket. He took out a one hundred dollar bill and waved it at me. My eyes almost popped out of my head. I never ever had one hundred dollars to myself at one time. I went to grab it, and he snatched it back and put it behind his back.

"You gonna buy me something?"

"Stop playing, boy," I said.

"No, I'm serious."

"Okay, okay. I'll get you something." I gave in, and Eric handed over the crisp one hundred dollar bill.

"You betta, or I'ma tell."

"Okay, okay, I promise," I said. I opened up the one hundred dollar bill and it read: "Go shopping on me until I get to New York. Love you, Dino." My heart melted.

I never did get a chance to buy Eric anything. The next morning my dad woke us up early to get back on the road. Tears rolled down my eyes as I left the small town that felt like home to me. I loved Kinston. I couldn't wait to go back. I met my first and second love there—boys and money.

My brother Kee and me, at age six, riding our bikes.

*O*n a beautiful, warm, spring Saturday morning directly following our trip to Kinston, I was up early, ready to go to dance school. I couldn't wait to go on my lunch break so I could hit the stores on Jamaica Avenue. I had a whole one hundred dollar bill to spend on myself!

All week I had been pondering in my mind about what I was going to get, and I still wasn't sure.

Maybe I'll buy an outfit and some shoes. No, I'll get some sneakers and a few record albums out of the music store. Oh, oh, I know! I'll get a pair of them Gazelle glasses and a pocketbook! I thought to myself as I brushed my teeth at the sink. *Today's gonna be a good day!*

"Good times, these are the good times, leave your cares behind, these are the good times," I sang out loudly as I put on my leotards and tights. I was funneling through my drawer, deciding what jeans and shirt I would put on over my dance clothes when my mother walked in the room.

"Jamie, you're mighty happy this morning. What's going on with you?"

"Nothing, Ma, I'm just ready to dance. You know my dance school recital is coming up in June, so they making up all the routines now. You know I got to practice hard. I want to be in the front row!" I replied, pulling up my indigo Lee jeans.

"Girl, I don't know how you manage to stay so competitive. I want you to do good in dance, but don't forget your statewide exams are coming up too in May. You got to maintain your grades, girl."

"Mom, I got this. School is easy."

"Don't be telling me nothing is easy. I want to see the black and white. Bring home the grades."

"Yes, Ma, don't I always?" I said in a sarcastic tone.

"Now, girl, I know you ain't gettin' smart with me."

"No, Ma, but you know I get good grades," I said in a gentle tone.

"I know, baby," she said as she rubbed my coarse, dark brown, medium-length hair. "I'm just a little worried. You got a lot on your plate. The choir anniversary is coming up in two more weeks, and, baby, you singing the lead song. Then you got your dance recital stuff, and you still got your schoolwork. I want you to succeed but, baby, this may be a little much. School is most important. Everything else is extra."

"Okay, Ma, but you know I do well in school. Besides, I want to be like them little kids on television. Maybe I can be like Tootie on *The Facts of Life.*"

"Now, girl, don't be getting besides yourself. That's a dream very few people achieve. Besides, you don't even know how to act!"

"Yes, I do, Mommy. When you don't be looking, I get in front of the mirror in the living room and I act out all the lines they be saying on television. You want to watch me?" I asked as she began to plait my hair in two cornrows to the back.

"What you talkin' about, Willis?" I said, as I balled up my face, imitating Arnold from the *Different Strokes* television show.

"Girl, you something else," my mother said laughing hysterically. "Girl, turn around so I can finish this hair of yours."

I hated getting my hair done. I had very nappy, coarse hair. It was so hard to comb through and even worse, it hurt. My mother would buy the Johnson & Johnson's No More Tangles hairspray to soften it up enough to comb through.

"Awe, you hurting me," I said as she began to part my hair and comb it.

"Now, child, I ain't even touch you yet. Come on so I can finish this."

"Okay," I responded in a disgruntled tone. I looked at the bottle of Johnson & Johnson's No More Tangles spray and saw the pretty white girl with two long, silky ponytails on the bottle.

"Mommy, why I can't have hair like hers? I want hair like that. I don't like my hair, Mommy," I said with tears in my eyes.

"Why it got to hurt like this?" I asked.

"Listen, baby, you are black. This is the type of hair we have."

"Well, yours ain't like that. Your hair is straight."

"Well, baby, I'm grown. When you get grown you can get a perm."

"That's not fair. All the grown people get to have everything. What about the kids?" I questioned as I jerked my head away from the comb that was hurting me.

"Well, you'll be an adult one day, but for now, you a child, and a child is to stay in a child's place. Now lean your head back so I can finish these damn braids."

I leaned my head back, and I took the pain. I hated my hair. I wanted pretty straight hair like the girl on the bottle and like my best friends, the twins, Renée and Michelle. Why did my hair have to be so nappy? Life wasn't fair!

My mother finished my braids. I finished getting dressed and got my pink ballet bag which was made out of a square cardboard with fancy plastic covering it, with a ballerina painted on the outside of it. I placed my tap shoes, my ballet shoes, my modern slippers, and a T-shirt to go over my leotards in the bag. I took the crisp hundred dollar bill out of my piggy bank and tucked it in my back pocket.

"I'm ready, Mommy," I called out, as I came down the stairs from my bedroom.

"Okay, I'm coming," she responded.

I grabbed a bowl out of the cabinet and loaded it with my favorite cereal, Franken Berry, poured my milk into the bowl, and guzzled it down.

After I finished eating, we left.

"Nelson and Kee, I'm gone. I'll be back," my mother shouted as she shut the door and locked it.

I jumped in the front seat of my mother's blue Mazda, rolled down the window manually with the knob, and turned on the radio. I fiddled with the stations, and I stopped as I heard the music. My song was on!

"Lodi dodi, we like to party, we don't cause trouble, we don't bother nobody. We're just a man who's on the mic, and we rock upon the mic, we rock the mic right," I rapped away with passion.

"What kinda music is that?" my mother questioned.

"Mom, this is rap music. That song is fresh."

"Fresh? I can't even understand what they are saying."

I paid her no attention; I was too mesmerized by the words and the beat of the music. Rap music was happening, and I liked it. I didn't care what my mother said.

We pulled up in front of the three-story building with the white awning on top that said in big, black, bold letters, "Bernice Johnson's Dance Studio."

I jumped out and kissed my mother. "See you later, Mom. I love you."

"I love you too, baby. Here's your lunch money," she said as she reached in her black pocketbook on the backseat. "Oh, and here's a quarter. Call me on the pay phone when y'all done. I don't feel like sitting around all day waiting for you."

"Okay, Mom," I said as I quickly grabbed the five dollar bill and the quarter she gave me. I took the money and slid it in the same pocket with my one hundred dollar bill.

Wow, I got one hundred and five dollars and a quarter! I thought to myself. I grabbed my bag and hopped out of the car and raced inside the dance studio. I was just in time for my first class, tap.

I had joined the pro class after Mrs. Johnson's recommendation and turned it up! Unlike the regular dance class, there were many talented girls in these classes, so it wasn't easy to stand out. This school was all about raising divas. When the teachers said, "Hit it," we had to be ready to go! We always had different celebrities showing up to the studio. As a result, we were often asked to do television appearances, movies, and music videos. I enjoyed the excitement of being around stars. It kept me on my game.

"Okay, ladies, put your bags and jackets on the back wall and put on your tap shoes," my instructor Lorna yelled. She was a pretty, light-skinned woman with freckles and straight, shoulder-length black hair. She had beautiful white teeth and an incredible smile.

I hurried up and took off my jeans and my shirt, stuffed them in my ballet bag, and took out my tap shoes and my T-shirt.

"Hey, Jamila," Renée greeted me as I was putting on my tap shoes.

"Hey, Renée. Where's Michelle at?" I questioned.

"She's on her way in here. She's in the lobby talking to Chris."

"Well, she better hurry up. You know how Lorna gets."

"Yeah, girl. She's all in love," Renée said as she changed her clothes.

"I'm in love too with T'chaka, but lately, he hasn't even been coming to dance school. I think he might be sick again."

"What's the matter with him? He's always sick!"

"Oh, you didn't know he got some disease. Um, let me think, it's something with sick in it. Sickapells or sickarells."

"You mean sickle cell?"

"Yeah, Jamila, that's it."

"Oh, my teacher was talking about that in class."

"He looks well to me, so I don't think it's bad," Renée said as Michelle came running through the door.

She had a huge smile on her face. "He loves me, he loves me not," Michelle said as she laughed. "You know he loves me!"

"Girl, you gonna be late for class. You need to be getting ready," I said to her in a feisty tone.

"You just mad 'cause you ain't got no boyfriend," she ranted flinging her bag down like a diva, and then she began to change.

"Yes, I do."

"Who, an imaginary boyfriend?" she joked, and the twin sisters laughed at me.

"Uh-uh, I got me a boyfriend, and he got money," I said in a fierce sister-girl tone.

"Who you kidding? Ain't nobody gonna want you. You tall and skinny with them big ole eyes and look at your nappy hair. Who wants that?" Michelle boasted.

I felt so terrible. Maybe she was right. I didn't have light skin and pretty hair like they did. Inside, I felt ugly and ashamed, but I couldn't let them know it.

"Brown-skin girls are all ugly," Michelle added.

"Oh, word? Well, Dino doesn't think I'm ugly, and he has more money than T'chaka or Chris. Matter fact, he gave me a hundred dollar bill, and I'm going shopping lunchtime with it!"

"Oh, please, girl," Michelle responded.

"Let me see the money," Renée said sarcastically.

"Oh, no problem," I said as I went into my ballet bag, took out my pants, and went into my pocket to grab the money.

"Look, a one hundred dollar bill. Do you see what it says in pen?" I asked as Renée quickly grabbed the bill out of my hand.

"Go shopping for me until I get to New York. Love, Dino," Renée read out loud. "Wow! She ain't lying, Michelle! Look."

"Oh, whatever," Michelle said as she acted uninterested.

"Let me get that back," I said as I snatched the bill out of Renée's hand and put it back in my pocket. "And by the way, I'm a brown-skin girl that got a boyfriend *and* some money. You a light-skin pretty girl who's broke. So now what?" I boasted back.

"Whatever," she said as she walked away.

"Okay, girls, now settle down. We have a new girl in the class. I want to introduce her to you. Her name is Chudney. She's gonna watch today, but the next class she gonna join in. We are getting ready for the recital so I mean business. There's no more game playing and showing up to class late.

"I'm going to start forming my lines. There will be three lines, and my best dancers will be in the front. Line up against the wall and each of you get a partner. Line up in sets of two. Okay, we are going to begin with heel toe, heel toe, heel toe, step, heel toe, heel toe, heel toe, step. Step, clap, clap. Step, clap, clap. Heel toe, heel toe, step, clap, clap. You got it?"

"No, can you show me it again," Shalon asked. She was a very slender, light caramel-skinned girl who was double jointed and very flexible.

"Okay, watch me closely. Follow my feet. Heel toe, heel toe, heel toe, step, heel toe, heel toe, heel toe, step. Step, clap, clap. Step, clap, clap. Heel toe, heel toe, step, clap, clap," Lorna instructed, slowly showing the class the dance steps.

"Okay, I got it," Shalon replied.

"Good, you and your partner go first. Five, six, seven, eight, and heel toe, heel toe, heel toe, step, heel toe, heel toe, heel toe, step. Step, clap, clap," Lorna instructed.

"Uh-uh, that's not it. Get to the back of the line. Next, let's go. Five, six, seven eight."

The pressure was on. We had to get these steps. Lorna was making cuts, and I wanted to be in the first line. I let like six sets of girls go ahead of me so I could pick up the steps. I practiced in my head as I waited my turn.

"Jamila, let's go, Five, six, seven, eight, and heel toe, heel toe, heel toe, step, heel toe, heel toe, heel toe, step, step, clap, clap, step, clap, clap, heel toe, heel toe, step, clap, clap. Okay again, and heel toe."

By the second time around, I knew I had it, and I was feeling myself. I was determined to make it to the front line. I pictured I was Diahann Carroll on the show I loved to watch, *Fame*. I strutted down the studio floor with pizzazz and energy.

"Yes, Jamila, you got it! Come sit here, up front," Lorna said as she applauded me. I caught the huffs and puffs of some of my classmates as they had to continue the drill until they got the steps.

Class was over and the new girl came up to me. "What's your name?"

"My name is Jamila. What's your name again?"

"I'm Chudney," she replied as Michelle and Renée approached.

"Where you from?" Renée asked.

"Oh, I'm from Connecticut."

"You came all the way from Connecticut?"

"Yeah, my mother says this school is good. My uncle Michael said I should come here."

"Wow, that's a long way! How long does it take for you to get here?" I asked as I grabbed my ballet bag.

"Oh, about an hour and thirty minutes."

"That's a long trip," Michelle said as we left the classroom.

"Well, it's not that long. It took us eight hours to get to North Carolina," I interjected.

"Well, that's all the way on the other part of the country," Michelle retorted in a feisty tone.

As we entered the studio lobby, Mrs. Johnson came running up to us. She was unusually excited.

"Chudney, Chudney, how are you, little darling? I'm Mrs. Johnson. I'm the owner of the dance school. Do you like the classes so far?"

"Yes, ma'am," Chudney replied.

"Oh, baby, you're going to have a wonderful time here. I assured your mom I will take good care of you. You will learn a lot here, darling," Mrs. Johnson said as she embraced Chudney.

This was strange to us so we looked at each other, puzzled. We never saw Mrs. Johnson act this nice to any kid.

"T'chaka, T'chaka," Mrs. Johnson shouted as he appeared out of nowhere.

"Yes, Grandma."

"This is Chudney. I'm good friends with her mom, and I want you to take good care of her."

"Yes, Grandma."

"Chudney, this is my grandson, T'chaka. He's in your class. He will look out for you and if you need any little thing you can tell me or him. Okay, darling?"

"Yes, ma'am."

Renée instantly became angry and very jealous.

"How she going to put T'chaka on this strange new girl? What's that all about? T'chaka is mine, and I ain't sharing him with nobody, and I mean that," Renée ranted.

"She didn't hook them up like that. Besides, she's okay, Renée," I said as we waited for our next class to begin.

"Did you see the look in her eyes when she saw T'chaka? She wants him. I know it, and she's pretty. Her hair is longer than mine," Renée responded.

"Listen, Nee, we are the twins, and ain't nobody gonna take what we got. We'll jump her behind first, sis," Michelle said in Renée's defense.

"Yeah, that's right," Renée said as she stared Chudney up and down from afar.

It was 11:55 a.m. Finally it was almost lunchtime. I couldn't wait for ballet class to be over.

All I could think about as I gracefully spun across the floor, doing my ballet moves, was shopping in the store with my hundred dollar bill.

"Hey, Ms. Thing, point them toes and hold in your stomach. Clean up them steps. I want to see them sharp.

"*Plié, pas de bourrées, relevé*, and hold. Y'all better do it right or there won't be no lunch. Y'all getting fat and out of shape anyway. It looks like you gotta go on a hamburger diet, honey child.

"I want my steps fierce, now do it again. Five, six, seven, eight, and one and two and three and four and five and six and seven and eight," my instructor Phillip said as he femininely waltzed across the floor. Phillip was a small-framed, caramel-toned man that could switch better than a woman.

"Chris and T'chaka, that is not it, Ms. Honies," Phillip said as T'chaka rolled his eyes. He and Chris hated dance school. They only went to appease their grandmothers.

"Y'all looking like faggots. I need to see strong legs and strong arms. Like this. One and two and three and four. Five and six and seven and eight," Phillip said in his highest, most irritable voice. When he talked you could hear his lisp. He snapped his fingers in the air as he switched his tall, skinny butt like he was on the runway.

"Okay, one last time. If you guys do this routine well, this time, you can go."

Everybody quickly got it together. I hated ballet. It was boring to me compared to the other classes. We were all ready to go so we performed our best.

"Five, six, seven, eight, and one, two, three, four and five and six and seven and eight," Phillip shouted rhythmically to the beat of the music as we danced.

We performed like we were on Broadway. Everybody danced in unison and on beat, barely meeting Phillip's high-performance standards.

"All right, y'all can go, but you better practice. The way it is now, everybody gonna be in the back line for the recital."

We quickly raced out of the class like we were running for our lives.

"Come on, Jamila," Renée and Michelle yelled.

"Okay, let's go," I hollered back.

"Wait one second. Where are Chris and T'chaka?" Renée questioned, looking around for them. Chudney was putting on her clothes, and T'chaka was standing there smiling and talking to her.

"Oh, uh-uh," Renée said as she stomped over to him.

"What's up, T'chaka? You going to McDonald's with us?" Renée asked sarcastically.

"Yeah, um, um. Yeah." T'chaka responded to her and looked back at Chudney. "So, um, Chudney, come on. We all gonna go to McDonald's. Let's wait for Chris," T'chaka suggested.

Shortly after, Chris approached.

"What's up, baby?" Chris said as he grabbed Michelle's hand.

"Nothing, babe. We wanna go to McDonald's," Michelle responded.

"Okay, T'chaka, let me get some money from my grandma," Chris said.

The two boys went to the front desk of the studio and Ms. Barbara took two twenty dollar bills out of the cash register and gave one to each of them.

"You boys be back here on time now. Your next class starts at 1:30," Ms. Barbara said, giving them a sharp look that meant business.

"Yes, Grandma," Chris quickly responded.

Although we were only kids at the time, we all were mature for our age. I simply followed the lead of the twins. They were considered a part of the "cool kids" in the dance school. I wanted to be down, so I made it my business to stay under them.

We all headed out the doors of the dance school. It was Renée, Michelle, Chris, T'chaka, Chudney, and me. Directly out front of the dance studio we spotted a black Town Car-style limousine parked. We all looked and stared at the tinted windows.

"I wonder who's in that car," I said while one of the back-tinted car windows came down.

"Chudney, baby, where are you going?" a brown-skinned woman asked.

"Oh, uh, we're going to McDonald's to eat," Chudney replied.

"Not by yourself, girl. Your mom will kill me."

"Please, I'm old enough to go to the store by myself."

"Oh, no, girl. You trying to get me fired?" the woman said nervously as she opened the car door.

"I'm coming with you," the woman demanded and exited the car.

Chudney sucked her teeth and rolled her eyes. "I can't ever do anything by myself," she shouted in a disgruntled voice.

"Y'all go ahead. I'm going to go eat with my nanny," she said as she waved us on and got in the car.

We all stood back in amazement, not understanding all of what just happened.

"Her nanny? What is a nanny?" Renée asked.

"Oh, that's a babysitter for rich kids," T'chaka replied.

"Who is that little girl? Is she famous?" Michelle questioned.

"Yeah, well, her mother is," Chris said as he grabbed Michelle by the hand as they walked next to each other.

"Her mother is Diana Ross," T'chaka interjected cutting Chris off.

Now it all started to make sense to me. "Oh, that's why she said her uncle Michael referred her to the dance school!" I said excitedly.

"Michael Jackson is this little girl's uncle?" Renée blurted out.

"Yeah," T'chaka said.

"You want to be starting something, yah got to be starting something. You want to be starting something, you got to be starting something," T'chaka sang passionately as he cut up in the middle of the street imitating the Michael Jackson moves. We all began to laugh.

I stopped and daydreamed how my life would be if I had Michael Jackson as my rich uncle! *Maybe I'll be able to meet Michael Jackson. That would be so awesome*, I thought to myself. I always watched him on television. I had his posters all over my bedroom walls and several of his pins on my jacket. I loved Michael! I was one of his number-one fans.

"Did you ever meet Michael Jackson?" Renée asked T'chaka.

"No, not yet, but I always meet celebrities. That's nothing. I'm the celebrity around here, now you gonna be the celebrity's wife?" T'chaka joked, grabbing Renée by her waist.

Renée laughed and chuckled in awe. She clearly wasn't mad at T'chaka any more.

We went to McDonald's and ordered our food and sat down and ate inside.

"Y'all, I'm ready to go. I want to spend this money my boyfriend gave me," I said proudly.

"Your boyfriend?" the boys both questioned, bewildered. It was clear I was the black sheep of the group.

"Yeah, that's right. I got a boyfriend too, and he gave me a whole hundred dollars to spend," I said as I whipped out my hundred dollar bill.

"Get out of here! You moving up in the world, Jamila. What you gonna buy?" T'chaka said as he grabbed the money out of my hand to inspect it.

"I don't know, but let's go find out," I said.

We left McDonald's on Jamaica Avenue and hit up the stores. We had already gone in a few stores, but I didn't find anything I liked.

"You want to go to the Coliseum Mall?" T'chaka asked me.

"What's that?"

"It's the new indoor mall on the other side of Jamaica Avenue. They got a lot of fly stuff in there."

"Wow, how far is it? Do you think we'll be back in time? It's already 1 o'clock!"

"Yeah, I got you. Come on."

We walked up Jamaica Avenue to the little brick street in the middle of the avenue and walked down the stone road until we approached this big building that wrapped around the block.

In big black letters I read, The Coliseum Mall. "This is it!"

"Yeah, come on," T'chaka said, and we entered the large building. There were a whole bunch of flea market booths set up side-by-side. The music inside was bumping hip-hop music, and we were drawn to this store that had graffiti shirts in the window. The store was called "Shirt Kings."

"Oh, oh, look, T'chaka," I said. "Look at these shirts!" They had the faces of people drawn on them. Some of the people were famous rappers.

"Yo, these are hot," T'chaka said as we flipped through a book of artwork.

"I want one of these. Mister, how much do they cost?" I said as the teenage boy that was spray painting a shirt looked up at me.

"They start at thirty-five dollars, and you got to buy your own sweatshirt," the man responded, reluctantly. "What y'all kids doing by yourselves? Go home and tell your parents to bring you back so you can buy one," he laughed. T'chaka rolled up on him, and I had his back.

"We got our own money, buddy, and I want to buy a shirt," T'chaka said as he took out a nice amount of money from his back pocket.

"Oh, and . . . um, sir, I want one, too." I took out my crisp one hundred dollar bill to show him we meant business. The man glanced at our money and said, "Yo, Nike, check out little man and his crew. These kids got money." The man he called Nike came from the back and took me and T'chaka inside his studio.

"What kind of pictures y'all want on your shirts?" Nike asked.

"I want my face on my shirt with my arms crossed. And on the bottom I want it to say, 'Paid In Full,'" T'chaka said.

"Okay, little man. Let me take a picture of you and pick out your colors," Nike said. "Shorty, what you want on yours?" Nike asked me.

"I don't know, sir," I said, puzzled. He looked at the one hundred dollar bill I had out and he said, "What does that say?"

I handed him the bill. "Go shopping for me until I get to New York. Love you, Dino."

"Who's Dino?" Nike questioned me after reading the message written on the bill.

"My boyfriend," I responded.

"Yo, Kasheem, Shorty is off the hook. You got a boyfriend?"

"Yeah."

"And how old are you?"

"I'm ten years old."

"Ten years old?"

"Yup," I said in a feisty tone.

"And how old is your boyfriend?"

"He's twelve."

"Twelve years old and he's giving you a hundred dollars to go shopping?" he said as he laughed and shook his head. "And where he live at? He says, till he gets to New York on the money."

"Oh, he's from Kinston, North Carolina, and he makes like four hundred dollars a day. He's gettin' money out there," I bragged.

"Yo, Kasheem, I told you them country dudes is getting money down South. Even the kids! We got to go down South, kid," he said to his partner, Kasheem.

"Okay, Shorty, what about I make you a female Dino with shopping bags in her hand?"

"What you mean? You don't even know what he looks like."

"No, Shorty. I'ma make the Dino character from the Flintstones, but I'ma make her a girl with door-knocker earrings, a Gucci bag, and jewelry on, with a whole bunch of shopping bags in her hands."

"Yeah, that sounds hot," I said as I pictured it in my mind.

"On the back I'm gonna write, 'Dino's Girl' in script."

"Oh, yeah, I'll like that a lot," I responded envisioning my shirt.

"I'm going to need a deposit and y'all can pick up your shirts in two weeks."

"How much you gonna charge us?" T'chaka asked.

"All right, since it's both of y'all, I'll charge you both forty dollars, and I'll supply the shirts."

"Cool," we both said. I gave Nike twenty dollars and so did T'chaka. I had eighty dollars left, and I still wanted to shop.

We went to a couple more booths. Then we approached the leather shop. They had some hot jackets in the store. I tried on several, and so did T'chaka.

The rest of the crew was downstairs playing in the arcade. T'chaka was caught up in to fashion just like me. He picked out a black Troop leather jacket, with Troop spelled out in red letters. I picked up a suede and black unisex letter jacket.

"Sir, how much you want for both of these coats? Give us a deal," T'chaka said.

The Arab man looked at us bewildered. We looked too young to shop on our own, but he said, "Give me seventy-five dollars apiece."

T'chaka pulled me to the side. "That's a good deal. I tried this coat on in a store in the mall, and they wanted one hundred fifty dollars for it. Let's get them."

I moved on impulse, not even thinking about the twenty dollars I needed to keep to pick up my Shirt King's shirt. "Okay, cool," I said as I took out my money, and he took out his. We paid the man and grabbed our bags.

I felt so good. I bought my own stuff with my own money! When we got back to the dance studio, I folded my new leather coat and hid it in my ballet bag. I knew I couldn't go home wearing this coat. My mother would kill me! This had to stay my little secret!

*G*rowing up, there was a few key people who captivated my attention. Being young, I was vulnerable to the influences of others. I wanted to be famous, and I wanted to be cool, so I followed all those who I felt possessed those two attributes.

I was sitting on the couch in the den watching television next to my brother. The show *227* was on, and we both were glued to the television.

"Kee and Jamie, my friend got tickets to see *Dream Girls,* and I really want to go so—" before my mother could finish, I interrupted her.

"Oh, oh, I want to go!" I said excited.

"Baby, I only got two tickets. This was a last-minute thing. My friend from work and I are going to go. You guys are going to go next door to Tanya's house. I'm gonna pay her, and she'll watch you guys tonight."

"Oh, man," my brother huffed and puffed.

"Mommy, I want to go with you," I whined.

"Well, you can't. I never get to do anything. I always got you kids with me. Now let Mommy enjoy her night."

"Okay," I said reluctantly, and my brother and I got our things ready to go next door.

We gathered our belongings and left and went to Tanya's. I walked up the brick steps to my neighbor's porch and rang the bell. Mrs. Verdi, my babysitter's mom, opened the door. "Hello, babies. How y'all doing?" she said welcoming us into her home.

"We're fine, thank you," we both replied.

"Tanya, Tanya," she called out as we entered the home that smelled like fresh Caribbean food.

Tanya opened her room door that was blasting with music. El DeBarge was playing on her radio.

"Oh, y'all can come in here," she said taking no real interest in us. Tanya clearly only babysat us to get extra money.

"Y'all want to watch some television?" she asked, and my brother quickly grabbed the remote.

Chapter Eleven

"Oh, shoot, they got cable," my brother said.

At that time very few people had cable. He flipped away on the television remote, and Tanya got on the phone.

"What's up, Simone, girl? How are you doing? . . . Yeah, I'm babysitting these little bad-behind kids from next door. Anyway, what's up with Todd? He gonna pick you up from school tomorrow? . . . Yeah, Curt coming to get me.

"Did you see them girls' faces when he pulled his Cherokee Jeep up in front of the school? . . . Yeah, that's right, we them fly chicks that got boyfriends with money. . . . Yo, when is Todd going back on the road?

"Girl, I saw his video. He is hot, girl. You got you a little superstar on your hand. I bet he gonna be buying you all types of stuff, girl. You hit the jackpot with this one . . . I told Curt I want them new Bamboo earrings. He said he's gonna get them for me so we gonna see."

I took in the entire call. Tanya was a fly chick. She was light-skinned with hazel eyes, and she dressed real nice. She had all the latest fashions. She had a whole bunch of jewelry, and she was only in high school. I really looked up to Tanya, but she paid me no attention. My brother and I were brats in her eyes.

"Tanya, the door," Ms. Verdi yelled.

"Okay, Mom, I'm coming," she shouted. "Simone, I'ma call you back. That's probably Curt," she said through the phone before she hung up.

"Jamie and Kee, I'll be right back," Tanya said, and she left her room, closing the door behind her.

I was so curious. I wanted to see who was at the door. Maybe it was her boyfriend Curt. Kee was busy watching television, so I slipped out of the room to see who was at the door.

I looked through the window and saw a white Cherokee Jeep parked outside and a tall, slender boy walk up to the door. He had on a big rope chain, a Kangol hat, and a two-finger ring like I saw the boys with in those rap music videos on television. My eyes lit up as I watched the scene.

"Hi, baby," the boy said, and he kissed Tanya on the lips.

"Hi, Curt," Tanya replied.

"I missed you, baby," Curt responded.

"I miss you too," Tanya replied.

"I got something for you."

"For real, baby?" Tanya said eagerly.

"Yeah, here." He handed her a small box. She anxiously opened it and pulled out these big door-knocker earrings, just like the girls in the music videos.

"Oh, Curt, thank you. Thank you *so* much," she said as she hugged him.

"Tell Simone, I ain't LL Cool J or nothing, but Curt get LL money." Tanya's best friend, Simone, was dating the famous rapper, LL Cool J. Today she is his wife.

Tanya laughed. "I'm babysitting the two kids next door, but I'ma call you as soon as I'm done, baby."

"Okay," he said and kissed Tanya good-bye. That was my cue to run back to the room.

Tanya came back in the house smiling from ear-to-ear. She put the big door-knocker earrings on, and she modeled back and forth in the mirror.

"Those are pretty," I commented.

"Yeah, I know," she responded sarcastically.

"Can I see them?" I asked.

"You see?" she said as she put them in my face but didn't let me touch them.

Man, these earrings were fly, and I wanted a pair. *Tanya has Curt like Monique has my cousin Donnell. These girls are living the life! Why couldn't Dino live in New York?* I thought to myself. Tanya quickly grabbed the phone, ignoring my brother and me.

"Simone, guess what, girl? . . . Yeah, it was Curt. He bought me them earrings I've been asking for. Yeah, girl, they are funky fresh! . . . Yeah, I think I might love him. Jerome trying to holla too, but he ain't got no Curt money! . . . Oh, by the way, Curt told me to tell you he getting more money than your boyfriend LL Cool J. . . . Yeah, girl, he was showing off. Make sure you tell LL what he said. He'll probably buy you something bigger to get back at Curt. Then, I'll go to Curt and get him to buy me something else. We gonna rock these dudes for all they got, girl! They really be thinking they doing something."

Tanya and her friends were pretty, and they had game. They were in the pockets of all the hottest dudes in the neighborhood. I couldn't wait to grow up and get a whole selection of get-money dudes of my own. *I'm going to show these chicks how to do it for real. I can't wait till I grow up!*

My cousin Donnell and me, at age ten, posing on the couch.

A few weeks had passed since I left my deposit on my shirt at Shirt Kings. I was up bright and early, ready to go to school. My mother had me tested and transferred to this gifted program at P.S. 26 in Fresh Meadows, Queens. I had to be up early to catch the bus that transported me to school.

I got dressed and washed my face and brushed my teeth. I had less than two days to come up with the twenty dollar balance I needed to pick up my Shirt King's shirt. I couldn't ask my mom for the money because I put the words "Dino's Girl" on the back of the shirt. Besides, she was gonna ask where I got the twenty dollar deposit from. *Oh, what am I gonna do? I got five dollars left, and my allowance is only ten dollars, so either which way, I'm gonna be short. Plus, I still need to buy stuff,* I thought to myself as I brushed my teeth.

I got the leather and suede coat out of my dance school bag and stuffed it in the bottom of my school bag. Then I grabbed a muffin and some juice and got ready to run out of the house.

"Bye, Mom and Dad. I'm going to the bus stop."

"Have a good day at school, baby," my mom replied.

"Bye, baby," my dad chimed in.

I raced out of the house, and when I got to the end of the block, I took my new coat out of my backpack and put it on. Then I walked two more blocks to the bus stop and waited patiently for it.

When I saw the bus approaching, I picked up my book bag and tossed it on my back. I got on the bus and spotted my friend Yolanda.

"Hey, girl," I said.

"Good morning, Jamila. That coat is fresh to death," Yolanda commented, checking out my new leather jacket.

"Thank you, girl. My boyfriend bought it for me," I replied proudly.

"Your boyfriend?" Yolanda questioned in disbelief.

"Yeah, girl, I met him down South. His name is Dino."

"Dino?"

"Yeah, girl, my boyfriend gets money, girl. He makes four hundred dollars a day."

"Ain't no little boys making no money like that. Stop lying."

Chapter Twelve

"Girl, for real. They be at this store hustling drugs, and they get money, girl! Big money."

"Wow, I want to go down there!" Yolanda interjected, finally believing my story.

As we wrapped up our conversation, we approached the school. We got off the bus and ran across the street to the candy store.

"Jamila, can you buy me some candy?" Yolanda asked.

"Yolanda, I only got five dollars left, and I got to get up twenty dollars to pick up my shirt."

"Yeah, well, if you buy me candy today, I'll pay you back double tomorrow."

"Double?" I questioned to make sure I heard her proposition correctly.

"Yes, double," she replied.

"Okay, here, take a dollar. Give me back two tomorrow," I said.

"Okay, cool," she agreed.

At that very moment, light bulbs went off in my head. This seemed like a great idea! I could take my whole five dollars and buy candy, then I could sell it for double the cost. I quickly went through the racks in the Korean stationery store and bought all types of candy and gum. I stuffed it all into the front pocket of my knapsack.

I waited for lunchtime, then I went into my new venture full force. I sold all my candy for double the price, cash money. The kids who couldn't go out to lunch but had money didn't mind spending it with me! That day I went home with eight dollars. And, the next day, Yolanda brought me back two dollars, so I ended up with ten dollars. I was only ten dollars away from my goal.

For a little over two weeks, I re-upped up on candy every morning. I bought exactly five dollars' worth of candy, and I sold it to the kids in the school yard for double. I made a little over fifty dollars on my own, and boy, you couldn't tell me nothing! I got my Shirt King's shirt, but I also got in trouble!

The principal from my school found out about me selling candy from one of the kids who I refused to sell candy to because he didn't know how to pay back on time! I was in the hot seat, and I almost got suspended.

Even worse, my mother had to come up to the school. And, oh man, she gave me the business, honey! She put me on punishment, but it worked out because I told her I bought my leather and suede jacket with the money I got from selling candy, so she let me keep it. I didn't have to hide my coat any more, but I still couldn't show her the Shirt King shirt that I rocked with pride. In my mind, I was Dino's girl, and I was proud.

My mother was mad at me, but I overheard her brag to her friend, "My daughter is a little business lady. She done figured out how to make money, Gladys."

"Yeah, that Jamie is something else. You better keep your eyes on that one," Gladys replied.

My mother should have listened!

W hen I was growing up, Ms. Gladys Mingo was one of my mother's best friends. She was like an aunt to me. Gladys had four children, two girls and two boys. Her youngest two were Sebastian and Keisha. Keisha was six years older than me and Sebastian was like ten years older than me. My brother and I looked up to them.

Ms. Gladys owned her own beauty salon, G&G's, in our neighborhood. That stood for Gladys and God as she told me. Ms. Gladys was a nice-looking, caramel-complexioned lady in her mid-thirties . She was heavy into fashion. My mother and I would go shopping with her and her daughter, Keisha, frequently. We would spend hours together in Abraham & Strauss, Macy's, and Alexander's. We would go up and down the escalators, from department to department, and I loved every ounce of the time we spent in the store.

Ms. Gladys loved to buy shoes. We went shopping at least twice a month, and every time she went, she bought a new pair of shoes. My mother wasn't much into fashion, but Ms. Gladys would convince her to buy new clothes for herself.

"Now, Liddie, you got to take care of yourself, baby. Come on, girl, let's buy some new suits and shoes for church. You be tearing them down, girl, when you put your heels on."

My mother would smile from ear to ear. "Yeah, Gladys, you think so?"

"Of course, girl. Let's treat ourselves. We deserve it."

"You sure are right, Gladys. Let's go!"

And that was that. We'd be in the mall until the doors closed. On a few occasions, they had to turn the lights out on us, and the security guard had to come usher us out of the store!

Ms. Gladys and my mother were inseparable. My mother would often stop by her beauty parlor, and we would be in there for hours. Ms. Gladys's shop was three doors down from our church. Many of the ladies from the church would get their hair done there, so the shop stayed packed with women. I loved visiting her salon because there was always something goin' on!

* * *

Chapter Thirteen

"Hey, Ms. Gladys," I said as my mother and I walked through her shop doors one day.

"Hey, Jamie. Hey, Liddie. What brings y'all by today?" Ms. Gladys greeted us.

"Oh, Gladys, I was just checking on you, girl. Did you eat yet?" my mother asked as I proceeded to run in the back and pull out her manikin doll to roller set the doll's hair.

"No, Liddie, I didn't eat yet. I didn't have a chance. All these kids have been in and out of here all day for the Sunbeam Choir Anniversary."

"Gladys, now you know you got to eat something! I'm glad I stopped by here. Do you want some Kentucky Fried Chicken?"

"Well, Liddie, I don't want to put you out yah way."

"Girl, please, what you want?"

"I don't know. I guess you can get me some chicken, some fries, and a biscuit."

"That's it, girl?"

"Yeah, I'm not that hungry."

"Okay, I know what to do. I'm gonna feed you right, girl, or you gonna be done passed out in here." My mother was always loving, caring, and protective of her friends. In my mother's eyes, neither Ms. Gladys nor her kids could do anything wrong. My mom was loyal to a fault.

"Girl, you crazy. I'm okay," Ms. Gladys said as she worked the perm in her client's hair.

"Jamie, come on!" my mother yelled.

"No, Mommy, I want to stay and put the rollers in the doll's hair," I protested in a disgruntled voice.

"Now, Jamie, don't play with me," my mother said in a serious voice which I knew meant business.

Then Ms. Gladys interrupted her. "Liddie, it's okay. Let her stay with me."

"Ma, please let me stay, please!"

"Uh, well," my mother said to herself.

"No, Liddie, it's okay."

"All right, Gladys, I'll be right back. I'm going to pick up Kee from his drum lessons and go get your food. You better be good, Jamie," my mother demanded as she walked out the door.

"I will, Mom." I proceeded to put the rollers in the doll's hair. I liked going to the beauty parlor and playing with the manikins. Ms. Gladys would let me wash and blow-dry the doll's hair, and I enjoyed doing it!

She had three hair stations in her shop with big long mirrors on the right wall. There was five hair dryers lined up on the left side of the wall, and two big hair sinks in the back.

The women would come in the shop looking busted and disgusted, but come out shining like a superstar!

"Hey, Jamie," my friend Nicole from church said from under the dryer.

"Hey, Nicole, what you getting done to your hair?"

"Oh, I just got a Kiddy Perm and Shirley Temple curls for the anniversary. What you getting done to your hair?"

"Oh, I don't know. I guess my mother gonna do something. But you said you got a Kiddy Perm. My mother said kids don't get no perms."

"Well, I just got one. Ask Ms. Gladys." Nicole scooted back the pillows which she sat on to reach the top of the hair dryer.

"Ms. Gladys, you gave Nicole a Kiddy Perm?" I questioned, remembering how my mother protested perms for kids.

"No, baby, it's not an actual perm; it's called a Vigorol."

"A Vigorol? What's that?" I asked.

"It's like a mild process that breaks down the hair."

"Ms. Gladys, I want that for my hair. Will it make my hair look like the white girl on the Johnson & Johnson bottle? I want my hair like hers."

"Now I don't know if it's gonna do all that, but it will make it straight. Like when I press it out for you with the hot comb."

"Oh, yeah, I'd like that. I want a Vigorol. Will you put one in my hair?"

"Now, baby, I don't know. You know how your mother is. I don't know if she gonna let you get one."

"Now come on, Ms. Gladys, help me out here. You know she will listen to you. Please help me convince her. Please, pleeeease!" I said giving her my best puppy dog face.

"Okay, Jamie, I'll try, but Liddie can be tough when it comes to you."

"I know. Tell me about it." I assembled the last roller in the doll's hair. Ms. Gladys had shown me how to roll and set the hair with the white end papers and the roller pins that looked like plastic toothpicks, to hold the mesh rollers together. I had gotten pretty good at it.

"Jamie, are you nervous about singing the lead at the choir anniversary?" Nicole shouted loudly from under the dryer.

"No, girl, I'm actually excited."

"You surprised me. I didn't even know you could sing," Nicole said.

"You can sing?" Ms. Gladys interjected in a sarcastic voice.

"I sure can, and I'm singing the lead part for our anniversary song on Sunday."

"Get out of here, little girl! Ya mother ain't tell me that. Oh, you know me and Keisha are coming," Ms. Gladys said as she suddenly took interest in my hair. "Oh, you can't sing no lead looking like this."

"I know," I said as I glanced at myself looking in the mirror. I didn't like my reflection. *If only I could have hair like Renée and Michelle, or even like the girl on the Johnson & Johnson bottle,* I thought to myself.

"Here you go, Gladys," my mother said as she swung open the glass door to the shop. My brother Kee was right behind her.

"Hey, Ms. Gladys. Is C.B. here?" my brother said in an excited tone. Sebastian, Ms. Gladys' son, was nicknamed "C.B."

"Hey, Kee. Um, I think he's back there. Go on and knock on the door in the back."

Kee wasted no time, and I ran right behind him. C.B. was in his early twenties. He lived in an apartment in the back of Ms. Gladys's shop, and he had a little baby son named Sean. I loved to play with the baby.

"C.B., open up. It's me, Kee," my brother said as he knocked on the door. Kee turned around and spotted me behind him. "Yo, why you following me?"

"I ain't thinking about you, boy. I want to see the baby," I said in a feisty tone.

"Man, for real, you get on my nerves. You always want to do what I do. I wish you'd get a life," Kee said to me as C.B. opened the door.

"Hey, Kee, and look at the pretty little girl. Hey, Jamie," C.B. said in a sweet passionate voice. C.B. was a short, light brown-skinned boy who was stocky and well built. He wore his hair in a low Caesar cut. You could always see his waves spinning in his smooth, fine-textured hair.

"Hey, C.B., is Sean here?" I asked.

"Yeah, he's in the back with Yvette."

I rushed to the back to go play with the baby.

"What's up, little man?" C.B. said to Kee.

"Nothing, man. I just came from drum lessons."

"I bet you are bad with them sticks, boy."

"Yeah, I'm all right with them," my brother said proudly smiling at C.B.

"Hey, Jamie. Hey, Kee," Yvette greeted us. Yvette was the baby, Sean's, mother. She was a slender, brown-skinned girl who always rocked her hair in long extension braids. Yvette was a fly girl who wore a lot of jewelry.

"Hey, Yvette," I responded as I reached out to pick up Sean. I loved this little boy. I used to rock him in my hands for hours and feed him his bottle. He was like the little brother I never had.

C.B. was just like Donnell. He had at least twenty pairs of Adidas shell toe sneakers lined up against the wall in his bedroom. He had about ten Kangol furry caps in all the colors and four pairs of Gazelle designer eyeglasses on the dresser. C.B. had Springfield Boulevard and a portion of Hollis Avenue on lock, along with his best friend Stretch. Like my cousin Donnell, C.B. was a hustler getting major money!

"Kee, I got some sneakers for you," C.B. said.

"Yeah?" Kee questioned as his eyes opened wide.

"Yeah, here, take those five pairs of sneakers over there. I already wore them twice. You know I don't wear no sneakers more than two times."

"Oh, thank you. Those right there go with my Lee jeans!" My brother acted as if he had died and entered sneaker heaven. He was mesmerized by C.B's style and all his clothes.

"Little man, you got a girlfriend yet?"

"Well, uh, I holla at a few girls, but—" Kee said as C.B. interrupted him.

"I'm going to teach you, little man, how to get your grown man on. You growing up now. What's up with you and school?"

"Well, it's okay, but these new boys came to my school, and they be trying to fight everybody."

"What you mean?"

"They be starting mess and stuff."

"They didn't say nothing to you, right?" C.B. asked in a more serious tone.

"Well, they be talking," Kee said when C.B. interrupted again.

"Look, li'l man, we don't take no shorts! You my little cousin, and you ain't nobody's punk. Yo, put yah hands up," C.B. instructed, and he started play boxing with my brother. "Yeah, hit like this, right, left, right. You hear me, boy?"

"Yes, C.B. Like this; right, left, right," Kee said as he mimicked C.B's moves.

"Yeah, like that but harder; right, left, right, boom," C.B. said as he demonstrated the fighting moves.

"Okay, okay; right, left, right, boom, boom."

"Yeah, little man, you got it! Stand like this and hold your hands up. Always block your face. Never let no one touch your face. You hear me, boy?" C.B. said.

Kee held his hands up to block his face as he was instructed. He caught on quickly. That day C.B. taught my brother to fight. It's been on and poppin' ever since then!

"C.B.," Yvette, C.B.'s son's mother, called. Like my neighbor, Tanya, she was a fly girl who rocked a lot of jewelry.

"What, Yvette? I'm showing Kee how to fight."

"Listen, I need some money."

"Some money for what? I just gave you money," C.B. responded with an attitude.

"Look, I want to go out tonight, and I want to buy the baby some more stuff."

"Go out? You ain't going nowhere! I don't know what type of dude you think I am. You should have thought about all that before you had my baby."

"C.B., it's nothing like that! My cousin is in town from down South and I want to take her to the mall and out to eat. Sean can come with me. I saw this cute sheepskin jacket with a matching hat for babies, and I want to get it for Sean."

"Yvette, you always want something."

"Baby, I just want to make sure the baby is okay. You know he's gonna look real cute in his sheepskin jacket," Yvette said as she gently hugged on C.B.'s shoulder.

"How much you need?" C.B. said glancing over at his firstborn son with admiration.

"Um, well, the coat is like a hundred and fifty dollars, and I'm gonna need money to shop and eat so give me like five hundred dollars, and I'm cool."

"Now you bugging. I just gave you three hundred dollars on Monday. I'm not giving it to you," C.B. said as he shrugged Yvette's arm off his shoulder.

"Baby, please, come on, you know I be holding it down for you. I'm yah ride-or-die chick. Please, Daddy," she said seductively grabbing him and kissing him on the cheek. She made eye contact, and C.B. smiled.

"Okay, baby, but this is it . . . for real." C.B. opened up a cereal box and pulled out a stack of cash. My eyes popped out of my head. This was the most money I had ever seen in my life! He quickly pulled off five one hundred dollar bills and passed them to Yvette.

"Don't ask me for nothing else," he said as he passed the bills off to her.

Here we go again. Another chick rockin' her man's pockets, I thought to myself. This was too easy! I couldn't resist taking my own shot at the apple.

"C.B., can I get some money to go to the store, please," I said in a sweet voice.

"Oh, yeah, let me give you some money to get some sneakers since I gave your brother some," C.B. said as he whipped out three twenty dollar bills and handed them to me.

"Thank you, C.B.," I said with a big smile. "I'm going next door to the shop," I said as I raced to the door. I swiftly ran through the apartment and opened the tall black door which led back to the beauty salon. My mother and Ms. Gladys were munching away on KFC chicken and laughing as they gossiped.

"Mom, I'm going to the store. C.B. gave me some money," I said, anxiously waving the money in the air.

"Money?" my mother questioned. By her voice I knew she was displeased.

"Yes, Mommy, C.B. gave Keith five pairs of sneakers, and he gave me three twenty dollar bills, see?" I said as I showed her the money.

"Uh-uh, Jamie, give him back his money!" my mother demanded. "He needs his money. He's got a young baby to feed."

"No, no, Liddie, it's okay. C.B.'s working overtime with his dad on some painting jobs. That boy is so responsible, Liddie. He just showing Jamie and Kee some love."

"Well, Gladys, I . . . I . . . I don't know."

"It's okay, Liddie. Let her have it, please."

"Well, okay, I guess. Jamie, give me the money. If he said to buy some sneakers, that's what you gonna do," my mother said reluctantly.

"Oh, no, Ma, I want to go to the store first," I shouted, irritated about parting with my crisp twenty dollar bills.

"No, I got a bucket of chicken, soda, and fries. Sit down and eat," my mother said as she took a soda out of the KFC bag.

"All right," I disappointedly responded.

"Liddie, she got the choir anniversary coming up. Our little girl can sing, huh?"

"Yeah, girl. She amazed me, Gladys. You know she thinks she's a little star."

"That's our baby girl," Ms. Gladys said as she touched my hair. "Liddie, we got to do something with her hair."

"Yeah, I'll probably braid it up tomorrow."

"No, I was thinking maybe we should give her a Vigorol."

"Vigorol? What's that?"

"It's a mild process, like a perm, but it won't damage her hair."

"Now, Gladys, I don't know about no perm, girl."

"Liddie, I just did one on Nicole. It will make her hair easy to comb through and manageable. Matter of fact, Nicole should be dry," Ms. Gladys said as she went to pull up the dryer. She unwrapped the hairnet that was tied on top of Nicole's rollers and took out one of the rollers to check her hair.

"Yeah, you are dry, Nicole; come out," she said.

"Look, Liddie, see how straight her hair is with no heat on it?" Ms. Gladys exclaimed as she took Nicole's hair out of the rollers.

"It is very straight," my mother said, examining the girl's hair.

"I'm telling you, Liddie, this will work out good for Jamie."

"Mommy, please, please, Mommy, please," I begged as I pulled on her hand, still crunching down on my chicken.

"I don't know."

"Mommy, you know you and I both hate having to do my hair. This will make it easy."

"And I'll keep it up for her, Liddie," Ms. Gladys interjected.

"Well, uh . . ." my mother grumbled.

"Please, Mommy, you'll be the best, best mommy in the whole wide world. Please," I begged and kissed my mother on the cheek.

"In the whole wide world?" she responded with a grin.

"Yes, Mommy, in the whole wide world," I said with a big smile.

"Well, okay, Gladys, when you wanna do it?"

"I can do it now. I don't mind."

"Right now, Gladys?"

"Yup."

"Okay, I guess so."

"Thank you, thank you so much, Mommy. I love you," I said as I grabbed and kissed her.

That day I got my first kiddy relaxer, and guess what? My hair wasn't nappy anymore! It was long, nice, and straight. I stayed in the mirror for hours just brushing and looking at it. *They ain't gonna tease me no more. My hair is straight like the girl on the Johnson & Johnson bottle. It's not as long, but I can work on that*, I thought to myself. *Watch out, world, 'cause here I come!*

*T*he Saturday before my choir anniversary, I was up early ready to go to dance school. I washed my face and brushed my teeth. Then, I unwrapped my new hairdo from underneath my silk scarf as I watched myself in the mirror.

"You sure are beautiful," I said to myself as I stared in the mirror. I couldn't wait to show off my hair at dance school. *I know they gonna love it!*

"Mommy?" I called.

"Are you ready to go, baby?"

"Yes, Mommy, but uh . . . Mommy, can I get the money C.B. gave me and go buy sneakers, please."

"Well, Jamie, that's too much money for you to be walking around with. Somebody might try to knock you in yah head. I don't think that's a good idea."

"Listen, Mommy, I'm getting older. Remember, I got my leather and suede coat myself. Please, Mommy. T'chaka and the twins shop all the time on our lunch break. I want to shop too, please!" I begged.

"Well, I don't think so. Why don't you let me take you to Green Acres Mall?"

"They have better sneakers on the avenue. Please, Mom. It is my money, right?"

"I guess so," she said contemplating. "I'm going to give you this money, but you better be careful, okay?"

"Yes, Mom, I will. I love you so much." I hugged her, and she reached in her bag and gave me the crisp three twenty dollar bills and five extra dollars for lunch.

I was so happy. Money made me feel good. I sat back in the car on the way to the dance studio daydreaming.

"I wish I had a boyfriend with a bunch of money, like Tanya, Monique, and Yvette have. I could buy anything I wanted. Even if Dino lived in New York, I know I would be straight. Money can solve all my problems. With money, I can get whatever I want, and if I have a problem, I can pay someone to solve it for me. I can't wait till

I get older. Then I'm gonna have all the money I need," I said to myself.

I arrived at dance school early and waited for tap class to begin. As I was changing my clothes, Chudney walked in.

"Hey, Jamila," she said.

"Hey, Chudney," I responded.

"Jamila, can you help me practice the steps in the routine?"

"Yeah, of course," I replied. I quickly changed my clothes and stepped in front of the large mirror that covered the whole wall inside the dance studio.

"Okay, it's like this: step, step, kick ball chain, step, step, kick ball chain. One, two, up and down and hit, hit, hit," I said to the rhythm of the steps as I watched myself do the steps in the mirror.

"Okay, do it with me. Five, six, seven, and eight and step, step, kick ball chain and step. No, Chudney, you got to use your left arm and your right leg, like this," I instructed, demonstrating the dance move.

"Oh, man! This is so hard for me," Chudney sighed in frustration.

"Just watch me. You can do it. Head up, chin straight, and left, right, left, you see?"

"Okay, head up, chin straight, and left, right, left," Chudney repeated as she did the dance move.

"Yes, that's it, Chudney. Now let's continue. Step, spin, clap, and up and down. Step, spin, clap, and hit, hit. Let's go. Five, six, seven, and eight and one and two and three and four, five, six, seven, and eight," I said as we danced together in front of the mirror.

"Okay, okay, I'm finally getting it," Chudney sighed in relief.

"Yeah, Chudney, you are going to be okay. Just watch the feet first and learn the steps, then you can work on the arm moves."

"Okay, that makes sense. Thanks, Jamila. Y'all are so good, and I just started so it's hard."

"Don't worry. We all been dancing together since we were three years old. So don't feel bad. Take your time and remember to watch the feet first."

"Feet first; yup, I got it."

"So, Chudney, what's it like to have a famous mother?"

"Well, it's okay, I guess."

"Man, I bet you get to see a lot of stars."

"I do sometimes."

"What you mean sometimes. Aren't famous people always around your mom?"

"Yes, I guess, but my mother is on the road a lot, so I often don't get to see her."

"Oh, for real? So who picks you up from school?"

"Well, my nanny."

"Oh, yah, nanny," I said as I thought to myself, *I wish I was rich and had a nanny.*

"Tell me about your house. Do you live in one of those great big houses on the hill?"

"Well, my house is pretty big, I guess."

"What about your room? What color is it?"

"It's pink, and I have a big bed with a canopy around it."

"Oh, my cousin Kanika has one of those. Do you have a lot of toys and stuff?"

"Uh, I guess so. My mommy always brings me stuff home from her trips."

"Oh, that's cool stuff I bet," I said as I sighed and imagined, *This girl has got it made. She's rich, and she can shop as much as she wants.*

My African teacher Sheryl clapped her hands as the younger girls, who were in the Tiny Tots class, filtered into the dance room. "Girls, girls, let's go! I'm ready to begin class. Today, we are going to start getting ready for the recital. I'm ready to do placements. Today, I'm going to have the Tiny Tots and the Super Tots classes together." Sheryl was a heavyset, brown-skinned lady with long, naturally curly hair.

"The Tiny Tots will start their routine and exit the stage, and then the Super Tots will come in. This is the way we will perform in the show," Sheryl said as the room filled up with both parents and kids.

Closer to showtime dance school got real serious. Preparing for the recital was like preparing for the biggest Broadway show ever!

Each year we had our recital at Avery Fisher Hall in Lincoln Center, which was huge. All types of famous people performed on that stage. All the parents of the kids that attended the school invited all their friends and relatives. I don't know who was more excited about the show, the parents or the kids.

Tickets would go on sale for the concert in April. Tickets were purchased on a first come, first serve basis. Parents would camp out overnight in front of the dance studio's door to be in line to get the best tickets, as if the tickets were for a rock concert. Some fistfights took place on the line about whose spot was first.

All types of famous celebrities would come to our dance recitals, including our old alumni. This year, everybody knew Diana Ross would be there because her daughter would be performing.

Parents started staying to watch the classes to make sure their kids would get a spot in the front row. They wanted their kids to be spotted and seen by other family and friends. This thing was real serious, and it was all about social politics!

"Okay, Tiny Tots, line up. Drummers, are you ready?" Sheryl said as she waltzed across the floor dressed in a bodysuit with an African garb tied around her waist. She placed her right foot up on a small wooden box in the front of the classroom.

"All right, I'm ready," the lead drummer Fred said.

"All right, boys, let's go. One, two, three, ready," Fred shouted as he led the five other drummers, who had their bongo drums tied across their chests. The drummers started with a drumroll, and their hands proceeded to go back and forth, hitting the bongo drums swiftly.

"Okay, ladies, five, six, seven, and eight," Sheryl said as the Tiny Tots began their routine.

"I need to see more energy," Sheryl yelled.

The little girls who ranged in age from three to six years old began to dance their hearts out. Sheryl walked around the class arranging the three lines. She was watching the girls to see who she would pick to be in the front line.

She picked out Devon first. Devon was a little short, stubby girl whose grandmother was one of Ms. Johnson's closest friends. This little girl had her pictures throughout our yearbook. She had at least five full-page ads. Her dancing was mediocre, but her connections always landed her a front-row spot.

"Devon, you stand here," Sheryl said as she led her to the front of the line. Devon quickly moved forward with a huge grin on her face.

Sheryl strutted about and roamed the room.

"Lift them legs up and arch them backs. I need more energy, ladies. Give me more," she yelled as she picked out Ashante next. Today, Ashante is a renowned R&B singer. Back then, she was a star in training.

Ashante's mother Tina was a part of the "Who's Who Club" in the dance school. Ms. Tina was very pretty. All the men in the dance school were on her. She had café-au-lait skin with beautiful Indian-textured curly hair that reached the middle of her back. Ms. Tina was a part of the adult dance classes. She stood on the sidelines of the class and winked at Sheryl as her child was picked.

The tryouts were clearly biased. The socialites' kids were always put in the front first, followed by the pretty light-skinned girls with long hair. Then whoever was left that danced the best. It was clear discrimination.

Sheryl finished picking the Tiny Tots spots, then it was my class's turn. "Let's hit it, Super Tots, five, six, seven, and eight," Sheryl prompted us as our drumroll came on. We all danced our best, hoping to gain a good spot in the front line.

I really got into it. I pictured myself on the stage at Lincoln Center with all eyes on me. I arched my back and pumped my arms as I performed as if I were a tribal dancer in Africa, but Sheryl paid me no mind.

"Chudney, come to the front," Sheryl said. Chudney smiled and made her way to the front line.

"Lift your legs higher. I need more energy," Sheryl shouted roaming the room, picking out her favorites. Renée and Michelle both got picked for front-row spots too, and so did the other socialites' children.

What kind of crap is this? I thought to myself. *I clearly dance better than all of these girls, yet she hasn't paid me one bit of attention. Okay, I'm gonna show this woman,* I said to myself as I gave it all I got. I danced my heart out and even caught the eyes of the drummers who started doing special drumrolls inspired by the energy I exerted.

"Oh, Jamila, you stand here," Sheryl said in a nonchalant voice as she stuck me in the second row. *Wow,* I thought to myself. *This is so unfair!*

We finished up the class, and it was time for lunch. I wasn't even excited about spending my sixty dollars that C.B. gave me. All I could think about was I had been cheated out of the spot I deserved. If I was light skinned and had long hair, or my mother was a dance school socialite, I would have made the cut. I was very disappointed.

"Hey, Jamila, you all right?" Chudney questioned.

"Yeah, I'm okay," I said in a I-don't-want-to-be-bothered tone.

"I made the front of the line."

"I see. That's nice," I said as I quickly gathered my belongings.

"Thanks for teaching me the steps," Chudney smiled.

"Yeah, okay," I responded. I took my clothes out of my ballet bag and began to put them on over my dance clothes.

"What's up, Jamila?" T'chaka asked as he approached me.

"Hey, Chaka," I said with a slight attitude.

"You want to come with me to the Coliseum? My grandmother gave me money. I want to go buy a chain."

"Oh, um, yeah. I got some money too! I want to go get some sneakers," I replied, feeling a little better about going shopping.

As we were talking, Michelle and Renée came over. They had stayed behind in the class as Sheryl showed them off to the parents.

"You see how cute they are, and they're identical twins. This one is the oldest, and she's the youngest," Sheryl would brag.

"Y'all going to McDonald's?" Renée asked us.

"No, we only got an hour today for lunch. We going to the Coliseum to go shopping. Y'all coming?" T'chaka asked.

"Shoot, I want to go to McDonald's," Renée pouted.

"Well, I'm going to buy my chain, so I'll see you when we get back," T'chaka said firmly. "You ready, Jamila?" he asked.

"Yeah, let's go," I said as I looked at Renée and Michelle and slid them both a smirk.

T'chaka and I headed down Merrick Boulevard, which was the street the dance school was on, and made a left onto Jamaica Avenue. Saturdays were a busy day on the avenue. The little stores in the downtown area were jam-packed with people. Nobody paid full price for anything. Everyone always negotiated a deal. I quickly learned how to talk the salesmen down too!

We passed the busy bus terminal. Almost every bus in Queens stopped at the Jamaica terminal. It was the central station in Queens. People flooded the streets with shopping bags.

I enjoyed watching the busy traffic. We approached the Coliseum Mall, and I could hear the music blasting as we opened the doors.

"My Adidas," by Run-D.M.C., was on the sound system. I began to bop my head as I walked in.

"You like this song?"

"Yeah, T'chaka, this is my joint," I replied as I began to do the whop dance.

"What you know about Run-D.M.C.?" he asked.

"I know a lot. First off, they from Hollis, Queens. That's my neck of the woods, and they talking about shell toe Adidas. My cousin C.B. got like twenty pairs in every color."

"For real? I got to get me a few pairs of those."

"Yeah! Well, C.B. gave my brother five pairs."

"Word? What's up with Kee?"

"I guess he chillin'."

"I don't see him come pick you up with your moms anymore."

"Well, he's all into watching videos all day and playing the drums."

"Oh, a'ight. Tell him I said what's up," T'chaka said as we walked down the Coliseum steps.

The Coliseum was filled with teenagers dressed in the latest hip-hop fashions. They had on gold teeth, leather jackets, Kangol caps, and Gazelles.

We got down to the end of the stairs and all you saw were clear glass booths surrounding the floor, filled with gold jewelry. There were at least forty booths packed up right next to each other with rope chains, door-knocker earrings, three-finger rings, and tons of bracelets. It felt amazing looking at all the jewelry.

"Come on, Jamila, we going over here to my man Benny's shop," T'chaka said as he grabbed my shoulder to follow him to the left.

"Hey, Benny," T'chaka greeted the store owner as we walked over to a large glass booth.

"Hey, Li'l Guy," Benny responded with a smile. Benny was a young Jewish jeweler in his late twenties. He was sort of stocky with black hair.

"What you looking for, Li'l Guy?"

"I want a rope chain, Benny."

"Okay, come over here and look at these," he said as he showed T'chaka the gold chains. While T'chaka was looking at the chains, I noticed the big door-knocker earrings Tanya had got from her boyfriend.

"Oh, oh, Benny, how much are these right here?" I asked pointing to the earrings in the showcase.

"Oh, those are two hundred twenty dollars, but they are too big for you. Come over and look at these right here," he said, and he pulled out some smaller door-knocker earrings, which were the same exact style.

"Oh, yeah, I like these."

"Come on. Try them on," Benny instructed passing me the big portable mirror to see myself in.

I tried on the first pair, and I liked them.

"How much are these, Benny?" I asked.

"For you, pretty girl, a hundred ten dollars."

"Oh, I don't have that much."

"Okay, look at these." He pointed at a smaller pair. "These are seventy-five dollars. Try them on," Benny said as he handed the smaller earrings to me. I put the earrings on and stared at myself in the mirror. *I look fresh to death, just like them girls I see in the music videos*, I thought to myself.

Then T'chaka approached me. "Jamila, those look hot on you. You look like one of them girls in the video."

"For real," I said and grinned at myself in the mirror.

"T'chaka, I only got sixty dollars. He wants seventy-five dollars for these," I whispered in his ear.

"Benny, let's make a deal. How much you gonna give me for the earrings and this chain right here?" T'chaka said as he pointed to a medium-sized rope chain that had a medallion in the shape of the letter "T."

"Okay, T'chaka, give me a hundred fifty dollars for the chain and seventy dollars for the earrings. That's only because it's you, Li'l Guy."

"No, Benny, I ain't got that much."

"What you got, Li'l Guy?"

"I got like a hundred seventy dollars."

"A hundred seventy for both? No, that's too low," Benny said in disgust.

"All right, Benny, we got to take our business elsewhere," T'chaka said as he grabbed my hand to leave.

"T'chaka, what you doing? I really want the earrings," I whispered low to him and hit his side.

"Trust me, watch this," T'chaka said, and he began to walk out of the store.

"Okay, okay, Li'l Guy. A hundred and eighty for everything right now," Benny said as we were walking away from the booth.

"No, a hundred and seventy-five," T'chaka yelled back.

"Man, you killing me," Benny said.

"Take it or leave it. I got the cash right here," T'chaka said as he pulled out his money.

"Oh, come on. Today is your lucky day," Benny yelled.

T'chaka took out a hundred fifteen dollars and I gave him my sixty dollars. Benny boxed the jewelry for us in two separate gold boxes.

"Benny, put them in different bags," T'chaka instructed.

"Okay, Li'l Guy," Benny responded. I grabbed my bag, and T'chaka grabbed his. We walked out from the jewelry booth and went over to the sneaker booth. The store had over a hundred different pairs of sneakers on display.

"Jamila, you like these?" T'chaka asked as he pointed out some white shell toe Adidas with a back stripe on them.

"Yeah, those are hot. They just like my cousin C.B.'s," I said. I started looking around the booth at the girl sneakers. I saw some all-gray Reebok, low-cut classics.

"How much are these, sir?" I asked the salesman.

"Give me thirty-five dollars," he said.

"How much you want for the both of these?" T'chaka questioned as he held up the shell toe Adidas.

"You know what? Give me seventy-five and you can take both," the salesman replied.

"Jamila, how much money you got left?"

"T'chaka, I only got five dollars left to eat, and I'm going to be in trouble. My cousin gave me money to buy sneakers, and I bought earrings instead. My mother is gonna kill me!"

"Okay, let's make a deal. Let me rock your leather and suede jacket, and I'ma buy you the sneakers."

"Okay, but what I'm supposed to wear?"

"I'ma let you wear my Troop jacket, and we can switch back next week. Your jacket goes hard with my new shell top Adidas."

"Okay, cool, you got a deal," I said as we interlocked pinkies to finalize our deal.

"Here, sir," T'chaka said, and he peeled off three twenties and a ten and gave it to the sales rep.

"This is seventy dollars, little boy."

"Yeah, that's all I got. I'ma come back next week and buy something else," T'chaka said to the salesman.

"Oh, all right, kid," the man said as he rang up the sneakers. He took the money and bagged the sneakers in two white bags that said I Love New York in black letters with a red heart on the bag. We grabbed our items and walked out of the store.

"Come on, let's get some hot dogs from the food court and hurry back to class. You know we can't be late," T'chaka said as he led me to the food court.

"Don't tell nobody about our deal," he said firmly.

"No, I'm cool. I got you." I took off my leather and suede coat. "Here," I passed him the coat.

He took off his Troop jacket and passed it to me, and I put it on. I also put on my brand-new door-knocker earrings. You couldn't tell me nothing. In my mind I was the joint. A fresh perm, fresh door-knocker earrings, a Troop leather jacket, and new Reeboks. I couldn't wait to go to school and show off my new wardrobe! I was only ten years old, but I was headed down an adult path. I was given a little room, and I was ready to score!

We ate and went back to the studio. As we entered the door, Renée and Michelle stared me down. If looks could kill, I would be dead!

"What took y'all so long?" Renée asked as we came through the door.

"Nothing, babe, we just went shopping at the store. Let me put my bags upstairs. I'll be right back," T'chaka said as he left me with the twins.

"Where you be getting all this money from?" Michelle questioned me.

"Not ya imaginary boyfriend, Dino?" Renée interjected.

"What?" I said with an attitude. "What, you mad 'cause I get money, girl?" I said as I sucked my teeth.

"No, you mad 'cause you ugly," Renée quickly responded back.

"You wish, girl! I'm cute, sexy, and I'm fly!" I said in a sassy voice as I snapped my fingers and held my hand on my hips.

"What you doing with T'chaka's jacket on?" Renée asked as she took notice of my jacket.

"We switched and what?" I snapped back.

"You just feeling yourself 'cause you got your nappy hair pressed," Renée snapped back.

"For your information, this is a perm so my hair won't be nappy anymore. It's straight now. So, boom. . ." I said as I threw my hands up like I was stopping traffic.

The twins both rolled their eyes and walked away. I felt good, and I looked good, all courtesy of my new friend: money! I knew as long as I had it I could buy whatever I wanted, including respect.

I t was on a beautiful Sunday in May, the day of the Sunbeam Choir Anniversary. I was up early, pacing back and forth in front of the mirror, practicing my solo for the program.

"Makes no difference what the problems . . . Church, I have this blessed assurance . . . I can call Him, when I need Him. Our Father up in heaven. I can go to God in prayer. I can go to the Lord in prayer," I passionately sang as I watched myself in the mirror.

"Jamie, are you nervous?" my mother interrupted me and asked.

"No, Mommy, not at all. I can handle this," I said confidently as I continued with my song. *"He can work it out, He can work it out."* As I sang passionately, I was interrupted by my brother this time.

"Shut up, you can't sing. You gonna make a fool of yourself," he taunted.

"You shut up, Kee, and leave your little sister alone," my mother scolded.

"He just mad 'cause he's stupid and can't do nothing," I taunted back at him.

"That's why you ugly and flat-chested," Kee retorted.

"I guess I would be—to a stupid, ignorant boy like you. Dummy!" I shouted back.

"Cut it out. You two are the worst. I can't take this mess early in the morning. Why must I have two kids who just can't get along?" my mom yelled furiously at us.

"Um, I can't stand you, you big-eyed ole dumb-looking fool," I said as I left the living room and stomped upstairs into the bathroom and shut the door. I sat on the toilet and began to cry. My brother's words cut through me like a knife. I got up and looked in the mirror.

Maybe I am ugly, and maybe I can't sing, I thought to myself as I wiped away my tears.

Then I began to pray. "God, please help me. I don't want to make a fool of myself today. Please allow me to sing well like Sister George. And, Lord, if You are listening, I don't want to be ugly and flat-chested. I want to be pretty, Lord. I know you can do anything,

Chapter Fifteen

so please make me beautiful, God. I want to be like them little kids on the TV, God. I want to be happy, successful, and rich. You said I can have whatever I ask You for, like Reverend Mixon said. Lord, I want to be rich and pretty and on television. Amen," I prayed aloud.

"Jamie, let me curl your hair, baby," my mother said, knocking on the door of the bathroom.

"Okay, Mommy," I said as I opened the door and dried my eyes.

"Mommy, do you think I'm ugly?"

"No, baby. Jamie, you are very pretty. Look at them dimples and look at that incredible smile," she said as she made me smile. "What would make you ask me that?"

"Well, Kee says I'm ugly, and Renée and Michelle too. I didn't make it in the front row at the dance school 'cause all the pretty, light-skinned girls with the long hair get to be in the front," I said as my mother interrupted me.

"What did you say?"

"Well, Kee says I'm ugly," I said, and she interrupted me again.

"No, no, I ain't talking about what Kee said. He is just joking with you. What happened at dance school?" she asked in a very disappointed tone.

"Oh, well, in African class, I didn't make the front line cause Chudney, Diana Ross's daughter, the twins, and the other light-skinned girls are in the front. I'm mad 'cause they don't dance better than me. Mommy, you know how I like African dance. They always be showing favoritism."

"Okay, well, I will deal with that on Saturday. But you don't worry, baby, Mommy ain't gonna let nobody shortchange her baby, and you can take that to the bank," she said as she began to curl my hair with the curling iron. "Baby, you can be whatever you want to be in this world. You are very smart and very talented. You are also pretty, baby. You are my little star."

"I'm your little star for real, Mommy?"

"Yes, baby," she said as she kissed my cheek. "Now you gonna knock 'em dead today at this anniversary, and you gonna do the same at the recital. You hear me, girl?" she asked as she stared in my big brown eyes.

"Yes, Mom," I responded.

"Always remember, baby, you are my little star."

"That's right, Mommy. I'm your little star!"

My mother gave me all the encouragement I needed that day. I knew she had my back, and I wanted nothing more than to make her proud. For goodness' sake, I was her little star!

* * *

We were all packed together in the small basement of Maranatha Baptist Church in Queens Village, New York. About fifty children were pacing around and four chaperones, including my mom. All the kids were putting on their maroon and cream-colored choir robes that touched the floor. We were all eagerly anticipating our grand entrance march for our choir anniversary.

"Quiet down, kids, let's get ready to pray. Hold hands and gather in a circle. Hurry up," Marvetta said as we quickly assembled into a circle. "Bow your heads and close your eyes.

"Father God, we thank You for another day to say thank You. Lord, we are assembled here ready to give Your name the praise, honor, and glory that You deserve.

"Lord, we ask that You bless our anniversary and that You allow Your Spirit to rest within each child in this building. Touch them, Lord, and allow them to perform for Your glory. We invite Your Spirit in now to take over. Show up, Lord, and show out! We give You all the praise, honor, and glory in Jesus' mighty name we pray. Amen," Marvetta prayed passionately.

"Amen," we all said in unison.

"Okay, listen up. I'm handing each of you a small flashlight. They are all different colors. Take the color I give you, and that's it," Marvetta said as she passed us the small pocket-size multicolor flashlights. We got our flashlights and lined up at the end of the steps, waiting to march into the church sanctuary.

"Good luck, guys," Marvetta said, and she left to go up to the pulpit. We made a double line, girls on the left and boys on the right. Then we headed up the narrow church basement stairs. As we climbed to the top of the stairs, we heard Marvetta say, "Now, here are the girls and boys of the hour. Now presenting . . . the Sunbeam Choir!"

The music began to play as the lights in the church sanctuary dimmed. *"This little light of mine. Oh, oh, oh. I'm gonna let it shine. Oh, this little light of mine. Oh, oh, oh. I'm gonna let it shine. This little light of mine. I'm gonna let it shine. Let it shine, let it shine. Let it shine,"* we sang passionately as we marched in the middle-size church flashing our flashlights from side to side.

The building was packed, row to row. People were even standing up in the back. Every other person had cameras out snapping pictures.

I quickly spotted Ms. Gladys and Keisha in the crowd waving as we approached the bridge of the song. *"This little light of mine, I'm gonna let it shine. This little light of mine. I'm gonna let it shine. This little light of mine. I'm gonna let it shine,"* we sang as we pointed the lights at the audience like Marvetta instructed us.

"Yeah, go, babies!" the voices in the crowd yelled. The energy in the building was off the hook, and I loved every moment of it! We finished marching in and assembled in the choir stand.

"I'm gonna let it shine," we sang as we slowly ended the song. We waited for Marvetta to give us the cue to sit down, then we sat down in unison.

"Good afternoon, church," Pastor Mixon said as he approached the pulpit.

"Good afternoon, Pastor," the congregation responded.

Reverend Mixon was a heavyset, light-skinned man who wore glasses and had a bald spot in the middle of his head.

"Is anybody glad to be in the house of the Lord?" he questioned.

"Amen. Yeah," the crowd responded.

"Uh-uh, I said, is anybody glad to be in the house of the Lord today?"

"Yeah, amen!!!" the crowd roared in a louder manner.

"I don't know about you, but I came to praise the Lord. Has anybody come to praise the Lord today?" he spoke louder to gain a better response.

"Yeah. Yeah. Amen," the crowd roared.

"He woke me up this morning and guided me on my way, and I'm happy that He did. Ain't ya glad today, church?"

"Yeaahhh."

"He didn't have to do it, but He did it anyhow! We got our beautiful children here today. Don't they look good?"

"Yeaahhh. Amen."

"Kids, stand up and show off your beautiful robes," he said as we stood up and the crowd applauded.

"It's important that we support our kids, church. Our children are our future. Let's take care of them, church. Is that all right?" Reverend Mixon said, as he waltzed across the pulpit. His long black robe dragged along the floor as he walked.

"Yeahh. Amen," the crowd roared.

"I said is that all right?"

"Yeah, Pastor, yeah, yeaahh, yeahh, yes, Lord."

"I feel like shouting today. Does anybody feel like me?"

"Yes, Pastor!"

"I said I feeel . . ." Pastor Mixon said as he dropped his voice . . . "like shouting. Does anybody feeeel like me?"

"Go on, Pastor."

"Yeaah, yeeeeaah," Pastor Mixon screeched as the church drums and organ started playing up-tempo shout music. The service hadn't even begun good, and the people were shouting already.

The first lady jumped out of her seat and ran to the front of the church and started doing her two-step dance. Even in the choir stand, the kids started clapping and stomping their feet loudly, and some of the older kids started catching the Holy Ghost.

Marvetta ran out in front of the choir stand as the shout music played. She led us in the song we sang when the Spirit of God came in the building.

"Fire, fire. Fire, fire. The Holy Ghost fire gonna set my soul on fire. On fire," we sang passionately and clapped our hands fast to the beat, and then the Holy Ghost hit.

Young and old were running around and dancing in the church.

Oh, Reverend Mixon knew just how to get this party started. From the top of the anniversary we had action. Even the grandmothers with their wide hats on their head and their long dresses were doing their two-step shout! The whole church was on fire for God!

It was intermission during the anniversary, and all our guests were downstairs eating cake and drinking punch. In my stomach I got butterflies. I was up next, right after the grand march, which was a Baptist church tradition. At anniversaries, the choir would march up to the pulpit doing special steps and dance moves.

My heart intensely started pounding. My friend Kim came up to me. She was an older girl whose brother was C.B.'s partner in the streets.

"Hey, Jamie, are you okay?"

"Yes, Kim, I am a little nervous."

"Don't worry, girl, you gonna do good. Look at your hair; it's so pretty."

"Thank you. I got a kiddy perm."

"I see. I like it, Jamie! Don't worry, you gonna rock the house, watch," Kim said with a friendly smile as she patted me on my back. Her words were comforting.

It was time to do our grand march. We had a whole routine prepared as we marched in the building and did something similar to the electric slide. The church was in an uproar! Everyone was clapping and taking pictures. We did that march, baby! You couldn't tell us nothing. From the older kids to the small ones, we turned it out!

"Now it's time for our choir selection being led by Sister Jamila Davis," the MC for the night announced.

We waited for Marvetta to give us the cue, then we stood in unison, and I came down from the pulpit and grabbed the microphone. The music began to play as I stared into the crowd. Every seat in the church was full. All eyes were on me.

I could hear in my mind my mother say, "Jamie, you're my little star."

I glanced over at my mother, and she smiled at me. That was all I needed!

"Makes no difference what the problem," I sang passionately.

"I can go to God in prayer," the choir sang, backing me up.

"Church, I have this blessed assurance," I sang as I took the microphone off the stand and walked closer to the crowd. The crowd began to cheer me on.

"Go ahead, Jamie!"

"I can call Him when I need Him. Our Father up in heaven. I can go to God in prayer. I can go to the Lord in prayer."

As I sang, I imagined myself being Sister George. This vision gave me confidence. I took command over the song and made it my own. Ms. Gladys got up and said, "You better go, girl," and the crowd backed her. At that moment I lost it. Something jumped in my spirit and took ahold of me.

"He can work it out!!! He can work it ouutttt. I know without a doubt!!! My God can work itttt outt!!!" I sang loudly in a peculiar tone.

"He put food on my table. My God, He is able. He's all right. He's all right. He alllllll right. He's all right," I sang as the audience joined in my passion.

The whole crowd was in an uproar! I was walking back and forth in front of the pulpit delivering this message that was deep inside me to the people. Even after I sang, they shouted for at least another twenty minutes.

Pastor Mixon yelled, "Encore, Jamie, come on back down here," and we sang again.

That moment was incredible! I discovered I had a unique ability to reach my audience through my spirit—I could rock the crowd! Everybody talked about that anniversary for months. Even the ones who didn't remember my name talked about the little girl with the grown woman's voice. Overnight, I became a hot topic in the church. *I can really sing!*

I woke up early Monday morning, ready to go to school. I was floating around on clouds, thinking about last night's anniversary. "Man, I really can sing," I said to myself as I stared in the bathroom mirror.

I took off my pajamas, grabbed the soap and my towel, and turned on the shower. I hummed softly to myself as I adjusted the water and put on my shower cap. I turned the knobs and closed my eyes. I pictured myself on a stage like Lincoln Center's Avery Fisher Hall.

In my mind, I was acting and singing like I was in a Broadway musical. Hundreds of people were staring at me intensely as I performed and the crowd cheered me on. "I'm going to be a star!" I said to myself.

I washed, jumped out of the shower, and wrapped myself in my towel. It felt good to be a star! I put on my lotion and my underwear. Then I went in my closet and pulled out an outfit that matched my new gray Reebok sneakers I bought. I got dressed and went back into the bathroom.

I unwrapped my new silky hair and gently brushed it down. Then I brushed my teeth and was washing my face when I remembered to take out my door-knocker earrings that I hid in the bottom of my ballet bag. I grabbed them and stuffed the box in the inside pocket of T'chaka's Troop jacket. Then I put the jacket on and headed downstairs.

"Mommy and Daddy, I'm leaving for school," I said as I turned to get out the door.

My mother came out of the living room.

"Jamie, you didn't even eat nothing. Fix yourself some breakfast. You still got time for the bus."

"Mommy, I'm not hungry. I ate so much yesterday."

"Baby, you really did good last night. I'm proud of you."

"Thanks, Mom," I said as I grabbed the knob of the front door.

"Baby, what's going on with you and T'chaka? Why y'all had to switch coats?"

"Mommy, I told you. He bought some new sneakers that match

my coat, that's all."

"You know I don't like you taking stuff from people."

"We only switching for a week. I'ma give it back to him on Saturday."

"Whose idea was it to switch coats, yours or his?"

"Mom, he asked me!" I said in an irritated voice.

"Well, I guess it's all right then. You getting a little too grown for me. Ask me before you take stuff from people," she said in a disgruntled tone.

"Yes, Mommy," I said as I walked out the door. "Good-bye. I'll see you this afternoon."

I walked down the street before I put my earrings on. As I walked, I felt like a million bucks. I looked fresh, and I knew it. I stood at the bus stop dreaming about all the things I would buy if I was rich like Chudney. As I stood daydreaming, the yellow school bus approached. I snapped out my daze when I heard the loud brakes on the bus squeal as the door opened up.

I climbed up the steps of the bus and walked down the center aisle. "Oh, shoot, that coat is hot, Jamila," one of the boys shouted.

"Look at her hair, girl," another another girl chimed in.

"Jamila, your hair is beautiful," Yolanda said as I slid in the row with her. "Look at your earrings. Are those real?"

"Yes, girl."

"Where did you get them from?"

"I got them from the Coliseum."

"You are incredible, girl. You making a lot of moves."

"Well, I try," I said in a sarcastic voice.

That day I got so much attention, and I loved every drop of it! I got compliments all day long, even from teachers. Everyone seemed to like my makeover.

My school was a predominately white Jewish school. About fifty of us were blacks bussed in from Jamaica, Queens. I was the only black person in the gifted program. At first, this didn't sit too well with me, but after a while, I got used to it. At that time, my white classmates weren't into the black hip-hop culture at all. While I was rocking door-knocker earrings, Lee jeans, Sergio Tacchini tracksuits, and Reeboks, they were wearing Champion sweat suits, leggings, and Keds.

Unlike my old school where the work was easy and I didn't have to study, in this school, I had to work hard to keep up with my class. These Jewish kids were very smart. I couldn't let them outshine me, so I really had to study.

Our classes were intense. In the fifth grade, we were doing work on an eighth-grade level. We had a special lab for our science classes, and we often went to the Queens Museum to complete our class projects. My classmates looked at me as if I didn't belong.

"Why is your hair like that? Where do black people live? Why do black boys wear their clothes so baggy?" were some of the questions I would get asked.

On the other side, the black kids looked at me like I was a nerd. "Why are you in that class with all them geeks? Why are you hanging out with white girls? Why are you acting like you are white?" were some of the questions I was asked by the black kids.

I was black, and I was proud! "Yes, I'm smart, but I'm fresh to death," I would respond. I made sure I stayed extra fly so nobody would question whether I was a nerd or not.

Often, all the fifth- and sixth-grade classes would come together for activities. We would all meet up in the gym or the auditorium. We got to sit anywhere we liked, so I would sit with the other black girls I was bused in with.

"Quiet down and take a seat, students," Ms. Portfolio demanded as we entered the auditorium.

We all filed in the auditorium, interested to see what announcement she had to make. "We are going to have a spring play on the story, *Oliver Twist*," she said with excitement. "Today, I want to start auditions. Everyone is going to have some sort of part. You'll either be in the play, or you'll help work on the activities for the play.

"I'm going to need singers, dancers, actors, artists to build the sets, ushers, ticket takers, greeters, food servers, and a bunch of other helpers. Let's take some time today so we can see who has what talent," she said as she instructed us to come up and start signing up. Ms. Portfolio was a middle-aged, short lady with auburn hair.

We all began to talk among ourselves. "Girl, *Oliver Twist*. That's wack," Yolanda blasted out.

"Yeah, that some ole white folks' Broadway play," my black friend Stephanie said.

"Why we can't perform *The Wiz* or something?" my other black friend Tamika blurted out.

"Guys, let's give it a chance," I said as I broke loose to go to the front to check out the auditions. "Broadway is okay. There's a lot of stars and celebrities that have big money who perform on Broadway. Don't knock it yet."

"Okay, can anyone here sing?" Ms. Portfolio asked. "I mean sing *good,* ladies or gentlemen," she asked as she looked over the audience.

"Yeah, I can sing," a white girl Anna said as she skipped to the front.

"I can sing too," another white girl, Rebecca, said as she stepped up to the front.

"Anybody else?" Ms. Portfolio asked as she looked down over her glasses.

"Yes, I can sing," Timothy, a white boy, said and came forward.

"I can too." Brad, also white, came forward.

"Anybody else?" Ms. Portfolio asked as she looked around.

"I can sing too," I said, reluctant of what my black friends would think.

"Jamila, okay, come on up," Ms. Portfolio prompted. By her facial expression, I could tell she was surprised by my participation.

I could see Yolanda and Tamika tapping each other and whispering.

"Okay, let's begin. Do all of you girls know the Annie song, 'Tomorrow'?" We all nodded our heads.

"Okay, well, let's begin. Who wants to sing first?" she asked as we all approached the piano.

"Oh, oh, me," Anna said anxiously.

"Okay, go up on the stage and listen for your cue."

"The sun will come out tomorrow, bet your bottom dollar that tomorrow there be sun. Just thinking about tomorrow," Anna began to sing like the little girl Annie in the movie. The whole auditorium began to stare in amazement at her as she sang the song, which didn't seem to faze her. Anna sang well, and she knew it.

"Okay, Anna, very good. Who wants to go next?"

Rebecca stepped up and said, "I will."

"Okay, please come up on stage."

Rebecca came onto the stage and sang in an opera style. She also sang quite well.

As I sat in my seat, waiting my turn, I began to feel nervous, and I didn't understand why. I'd sung in front of the whole church before, and I danced in front of hundreds of people in Lincoln Center. Why would I be nervous to sing in front of about a hundred of my schoolmates?

You're my little star, I kept hearing my mother's voice repeat in my head. "Yes, Jamila, you are a star; you can do this!" I said to myself for encouragement.

Rebecca finally finished, and it was my turn.

"Jamila, are you ready?"

"Yes, ma'am," I said as I approached the stage. I looked out at the audience and everybody began to stare dead at me. I looked up at the clock and closed my eyes as I listened for my cue.

"The sun will come out tomorrow, bet your bottom dollar that tomorrow there be sun." I sang as I envisioned myself as the white Annie on television, yet I sang with a deep soulful voice. *"I think of a day that's gray and lonely. Then I pick up my chin and grin and say,"* I sang, and as I was getting into this thing, clearly, my audience was too. I could see some children tapping each other and others smiling. I knew I had them.

At the end of the song I paused and I grabbed my heart, and stared like I saw them do in the movies. Then I belted, *"You're only a day away!"* I ended my song holding the last note for as long as I could.

My black friends stood up. "Yes!" they cheered, and they began to applaud.

"Settle down, children. Now settle down," Ms. Portfolio shouted.

"Timothy and Brad, do you both know the song, 'If I Only Had a Brain'? from *The Wizard of Oz*?"

"Yes, I know it," Timothy said in an excited manner. Timothy was a prime example of a typical overachiever grade-school student. He was a white boy who was sort of heavyset, tall, with short blond hair and blue eyes. Timmy excelled in sports and academics. Whatever was happening in school, he was all in it!

"Okay, Timothy, you can start first," Ms. Portfolio said as she began to play the chords on the piano. "Come up on stage."

Ms. Portfolio finished her introduction on the piano, which took us all back to being in the center of Oz. Then she gave Timothy his intro cue on the piano.

Timothy sang that song like he was on a Broadway stage, and we were all in it with him.

"Oh, I can tell you why the ocean reaches the shore," Timothy sang passionately as he reached out and showed us the ocean water he was singing about with his hands. He waltzed back and forth on the stage just like the people on Broadway. Even his expressions matched the song! This kid was great!

"If I only had a brain," Timothy sang passionately as he ended the song. Everybody in the auditorium stood up and clapped, including the teachers.

Timothy wasn't modest at all. He threw his hands in the air, and then crossed his right arm in front of him as he took a bow.

I turned over and looked in Brad's eyes. I could tell he was nervous. Going behind Timothy was gonna be a tough act to follow, and Brad knew it!

"Okay, Bradley. Let's go. It's your turn," Ms. Portfolio said with anticipation. Bradley's face was beet red as he walked up the steps of the stage.

"Go on, Bradley. You're going to do just fine." Ms. Portfolio tried to comfort him detecting his slight fear. She began to play the chords on the song. It was Brad's cue, and he missed it.

"Come on, Bradley, this is your cue." Ms. Portfolio played it again.

Bradley looked out at the audience who were all staring with anticipation, and then he opened his mouth . . . but nothing came out.

"Bradley," Ms. Portfolio said.

But there was no response.

"Bradley," Ms. Portfolio said once again as Bradley stared deeply at the audience.

"Oh, oh, I'm sorry, I can't do this!" Brad said as he ran off the stage and out of the auditorium.

Mr. Greene, one of the fifth-grade teachers, followed him out of the auditorium. The whole auditorium followed Bradley with their eyes. Several laughs came from the audience as children pointed at him.

"Now settle down, kids. I don't see any of you with the courage to get on this stage, so shut your mouths!" Ms. Portfolio scolded, and everyone began to settle down.

"Okay, Timothy, it looks like you are going to be *Oliver Twist*," Ms. Portfolio announced.

"Yessssss!" Timothy said as he jumped out of his seat, and the crowd cheered him on.

"Okay, girls, we have three of you. Rebecca, Anna, and Jamila. Can any of you dance?"

"I can," Anna shouted loudly.

"Oh, I can dance too!" I said as I stared Anna up and down, letting her know this competition wouldn't be easy.

"Can you dance, Rebecca?" Ms. Portfolio politely asked.

"No, ma'am, I can't," Rebecca said in a sad tone.

"Okay, well, I am going to need someone who can dance for the girl's leading role. You will still be in the play, but not for the leading role. Sit down over here," Ms. Portfolio instructed and Rebecca dropped her head and sat in the second row.

"Ladies, there's only you two left. I'm going to need to see you dance," Ms. Portfolio said to Anna and me as she stood up from the piano.

"Oh, oh, oh, I want to go first!" Anna shouted.

"Go up onstage and let me see what you've got," Ms. Portfolio said as she coaxed Anna along.

Anna was a slender girl, with long blond hair separated into two long ponytail braids. She was a "cool kid," who was very popular in school.

Anna got up on the stage. "What do you want me to dance to?" she asked excitedly.

"Okay. I want you to sing a song and dance at the same time."

"Cool, what song?"

"Whatever song you like."

Anna stopped and paused, then she began to sing Tiffany's "I Think We're Alone Now." This was a hit pop music song on the music charts at the time. Anna began to do a sort of ballet-type dance as she sang.

"I think we're alone now. There doesn't seem to be anyone around. I think we're alone now. The beating of our hearts is the only sound," she sang passionately away as all the white children in the auditorium began to sing the song with her.

As Anna got more and more attention, she started spinning and dropping, and really getting into the song. I had to admit, Anna was pretty good, but she was no threat to me.

"And then you put your arms around me, and we tumble to the ground, and then you say, I think we're alone now," Anna sang as she changed her voice to go with the words of the song and jumped on the floor to show she was tumbling down, and the crowd went wild.

"Oh, she got it in the bag. She's gonna win," I heard the voices of the children behind me saying. The song ended, and it was my turn.

I approached the back stage area and heard in my head my mother saying, *"You're my little star." The odds are against me, but I have to make a comeback,* I thought to myself.

"Jamila, are you ready?" Ms. Portfolio asked.

"I can do any song, right?" I asked.

"Yes, Jamila, whatever you like."

"Okay," I said as I cleared my throat. I looked out into the audience and all eyes were glued on me. You could hear a pin drop in the building. It was so quiet!

"Home girls, attention you must pay. So listen close to what I say. Don't take this as a simple rhyme, 'cause this type of thing happens all the time," I rapped passionately to the rap song, "Tramp," by Salt-N-Pepa. I did all the moves I watched the girls do in the video. I rapped passionately as if I were in the video.

All the black kids in the auditorium got out their seats and started dancing. I could see Yolanda doing the Whop dance and Tamika doing the Roger Rabbit dance. They were in the back cutting up while the white kids looked in awe, tapping and whispering to each other.

"What you call me? Tramp!" I rapped hard as I ended the song and crossed my hands on my chest and nodded my head like the rappers in the videos do, and I paused.

"Yes!!! Yeah!!!!!" I got a good response from the blacks and the whites in the audience.

"Okay, that was nice, but Jamila, this is a musical. I need to see you sing for real and dance," Ms. Portfolio said as I caught Anna's eyes. She gave me a smirk like, let me see you outshine me with *real* singing.

"Okay, I got this," I responded. I gathered myself together and took a deep breath.

"Everything must change. Nothing stays the same. Everyone will change, no one stays the same. The young become the old, and mysteries do unfold," I began to sing passionately, Quincy Jones's song, "Everything Must Change." I sang and danced my heart out. Sharp spins, pirouettes, and precise moves with feeling, just as I did in my

dance recital the year before. The song was a passionate song, and I felt every word, so I expressed what I felt in the bottom of my soul with my voice and my movements.

Anna's mouth dropped, and Ms. Portfolio stared at me in awe. Not quite what they expected from this little black girl!

"Everything must change," I sang passionately as I did a riff with my voice and gently ended the song on my knees. The whole audience was up on their feet, clapping.

I bolted off the stage proudly and returned to my seat where Yolanda met me. "Oh my God, Jamila, you was wonderful," she said as she hugged me.

"Jamila, give me a high five," a white boy behind me said to me as he slapped my hand.

"Yo, I ain't know you can dance and sing like that," Tamika said as she snapped her fingers and put her hand on her waist.

That day I gained the respect of the whites and blacks in the school.

"Okay, guys, on that note, let's take a short break. I'm gonna need to decide this with the rest of the teachers," Ms. Portfolio said as she and the other teachers gathered together to decide.

Anna came up to me. "Jamila, you was great. Where did you learn how to dance like that?" she asked as she patted me on my back.

"I go to Bernice Johnson's Dance School. I've been dancing since I was three."

"Oh, cool. I've been dancing since I was five years old. I take ballet, tap, acting, and jazz," she said excitedly.

"Oh, I take ballet, tap, jazz, modern, and African."

"Wow, African dance. I would love to try that."

"Yeah, it's my favorite class!"

"Hey, listen, you think you can show me some of them rap moves? I think it's kind of cool!"

"Yeah, and will you show me them pop moves? I kind of like that song you sang too."

"Bet! Let's meet in the school yard for lunch tomorrow."

"Cool."

The teachers finished talking, and Ms. Portfolio came over to Anna and me.

"Do you both know how to act?" she asked.

"Yeah, I've been taking acting classes since I was five," Anna responded. Then Ms. Portfolio looked at me.

"Well, I watch the actors on television. I don't have any real training though," I said.

"Okay, I'm going to have you both read a few lines from the play," Ms. Portfolio said as she unraveled the script from her bag. She gave us the lines to read, and Anna blew me out of the water. This girl could act!

Anna ending up getting the leading role, and I got a small part in the play. I knew after that day I had to get some real training in acting if I ever want to be a star and get on television. I went home and told my mother what happened. I was devastated!

"Mommy, mommy, I didn't get the part," I said with tears in my eyes. "Anna got it 'cause she knows how to act."

"Jamie, you can't be in everything. You got to give other people a chance, too," she said as I buried my head in her lap.

"But, Mommy, I am supposed to be your li'l star," I said as I rested my head on her breast.

"You are always going to be my li'l star, baby, no matter what," she said as she rubbed my hair and dried my tears with her hands. My mother continued to comfort me. "Listen, I'm going to find you a good acting school, baby, and you know my baby is a quick learner. You gonna get that part next year. Don't cry, baby."

"Yeah, Mommy, acting school. That sounds good," I said as I imagined how it would be in my mind. I abruptly stopped crying. "Yup, I am a star, and I'm going to be on TV, Mommy. You watch and see!!!"

"I know, baby, you're Mommy's Li'l Star!"

Me, at age ten, posing for the camera at 60 Minute Photo.

*I*t was a rainy, Saturday morning. I was up early, as usual, in front of the mirror practicing my steps for dance school.

"Jamie, are you ready to go to dance school?" my mother asked me as she peeped into the living room.

"Yes, Mom, I'm just practicing," I said as I continued to do my dance moves.

"Okay, let me hop in the shower and get dressed. I'm coming to dance school with you today," she said as I stopped and looked at her with a puzzled face.

"You are?" I spoke in a dumbfounded voice.

"I sure am! I'll be ready in a minute." She tightened her housecoat around her waist and walked in the restroom.

Oh, shoot! I thought to myself. I had no clue what I was in for. My mother had a made-up mind. She was going with me, and there was nothing I could do about it.

The ride to dance school was silent. I listened to the music on the radio and tried to envision what was going to happen. With my mother, anything was possible!

We arrived at dance school. When I walked in, most of my classmates were already there. I hurried in on my best behavior, knowing my mother was watching.

"Hey, Jamie!" Renée greeted me.

"Hello, Ms. Davis," Renée said as she greeted my mother.

"Hey, baby, where is your sister?" my mother asked.

"Oh, she's in the bathroom getting changed."

"Okay. How's your mom, baby?"

"She's okay."

"Tell Lorna I said hi, okay?"

"Yes, I certainly will."

"You kids hurry up and change so you can get to class on time."

"Yes, Mommy."

"All right, Ms. Davis," Renée said as she grabbed me by the hands and whispered in my ear. "What is your mother doing here?"

"I'm not sure. But I guess we gonna find out," I said as we entered the dance classroom.

Chapter Seventeen

"Okay, ladies, let's go. We ain't got no time to be playing. The concert is around the corner. Let's go! Tiny Tots, line up on the right. Super Tots, line up on the left. Let's go!" Sheryl, my dance instructor, said as the dance class became jam-packed with students and parents.

My mother entered the classroom and slid past the other parents to the front. She had a very serious look on her face. She didn't crack a grin or a smile.

"Five, six, seven, eight. Hit it!" Sheryl said as the drums played away. The Tiny Tots came out and danced, and then it was our turn.

"Super Tots, get ready! Five, six, seven, eight, hit it!"

We came out on the floor in a sliding dance move Sheryl taught us with our hands stretched straight out across. "And one and two and three, hit, step, step, step. Kick. Step, step, up, down. Let me see your energy! Give it to me, girls!" Sheryl yelled as we danced our hearts out to the music.

I danced away, and I watched my mother's face. She was clearly disappointed. Chudney began to stumble and messed up on steps. Other girls in the front row also messed up on steps. My mother began to shake her head.

"Girls, you got to keep up. Come on, let's get this right, ladies! Matter fact, stop the music. I want y'all to start from the top," Sheryl said in an annoyed tone.

My mother stared Sheryl up and down like she was about to jump on her. Sheryl eventually caught her eyes and quickly looked away.

"Okay, ladies, five, six, seven, eight, hit it," Sheryl said as we started the routine from the top. As we did the routine again, the girls in the front row continued to make mistakes. My mother was bursting with anger. It was clear by the expression on her face.

"Excuse me, Sheryl, can I talk to you for a moment?" my mother said in a feisty voice interrupting the class.

"Miss, I'm teaching a class. You can see me after class," Sheryl said as she rolled her eyes and paid my mom no attention.

"I don't know what the hell kind of stuff y'all got going on in this dance school, but there is clearly a problem. The ones in the back dance better than the ones in the front. I pay my money each week just like their parents do. Y'all gonna treat my child right, and I mean that!" my mother said as she stormed out of the class.

"Are you threatening me?" Sheryl screamed at my mother right before she reached the door.

"Baby, that's not a threat—that's a promise!" my mother yelled back, and she walked out the door.

I was so embarrassed! All the parents were huddled in the corner, whispering, and my classmates stared at me with a startled look. I continued to dance as if it didn't faze me, but deep down inside, I was nervous.

"This is my class. I make up the rules around here. I place people where I want to place them. Matter fact, Jamila, get in the back. You are going to be the last person seen in this concert, Ms. Thing," Sheryl yelled at me, and I couldn't control my tears. I stepped to the back line and tried to hold my composure. I was so mad. This just wasn't fair. I stopped pouring my heart into the dancing and just blended in with the dance moves of the girls in the back.

Half an hour later, my mother came back into the class with the dance school owner, Ms. Johnson. When that door flew opened, I knew it was on! My mother spotted me in the back row and began to whisper vigorously in Ms. Johnson's ear.

"Okay, ladies, five, six, seven, eight, hit it!" Sheryl yelled as she watched Ms. Johnson from the corner of her eye. She was visibly nervous.

It was on now! I knew I had to perform my best. I took a deep breath and gave it all I had. I outshined just about everyone in the class.

"Jamila, you come stand up here," Ms. Johnson said as she instructed me to come stand in the front line. She made a bunch of changes that day, placing us all according to our dance abilities. Chudney got to stay in the front row, but Renée got kicked to the third row. All the darker-skinned girls that could dance were so happy! Sheryl was devastated as her decisions were undermined by the true boss, Ms. Johnson! She just stared in dire embarrassment.

To this day I don't know what my mother said to Ms. Johnson, but I never had any more problems in that dance school. Teachers and students alike respected me! My mother was serious about me and my success, and she didn't mind letting the whole world know it! I was Jamie, her little star!

My mother, my brother and me, at age ten, posing for the
camera at 60 Minute Photo in Green Acres Mall.

*O*ne afternoon after school I followed my daily routine. I intensely watched each video on the show *Video Music Box*, a popular TV show in the late '80s. Standing in front of the television I would mimic all the latest dance moves I saw. I studied the outfits the girls had on at the nightclubs, as Crazy Sam and DJ Ralph McDaniels passed the girls the mic so they could give their shout-outs to the audience. The hosts interviewed different women at the hottest nightclubs in New York City between every other music video.

"I want to give a shout-out to my sister Theresa and to my man Kendell. Brooklyn in the house!" one of the girls shouted at the camera.

Whoa, I want to go to the club and give a shout-out too! I thought to myself. *I can't wait to grow up. First thing I'm gonna do is go to the club and be in the videos!*

As I was watching the show, my mother entered the room. "Jamie, your aunt Hattie has set up an audition for you to try out for this really good local theatre group. If they accept you, you can attend and take acting classes there."

"For real, Mommy?" I questioned anxiously.

"Yes, baby. Your cousin Kanika just got in, and I think you'll get in too."

"All right. What I got to do?" I said in an excited tone.

"They have practice tonight in Laurelton. Hattie told me to just bring you down there, and she'll get the lady to audition you on the spot. The place is called The Laurelton Theatre of Performing Arts. The owner is some lady that's been in a lot of movies and all over Broadway. I think she said her name is Mrs. King."

"Oh, boy, Mommy. I'm gonna be on TV. I just know it!" I said as I jumped up and down in excitement.

"Okay, calm down, Jamie. You got to get in first!"

"Mommy, I got this! I'm your li'l star, right?" I said as I gave my mother my puppy dog smile.

"Yes, baby. Knock 'em dead, girl!" my mother said unable to resist my smile, and she kissed me on the cheek.

Chapter Eighteen

"I sure will," I responded with confidence and smiled.

We jumped in the car and headed to the theatre. I didn't even turn on the radio as I normally did. I was too busy trying to prepare for the audition.

"Oh, Romeo, oh, Romeo, where doeth thy heart go?" I said as I attempted to act.

"Listen, Jamie, you ain't got to act like no fool. Just be yourself. I used to act when I was in college."

"Oh, that's right, Mommy!"

"Yeah, I could act, but I couldn't sing to save my life! That limited what I could do. You can sing so you have an advantage. Listen, just put yourself in your mind in the shoes of the person you are portraying. I want you to feel like they feel, do what they would do, and act as they would act. You got that?" my mother instructed.

"Yes, Ma, I got to put myself in that person's shoes. I'm gonna feel like they feel, do what they would do, and act as they would. Right, Ma?"

"Yes, baby. That's all you got to do!"

"Okay, Mom. I can do that!"

We pulled up on the busy street, Merrick Boulevard, which was the same street as my dance school, but it was way down further in Laurelton, Queens. As we approached the store-front theatre, my aunt Hattie was waiting for us outside the door. Aunt Hattie was a tall, light-skinned lady with long Jheri curls and glasses. She was my father's younger brother's first wife.

"Hey, Liddie, hey, Jamie," she said anxiously. "Now listen, Ms. King don't know you gonna show up. Just follow me, baby, and I'm do my best to get you in," she said to me as she patted my head.

"Now you go with ya aunt Hattie, baby," my mother instructed, and Aunt Hattie led me into the theatre.

Aunt Hattie opened the doors, and we walked into a small waiting area that led into this huge classroom that was covered with large mirrors. There was a ballet bar on the right wall and a grand piano on the left side of the room. A heavyset, dark chocolate woman, who wore a curly, coarse wig, and heavy foundation makeup, lighter than her skin tone, sat behind the piano. A group of people surrounded the piano, both young and old. They were practicing for an off-Broadway play called *Mahalia Lives*. It was about the deceased famous gospel singer Mahalia Jackson.

A dark-skinned, heavyset lady was at the edge of the piano singing, *"Oh, tell it, tell it, tell it over and over of Jesus more, more. Till the soul can't tell it anymore. Oh, tell it, sing it, shout it everywhere,"* she sang the gospel song passionately. She sounded like Sister George, but she was even better!

"Okay, everybody, sing," the lady on the piano shouted out.

"Tell it, tell it! Over and over of Jesus more and more. Till the soul can't tell it anymore. Oh, tell it, sing it, shout it everywhere," the group sang with zeal. It sounded amazing to me!

Everyone sang in unison on the right key. They sounded like professionals on Broadway. After the song ended, I watched my cousin Kanika, who was one year older than I, get into her lines. She was playing the role of Young Mahalia. I didn't even know she could sing. *"God, if you're listening, if there is a little doll left over from Christmas, may I have it, please?"* Kanika said her lines as the piano began to play.

"Sometimes I feel like a motherless child. Sometimes I feel like a motherless child. Sometimes I feel like a motherless child. A long ways from home. A long ways from home," my cousin sang with soul and passion. I could feel every word she sang, so much that I wanted to cry.

"Very good, Kanika. You are almost ready for your first live show. We still have to find an understudy for you for the dates that you can't make."

"Um, Ms. King. This is my niece, Jamie. She sings and dances really well. She hasn't acted before, but she learns quickly. I think she might be a perfect understudy for Young Mahalia," Aunt Hattie said as she interrupted Ms. King and ushered me up to the piano.

"Hey, little girl. My name is Mrs. Coretta King," she said as she came from behind the piano and shook my hand.

"Hello, ma'am," I said as I greeted her with a smile.

"So you can sing and dance?"

"Yes, ma'am."

"Do you have any formal training?"

"Well, I've been dancing at Bernice Johnson's since I was three years old. I'm in the pro class, and I take African, jazz, tap, ballet, and modern."

"Oh, I know Bernice. Let me see you do the Time Step," Ms. King instructed as everyone in the theatre watched me.

"Okay, ma'am," I said as I moved out to the center of the floor.

"Five, six, seven, eight," I said as I tapped the Time Step and jazzed it up like Lorna taught us in tap class. "Fall, slap, step, step, fall, slap, step, step, fall," I said as I added on extra dance moves.

"Okay, I like that! Let me see if you can do the song for the play. Here are the words to the song and the script for the part of Young Mahalia. Go in the back and practice with your cousin, and I'll call you back out in about half an hour."

My cousin and I went to a small studio in the back of the theatre, and she taught me the song and the lines to one of the scenes. As I learned the words, I thought about what my mother had taught me: "Put yourself in that person's shoes, feel what she feels, and act as she would act." My mother's words kept racing in my head. Our time was up, and Ms. King called me out to the front.

"Okay, darling, I want you to say the monologue and go right into the song," she instructed as she sat down at the piano. I took a deep breath and transformed in my mind into Young Mahalia.

"Lord, I don't know why my auntie be so mean to me. She don't let me do the things the other kids do. Ever since my mother died, I feel all alone. It's like I ain't got nobody, Lord, except for You . . . And, Lord, if You still listening, if there's a doll left over from Christmas, may I have it, please?" I said as I ended my lines, and the piano began to play. *"Sometimes I feel like a motherless child, sometimes I feel like a motherless child."* I dropped the script I had in my hand and walked out onto the center of the floor, as I sang passionately. I played the role envisioning myself to be Young Mahalia.

"A long ways from home, from home, a long ways from home," I sang passionately, and I began to cry, feeling the loneliness of the character Young Mahalia. *"A long ways from home,"* I sang holding the note as I ended the song, and I held my head and began to cry profusely.

The theatre group applauded, and Ms. King jumped to her feet. "I love her! She's a natural," she said as she walked over to me from the piano.

"You got the role, young lady," she said as she patted my back. "Hattie, is this her mother?"

"Yes, ma'am," my mother replied, speaking up. She stood very proudly next to my aunt Hattie.

"Okay, well, we have practice every Wednesday night at 7 o'clock," Ms. King advised.

"No problem, I'll have her here on time," my mother replied anxiously.

On the way home that night, I got in the front seat of the car and leaned the chair back. I was in a daze. I saw myself on Broadway. I was officially a part of a real theatre group, performing in different states and cities! *Wow, I had landed the jackpot!* I thought to myself. *Watch out, world, I am the next little star coming through!*

Chapter Nineteen

It was approximately 4:30 in the afternoon, and I had just arrived home from school. My mother was already home, as usual. The junior high school she worked at let out at 2:15 each school day, so my mother was always faithfully home by 3 o'clock, waiting on my brother and me to arrive home. I was in grade school, and my brother was in junior high school. I rode the yellow school bus home. Kee rode the city bus, which was public transportation.

"Hi, Mommy," I said as I walked through the door.

"Hi, Jamie, did you see Kee down the block?"

"No, Mommy."

"You know I'm sick of him playing with me. I want y'all both to come straight home from school. He should have been here already," my mother said angrily as she paced back and forth.

"Mommy, it's still early. He probably went to get something to eat."

"I don't want to hear no excuses. When I tell y'all something, I mean what I say! There's so much happening in the streets, and my spirit doesn't feel good. I had a bad dream last night, and I don't want y'all roaming these streets. You hear me?" She glanced at her watch again, checking the time.

"Answer me when I talk to you, girl," my mother spoke sharply. She was visibly irate.

"Oh, I'm sorry, Mom, what did you ask me?"

"I said I want you to come straight home from school."

"Yes, Mom. I'm here, and I hear you," I said in a soft tone so I wouldn't piss her off any further.

I left the kitchen and went into the den where I turned on the television to watch music videos. Before I could settle in good I could hear my mother grumble.

"Here goes that hardheaded little boy now." My mother immediately got up from the kitchen table and raced out of the house to the front porch. My brother was walking up the street with his two friends, Matt and Chris. They were fraternal twin brothers.

My mother was outraged! "Where the hell you been at, Kee?

Didn't I tell you to bring your butt straight home from school?"

You could tell by the look in my brother's eyes he was so embarrassed. "Yo, Mom, chill. I'm coming inside," Kee said. Matt and Chris began to tap each other and laugh.

"What the hell you laughing for, you peanut-head fool and you tall, slinky, high-butt bastard?" my mother shouted, and the two boys quickly stopped laughing. "I can't stand y'all both. I wish you'd stay the hell away from my child!"

"Yo, your Moms be wilding," Chris commented, shaking his head in disbelief of my mother's rudeness.

"Yo, what's the matter with her?" Matt said in disgust.

"Yo, I'ma check y'all tomorrow. I'll meet you at the bus stop in the morning. Don't walk down this block. Meet me on the other side of Springfield," my brother whispered to the twins as he opened our fence.

"Yo, Mom, why you always got to embarrass me?" Kee said as he walked through the door.

"You don't listen. Didn't I tell you to bring your butt straight home?"

"I know, but—" Kee said as my mother interrupted him and slapped him on his head.

"But hell. When I tell you something, you listen and that's that. I don't like them two damn boys. My spirit don't agree with them. They not good for you, Kee! You better listen to me, boy! Them boys don't mean you no good," she yelled.

"Mom, listen, you don't even know them. Why are you acting like that?"

"I ain't got to know them. I know what I see and feel. They ain't no damn good, boy. Now you better listen to me. I don't want you hanging out with them. If you do, I'm gonna fix both you and them. You hear me?"

"Yes, ma'am," my brother said as he sucked his teeth and walked away.

"Keep testing me and you gonna get a taste of what these two hands are made of," Mama muttered as she waved her two fists in the air.

"Mommy, I ain't no little boy. Let me grow up. For goodness' sake, I'm in junior high school," he said as he closed the door and walked upstairs to his room.

My mother was on fire. Whatever it was about them two twin boys, she didn't like them, and she didn't want my brother around them. My mother always had a sixth sense about certain people. She just knew when something wasn't right about a person.

I was in the den watching videos when the telephone rang.

"Hello," I said as I answered the phone.

"Jamie, Jamie, is your mother home?" Ms. Gladys said in a tearful voice.

"Yes, Ms. Gladys. Are you okay?"

"Yes, baby, please put your mother on the phone. It's urgent!" Her voice sounded tense.

"Mommy, mommy, get the phone. It's Ms. Gladys, and she crying! Hurry up," I yelled.

"She's crying? What?"

"Mom, hurry, pick up," I said as my mother picked up the phone in her room. I couldn't hang up. I had to hear what was going on.

"Gladys, what's wrong, baby?" my mother said in a concerned tone.

"Liddie, Liddie," Ms. Gladys said, crying.

"Yes, Gladys, what's wrong?" my mother responded, and she began to cry too.

"They done shot C.B. three times."

"No, Gladys, no!" my mother screamed.

"He was standing out on Hollis Avenue, and somebody shot him!"

"Oh, no, Gladys," my mother sobbed.

"He's still alive. They put him in the ambulance. He's at Mary Immaculate Hospital. I need you to take me there!"

"Okay, where are you?"

"I'm at home."

"I'm on my way right now," my mother said as she quickly hung up the phone and grabbed her car keys.

I was so outraged and shocked. I held the phone to my ear even after they hung up, and I also began to cry. I didn't know what to think.

"Kee and Jamie, get your stuff. We got to go!" my mother yelled in a tearful voice.

"Kee! Kee! I'm calling you," she yelled up the steps.

"Mom, what?" my brother responded with an attitude.

"They done shot C.B. Come on, I got to take Ms. Gladys to the hospital."

"What?" my brother said in disbelief.

"They done shot—" and before my mother could get the rest of the words out of her mouth, my brother lost it!

"Oh, what? No, no, Ma, no, they didn't!" he hollered and screamed as he punched against the wall. I never saw my brother act like this before. He frightened me.

"Oh, they want war, that's what they want," he yelled. "Right. That's it. Oh my God," he shouted. Then, he broke down and cried.

"Kee, it's gonna be all right," I said as I rushed to comfort him. "He still living. Come on. We got to go to the hospital." I grabbed his arm to come on.

Alarmed, we raced out of the house and jumped in the car to get Ms. Gladys, who was already waiting outside. My mother raced to the hospital emergency doors, and Ms. Gladys hopped out. My mother found a parking space, and we quickly went through the emergency room doors together. All I saw were doctors and nurses all over the place. The hospital was pretty busy that evening.

We approached the emergency room nurse's station, where a black, heavyset nurse sat at the desk.

"Ma'am, I'm here to see Sebastian Mingo," my mother said in a nervous voice.

"One second, ma'am," the woman responded as she looked in the computer. "Oh, he's in critical condition in the Intensive Care Unit. Only one person is allowed in at a time, and someone has the pass already. The kids can't go in there, okay, ma'am?"

"Yes, thank you," my mother said, and we sat down in the waiting room.

We waited for Ms. Gladys to come down, but Kee couldn't sit still. He had this strange look in his eyes as he paced back and forth.

"Yo, they gotta pay for this, man! For real," he kept saying.

"Calm down, Kee, just pray. Pray, okay?" my mother advised.

"Mommy, they playin' with people's lives," Kee rebutted.

"God don't like ugly, boy; just pray," my mother said as she rubbed his back, in an attempt to calm him down.

Ms. Gladys came down like an hour later. "Liddie, Liddie," she yelled.

"Yes, Gladys."

"He's okay! They did surgery on him and took out the bullets, but one landed in his intestines. The doctor said if it landed one inch over, he would be dead."

"Oh, thank You, Jesus, oh, thank You, Lord," my mother cried out in relief.

"Listen, Liddie, I got the pass of the old man in the bed next to C.B. He's up on the third floor. Take this pass and come with me. The kids can stay down here," Ms. Gladys instructed, and she passed my mother the large pink plastic hospital pass.

"Okay. Y'all, I'll be back. Don't move. Sit down and relax," my mother instructed as she quickly got up and followed Ms. Gladys.

We sat in the waiting room for about another half hour, and my brother kept pacing back and forth. I had settled down already after I heard C.B. was okay.

"Jamie, I'm going up."

"But how, Kee? They said no kids can come in!"

"I don't care; I'ma take my chances," he said as he got up out of his seat to approach the elevator. I quickly followed behind him. The elevator door opened, and as the people went out, my brother and I snuck in.

"Kee, we don't know where he's at."

"Listen, Ms. Gladys said the third floor," he said as he pressed the elevator button marked "3."

The elevator door closed and opened again on the third floor, and we followed the signs that said Intensive Care. As we walked down the hallway, we stuck our heads in the first room, where we saw a man who was wrapped in bandages. He had a tube coming out of his mouth.

"Wrong room," my brother whispered to me. Then we heard my mother's voice and followed her voice to C.B.'s room.

We walked in the room and C.B. was hooked up to a machine with tubes. He sat up in the bed fully conscious, talking to his mother and my mom.

"What are y'all doing up here?" my mother yelled. My brother didn't even seem to hear her. He approached C.B.'s bed and grabbed his hand.

"C.B., you all right?" he asked as tears rolled down his face.

"I'm all right, li'l man," C.B. said in almost a whisper.

"I don't like what they did to you, C.B. You taught me not to be no punk. We ain't no punks, man. Why did they do this?" my brother asked.

"Look, Kee, calm down. I'm going to be okay. I got this," C.B. replied.

"No, C.B., this can't go down like this."

"Kee, chill, chill out! Listen, Mom, Ms. Davis and Jamie, give us a minute, please," C.B. asked in a little louder voice.

"Huh?" I said confused.

"Come on, Jamie and Liddie, let's go outside for a second," Ms. Gladys instructed as we left the room.

I didn't know what they discussed in that room. I just know from that very day my brother was no longer a little boy. He grew up before my eyes and became a man! My mother didn't pay much attention, but I did!

I guess she just felt that Kee loved C.B., and he was hurt. I knew there was something else to this equation, but it took me a long time to figure it out!

My dad and me at my Sixth Grade Graduation, at P.S.
26 in Fresh Meadows, Queens-New York.

"Ladies, it's showtime! Let's go," one of the instructors said as he opened our dressing room door at Lincoln Center's Avery Fisher Hall. All the instructors had on headphones and walkie-talkies in their hands. "Ten-Four, the Super Tots are on the way down," the instructor spoke into his walkie-talkie as he closed the dressing-room door.

My classmates anxiously lined up, and the stage mothers led us down the hallway to the elevator. We all packed in the large commercial elevator and headed down to the stage.

All types of important figures surrounded the backstage area. You could see people running back and forth in a frenzy, to ensure that the concert was a success. This was the real deal! They treated this concert like it was a premiere show on Broadway! We watched the class before us perform on stage. The song ended, and they bowed. It was our turn, and my heart began to race.

"Lights, camera, action, ladies, let's go!" Ms. Johnson screamed from backstage as we stood with anticipation.

The stage lights blacked out and we raced on the stage and took our positions. The lights brightened as the "Bugle Boy" song blasted from the grand state-of-the-art theatre system. The Avery Fisher Hall auditorium was packed. Hundreds of people filled their seats staring with anticipation. From the floor seats to the large balcony area, and even in the box seats above the stage, it appeared that all eyes were on me. I was only ten years old and standing in the spot that many successful performers have stood, and it felt amazing! I got a rush from the energy. It inspired me to jump right into character.

The crowd cheered as the curtains opened. We were dressed in military-style outfits. We wore short green skirts with a button-up short sleeve green blouse that had army patches on it. We had on small green army-style caps that propped up on top of our heads. Our legs were dressed in black fishnet stockings with diamond-cut holes, and we wore black tap shoes on our feet. We each stood behind a stool which we used as our props as we tapped around the stool acting out the words to the song.

Chapter Twenty

We also had fake bugle-style trumpets that we used as props as we danced. The crowd went wild when we pulled the bugles out! We changed positions with each other on the stage, moving the chairs and the props to the back of the stage where we danced. Then we formed a huge circle; each of our arms connected us as we kicked up our feet and moved about in a circle like the Rockettes at Rockefeller Center, during Christmas time. The crowd ranted and raved throughout our routine. We ended our routine in a pyramid line position on the stage. We each struck a different pose and froze as the audience stood and cheered.

The studio lights darkened, and the curtain closed. We quickly ran off the stage and hurried back to our dressing room. I felt like I just performed for the biggest Broadway show ever! My heart raced with excitement!

"Jamie, you did so good!" my mother said as she greeted me backstage.

"Thank you, Mother, I try," I said imitating a movie star in her prime. My head was in the clouds, and no one could tell me nothing! In my mind, I was a star for real.

Next, we quickly got ready for our jazz performance. We changed into our costumes, touched up our makeup, and fixed our hair. There was a knock on the dressing-room door.

"Super Tots, you're up in ten minutes. Let's go!" the instructor shouted as he peeped his head in.

We lined up and got ready to perform once again. This time, I was no longer nervous. I was anxious to show the crowd what I was all about—"show biz!" We crowded in the elevator and headed for the stage.

"Super Tots, stay right here. We are almost ready for you," Lorna said as she met us backstage. The Tiny Tots were onstage performing their jazz routine. They looked so cute! Devon and Ashante had a solo with two little boys in their class. The crowd roared as the little boys lifted the girls in the air, doing dance moves and spins just like the adults do. All of the routines were choreographed to perfection. Ms. Johnson wanted to make sure that her show would always be talked about!

"Okay, ladies, get ready. Five, four, three, two, one, action!" Lorna yelled as the stage lights darkened. The Tiny Tots ran offstage, and we took our positions. The lights came on and the stage curtains opened.

We were dressed in red lingerie outfits, with fishnet stockings and red dyed jazz shoes. The song "Hey, Big Spender" came on as the stage curtains opened. We began to dance seductively to go with the words of the Broadway-style song! We all danced around the boys in the class who had on tuxedo-style costumes with top hats and canes. They played the role of the big spenders, and we played the role of old-school hookers, or street ladies of the night.

"The minute you walked in the joint I could see you were a man of distinction, a real big spender. Good lookin', so refined Say, wouldn't you like to know what's goin' on in my mind?" The words to the song played loudly on the state-of-the-art music sound system. We danced around the boys seductively, and they walked around us and stared with admiration, acting out the words of the song. The audience pointed, laughed, and stared as you wouldn't expect this type of performance from ten-year-old children. Cameras flashed everywhere!

It was almost time for the grand finale. The class danced off the stage, and the four boys stayed on stage, performing their solos. Four girls greeted them, including myself, and we grabbed our partner's hands and did a waltz-type of spin. We danced to the music with passion as the boys lifted us up in the air and spun us around. Then they let us down on the floor, and we began to dance on our knees as the boys danced over us. The crowd went wild! We ended our routine, and the lights went out! My heart began to race with adrenaline from the excitement. I was in my glory on the stage! We ran off the stage and hurried to make our next performance, which was only fifteen minutes away!

"Come on, Jamie. We got to go!" my mother shouted as she escorted me from backstage.

My classmates had already gone back to the dressing room. I stayed behind with the other solo performers. We stood at the elevator, but it was taking too long to come, so we raced up the back stairway.

By the time we got to the dressing room, everyone was already getting ready for the African performance. I ran to get my suitcase when the knock on the dressing-room door came.

"Super Tots, y'all got ten minutes to showtime," the instructor announced.

"Ten minutes. Mommy, I'm not even dressed!" I cried.

"Where the hell is your suitcase?" my mother responded as we looked for the suitcase in the spot I left it.

"Mommy, mommy, my suitcase isn't here!" I cried.

"What do you mean? It was right over here," my mother responded as she checked the spot we left it in.

"Oh, hell, no! Who got my daughter's suitcase?" my mother questioned as everyone was lining up to leave the room. No one paid us any attention. We ransacked the room as the instructor came back.

"Five minutes, ladies, let's go."

My classmates started to leave the room and I wasn't even dressed! I began to cry profusely. "Mommy, I practiced all year for this, now I can't perform 'cause I don't have my suitcase." After the girls left the room, luckily we found my suitcase on the other side of the room.

I quickly opened the suitcase to discover there was no African costume inside of it! Thinking on her toes, my mother quickly went through the other suitcases in the room and discovered another black suitcase that looked just like mine. She opened it and found an African costume in it. The outfit was a little big for me, but my mother tied the African garments around me as tightly as she could. She grabbed my hands, and we ran down to the stage through the back stairway.

I was out of breath as we approached the stage. The drummers were already on the stage in their beautiful African garments.

The drumroll came for us to start, and I quickly ran straight out on the stage. My adrenaline was already going wild because of what I had just gone through, so I released my frustration in every step of my African dance. I danced with every ounce of energy that I had left in me!

It was time for my solo, which was about thirty seconds. I came out on the stage again and rocked it! I performed my African jumps, and I spun my head around in circles as fast as I could, while my class was on their knees in a circle around me, clapping. The audience cheered wildly as I performed my heart out. The cheers made up for the pain of me not having the right costume on.

My performance ended, and my mother picked me up at the stage exit. "Okay, baby, come with me. You did awesome, by the way," she said as she led me to the back stairways.

"Why are we not taking the elevator, Mom?" I said bewildered.

"'Cause I need to get back upstairs before your class makes it back."

We hurried up the stairs and beat the class back to the dressing room. My mother grabbed my black suitcase and the suitcase she got the African costume out of. She waited for the girls to come claim their suitcases, and we noticed Shantey and her mother looking for her suitcase.

"Is this what you looking for?" my mother said in a nasty tone as she pulled out the suitcase.

"Yes, what you doing with my daughter's suitcase?" Shantey's mother scolded.

"Take a look at your daughter's African costume. Doesn't it look too small to you?" my mother screamed as the woman checked out her daughter's outfit.

"That's because that's *my* child's outfit! Look at the tag. I wrote her name in it!" my mother shouted as the lady checked the tag on the costume Shantey had on. My name was written on the tag in big black letters.

"Oh, man, I'm so sorry," Shantey's mother apologized.

"I don't understand. Y'all stuff was all the way over there on the other side of the room. Why would you come and pick up Jamila's things? She almost missed the performance behind that!"

"I'm sorry again, Liddie—all the excitement and the race for time."

"Well, okay. Please, please, please, don't y'all touch my baby's stuff again," my mother shouted loudly, and the entire room felt her force!

My mother meant business when it came to me. She wasn't going to let anyone ruin my success! I got dressed for my next performance. The room was silent after the commotion. We had two more performances left. My mother made a special little corner for me to get changed in as she grilled the other parents and murmured under her breath.

"I don't know what these people trying to do to you, but, baby, God got you, and He always gonna take care of you, baby," my mother said as she helped me get dressed.

"Mom, I know, it's okay. I think it was a mistake."

"People don't make mistakes like that. That costume was way too tight for that little girl! Her momma ain't crazy, but I got something for them if they keep playing with you."

I didn't understand why my mother took this so personal, but as I thought it over, it didn't make sense how they mixed my stuff up with Shantey's. Maybe they did want me to miss my African solo!

The night was a success. We completed all of our performances well. I quickly got dressed with the anticipation of watching the rest of the show. The best performances and the tribute were always saved for the last part of the show. I packed my costumes, and my mother and I went out to sit in the audience with the rest of my relatives who were enjoying the show.

"Oh, baby, you did so good," my father said, and he embraced me as we took our seats.

"We got you on camera, baby," my aunt Carolyn cheered.

I sat down in my seat and watched the rest of the performance. Oh, the show was so good! I enjoyed every moment of it!

There were quite a few duet performances done that night with a male and female dancer. They were so amazing! The one in particular I liked was done by two alumni students that was performed to Shirley Murdock's "As We Lay." The two dancers danced so passionately. They hugged, and the man spun the woman around as they dipped and fell on the floor together. Then they rolled and rolled, acting out the words to the song in their dance. The audience members stood up and applauded at key points in the routine and snapped photos. You could hear the "oh's" and "ah's" of the audience members. There was so much heat and passion on that stage!

The stage lights went dark, and when they came back on, Ms. Johnson stood on the stage in a beautiful long sequined black gown with a mic in her hand. The audience cheered as the spotlight came down on her. She looked stunning, just like a movie star.

"Good evening, ladies and gentlemen. Have you guys enjoyed the performance thus far?" she asked as the audience cheered and applauded for her.

"Well, we're at the grand finale. I told you all we have a special tribute tonight. We would like to honor someone whose music has truly influenced this generation. His name is Michael Jackson, and guess what? He's here!" she yelled as the crowd went crazy, and the spotlights flashed the box seats on top of the stage where he sat.

Michael Jackson stood up and waved and blew kisses at Ms. Johnson as the audience applauded. The crowd was in such awe that they gave him a standing ovation.

"I have to thank my special friend, Ms. Diana Ross, for making this all possible. Diana, stand up and wave at the audience, please!" Ms. Johnson said as Diana Ross, who was sitting next to Michael Jackson, stood up and waved. The crowd also stood up and clapped as they cheered for Diana Ross too.

"Ladies and Gentlemen, we had a special treat this year at our dance school. Diana's daughter performed with us in the Super Tot class. I love you, Diana, for entrusting us with Chudney. Now, ladies and gentlemen, let's no longer delay tonight's special performance," she announced and exited the stage.

The curtains opened and Michael Jackson's *Thriller* music came on. The crowd went wild! The tap pro class was dressed in cemetery clothes and wigs just like in the Thriller video. They had tombstone props and everything. It was incredible. Edgar, one of the studio's premiere alumni, played Michael Jackson. He had the red and black Thriller jacket and the black high water pants like Michael Jackson wore in the video. It was sensational! Even Michael Jackson enjoyed it. He stood to his feet clapping, holding Emmanuel Lewis in his arms.

After that night, you couldn't tell me anything! I told the whole world Michael Jackson, Diana Ross, and Emmanuel Lewis, the lead character in the popular 80's T.V. show, *Webster*, came to my dance recital! My world was transformed after that night. In my eyes, I was truly a little star!

"Mom, I'm ready," I shouted as I dragged my suitcase down the steps.

"Okay, baby. Let's go," she said, and she grabbed her travel mug filled with coffee and her car keys.

We rode two towns over to the Laurelton Theatre, where we met the cast members of the play *Mahalia Lives* standing outside of the theatre with their luggage. I anxiously gathered my luggage and kissed my mom.

"Now, Jamie, here's some money. Call me as soon as you get back, and I'll come pick you up. Don't get in any trouble."

"Yes, Mommy."

"And Jamie, knock 'em dead, baby girl!" my mother said before I shut the car door.

"I sure will!"

I joined my fellow cast members waiting in front of the theatre for the bus.

"Hello, Young Mahalia," Mrs. King greeted me as I approached the theatre.

"Hi, Mrs. King," I said with admiration.

"The shuttle bus should be here any minute. Would you like some breakfast or hot chocolate from the store?" Mrs. King asked as she sipped her coffee and ate her buttered roll.

"No, thank you, ma'am," I replied. "What time will we get to D.C., Mrs. King? Is it far?"

"Let's see, we should be gone by 8:30 and reach there no later than 1 p.m. The show starts at 7 o'clock, so we have plenty time to check in the hotel and get ourselves ready for the performance."

"So you never been to Washington, D.C., before?" Mrs. King questioned.

"No, ma'am."

"Okay, maybe we'll have a little time, and I'll take you to see the White House."

"Wow, the White House! Where the president lives, right?"

"That's right. Did you know Mahalia Jackson sang in Washington, D.C., at the March on Washington led by Dr. Martin Luther

Chapter Twenty-One

King?"

"No, I didn't know that."

"That's right, young lady, and I'm gonna take you to the place where she stood and sang."

"Oh, wow. I'm so excited," I said as I daydreamed about Dr. King and Mahalia Jackson.

I envisioned Mahalia Jackson standing in Washington, D.C., at the March on Washington, singing while hundreds of people stood in the streets and watched. Now I was performing in the play as Mahalia and going to the city where she sang. I was so excited. I was eleven years old and the youngest cast member in the play. I was the understudy for my cousin, Kanika, who couldn't make it to the performance. The second youngest was "Teen Mahalia," who was played by a sixteen-year-old named Kenya.

The shuttle bus arrived, and the entire cast loaded in. There were about thirty of us in total, including cast members and band members. We boarded the luxury bus that had TVs, recliner seats, and a minijuice bar. I found a nice comfortable seat in the back of the bus and went to sleep.

"Hey, Jamila, would you like to eat with me?"

"Okay, ladies and gentlemen, we are here!" Mrs. King announced.

The time seemed to have flown by as I got caught up in my dreams. We quickly gathered our luggage from the bins on the top of the bus and headed into the hotel. I instantly felt like a celebrity as the bellhops greeted us and carried our luggage. We entered the large busy hotel lobby, and Mrs. King checked us in and got our room keys.

"Okay, Kenya and Jamila, you'll be rooming with me," Mrs. King said.

We loaded into one of the hotel elevators and went up to our room. The cast had several rooms, all on the same floor.

Our hotel room was a nice double-bed room with a lounge area and large bathroom. I anxiously entered the room to check it out. I dived onto the bed to check out the softness of the mattress. Then I raced over to look out the window to catch the view. The view was incredible! I could see all the tall buildings in the busy downtown area.

"Mrs. King, will you still take me to see the White House?" I asked very politely.

"Okay, Jamila, we still have a few hours before showtime. Kenya, would you like to go?"

"No, Mrs. King. I'm tired. I just want to relax," Kenya replied. Kenya was a pretty light-skinned girl with medium-length hair who was extremely talented.

"Well, all right, but listen, Kenya, you are not to leave this room. I am responsible for you. I told your mother I would take good care of you."

"Yes, Mrs. King, I'm not going to go anywhere. I promise."

"Well, okay. You have the phone if there are any problems."

"Yes, ma'am."

Mrs. King and I left the hotel, and the bellman flagged us down a cab. We sat in the backseat of the cab, and the cabdriver set the meter. I watched the scenery in the downtown area out of the window of the cab and was mesmerized by what I saw. Mrs. King became my tour guide, telling me what historical landmarks we were passing.

"Hey, there goes the White House, Mrs. King!" I said excitedly as we approached the building.

"You are right, darling. Here we are!" she replied.

I intensely stared at the big white building with beautiful large columns. I had seen it before in my textbooks and on television, but never in person. I was mesmerized.

"Cabdriver, you can let us out here," Mrs. King requested, and we exited the vehicle.

"Darling, you are standing in the place where so much history has taken place. So many great people have stood where you are standing. This is the place that the entire world heard the message of Dr. Martin Luther King. 'Let Freedom Ring!' That's what he said, darling. Back in my day, white folks and colored folks didn't mix with each other. As a singer and actress growing up, I had to perform for white people and black people separately. Some of the places I performed for white folks I could only enter because I was performing. Even after I performed, I couldn't use their bathrooms or their water fountains.

"Jamila, your generation is so blessed. The way has been paved for your generation to excel. Times were rough for black folks in my day. We had to struggle and work very hard to get everything we got! We didn't have the opportunities that you have now. Jamila, you have a lot of talent. You can be whatever you want to be in life. You are very special," Mrs. King said as she walked me past the historical monuments in Washington, D.C.

"You really think I'm special, Mrs. King?" I asked in awe.

"You certainly are, baby. I recognized your talent as soon as you walked through the doors of the theatre. You are going to become someone who is very powerful and successful one day, and you remember I told you so, young lady. Okay?"

"Yes, ma'am, I'll always remember what you said to me."

"Now let me see that beautiful smile."

"Like this?" I said as I stopped and gave my biggest smile, showing all my teeth.

"No, darling, when you smile, I want to see your entire face smile! That includes your eyes. Now watch me, baby," Mrs. King said as she taught me how to liven my entire expression when I smiled.

"Mrs. King, like this?" I asked as I mimicked her.

"Yes, darling. You catch on quickly! I'm going to teach you how to be a fine young lady. Is that okay with you?"

"Yes, ma'am," I said as I sucked up all the attention she gave me.

The conversation I had with Mrs. King boosted my self-esteem! My mother always told me I was her little star and I was special, but now, Mrs. King said it too! *Maybe I really am special. Maybe I will be someone great like she told me*, I thought to myself.

We enjoyed our entire afternoon together, walking up and down the busy downtown Washington, D.C., streets. Mrs. King covered the areas of black history that unfolded in the midst of Washington, D.C. I left her with a newfound understanding of the expression, "I'm black, and I am proud."

We headed back to the hotel in time to freshen up and prepare to leave for the evening show. As I got dressed, I repeated in my mind all the struggles Mrs. King went through as a black singer and actress. She told me I should be grateful for my opportunities, and, even more important to me, she said I was special. I wanted to show Mrs. King I was grateful, and I wanted her to see me shine!

The evening approached, and the shuttle bus met us in front of the hotel. We all loaded in. I placed my suitcase above in the luggage rack, and I stayed to myself in the back. I went over my lines in my head, and I began to daydream. I saw the audience staring and clapping, as I pictured myself as the star of the show.

"Jamila, c'mon, girl. We here!" Kenya shouted as she nudged me.

"Oh, okay," I said as I awoke from my daydreaming. I got my luggage and headed out of the bus. We entered a large church auditorium where we were led up the back stairs to our dressing rooms. I shared a dressing room with Kenya.

I got dressed and roamed around the halls of the backstage area. All the cast members were practicing and getting into their roles. Everyone was serious. There was no more joking and playing like we were accustomed to at rehearsals. It was showtime!

I made my way to the stage and peeped out from the curtains. The auditorium was packed with church members. The women were all dressed to impress in their fancy church dresses and their large hats. The people were all talking and loading into the busy auditorium, anxiously awaiting the play to begin.

Mrs. King's productions were highly sought after. She generated a lot of attention and a great buzz, especially in the African American churches throughout the country. After one person would see the play, they would brag and tell the next person, who would then make arrangements to book us.

"Jamila, what are you doing?" Kenya asked as she tapped me on my shoulder.

"Nothing. I just wanted to check out this place," I responded with an attitude.

"C'mon, Jamila. Mrs. King wants us to get ready for prayer."

We left the backstage area and headed into a large room where we all held hands, and Mr. Smith, who was not only a cast member in the play but also a minister, led the prayer. He was a heavyset black man with dark brown skin and had a bald head.

Mr. Smith prayed passionately.

"Father God, we come to You today in the mighty name of Jesus. The name that is higher than any other name. Lord, we invite Your presence and Your Holy Spirit into this place right now. We ask that You touch us and fill each and every one of us with

Your precious Spirit. Give us the ability to do what we cannot do in our own strength. Lord, we lend You our vessels so You can be glorified today. Touch hearts and minds so our performance will help save the life of someone who sits in this audience. Cover us, Lord, keep us, and guide us safely home to our families. In Jesus' mighty name, we pray. Amen."

"Amen," everyone said in unison. We ended our prayer, and it was showtime.

I played the part of Young Mahalia, so I was up first. The narrator came onstage and introduced my scene. I quickly transformed into my role. I came out in an old-fashioned dress with Mary Jane shoes on. I was cleaning up the living room on the set, and I stopped and looked about to see if anybody was around. Then I popped an old blues record into the record player, and I began to dance and sing away to the tune. As I was singing and dancing around, my aunt appeared out of nowhere and tapped me on my shoulder.

"Mahalia, what in the world are you doing?"

"Oh, Auntie, I was just . . . um . . . I was . . ."

"What did I tell you about that heathen music? I don't want that stuff in my house."

"Uh, yes, yes, ma'am."

"Give me that record," she said as she grabbed it and broke it in half.

"This is the Lord's house, and in the Lord's house we play His music. You hear me, little girl?"

"Yes, ma'am."

"Now you go and get ready for church," she said, and she left the room.

"Yes, ma'am," I responded. Feeling lonely and hopeless, I began to pray.

"Lord, things sure have been rough since my mommy left me. She would have never beat on me or mistreated me like my auntie do. Lord, I don't know why my auntie be so mean to me. She don't let me do the things the other kids do. Ever since my mother died, I feel so all alone. It's like I ain't got nobody, Lord, except for You. Do You love me, Lord? If you do, please help me. Touch my auntie's heart. Please help her treat me better. I want to enjoy my childhood, Lord, and do fun things like the other kids do. And, Lord, if you still listening, if there's a doll left over from Christmas, may I have it, please?"

The piano began to play, and I sang, "Sometimes I Feel Like a Motherless Child." As I sang I felt the energy of my audience. I also felt the pain of my character, Young Mahalia, and I began to cry. I thought of how lonely Mahalia had to feel without her mother. I thought of how life would be for me without my mother, and I cried intensely. I almost couldn't get through the song. The people in the audience began to cry too. I saw tissues being passed back and forth. I ended my scene, and the audience applauded as I left the stage. Mrs. King greeted me as I walked off.

"Good job, Jamila! You even had me crying, darling. I told you, baby, you have a gift. We've got to work on it. That was absolutely fabulous!" she said.

Kenya was up next. She walked on the stage as I walked off.

There was nothing like the high I got from performing. Inside, I was on fire. Participating in this play made me feel closer to my dream of one day being a star. After the show, I stood taking pictures and signing autographs with the audience members.

"Little girl, you are amazing! You had me crying. You gonna be a big actress one day, I bet," a little old lady with gray hair said to me as I signed my autograph on her program. I felt very special. I loved show biz, and it looked like show biz loved me, too!

It was a humid July day, in 1989, and I was preparing for my twelfth birthday party. I decided to go into my brother's room to look for his friend Urnesto's number, who I wanted to DJ at the party. I went in his room looking for his phone book and opened his top drawer and noticed a knot of money wrapped up in a rubber band. *How in the world did he get this much money?* I thought to myself as my eyes opened wide in awe of the money. *Oh, he gonna give me some of this, or I'm going to tell Mommy!*

I paced the floor in my room trying to figure out the source behind my brother's fortune. He was out playing ball, but I anxiously awaited his return. I imagined all the stuff I was going to buy with the money I was going to blackmail him for!

Nighttime drew near, and Kee finally returned home. Before he could get upstairs, I stopped him. "Hey, Kee."

"What?" he replied, clearly not wanting to be bothered.

"You in trouble," I said as I pointed my finger at him.

"Yo, what did I do?" he asked nervously.

"Come here," I said as I led him into his room and opened the drawer.

"Yo, what you doing?" he said as he tried to grab my hand. I shoved him away and opened the drawer and grabbed the money.

"What's this?" I asked as I held up the money.

"It's none of your business!" he said as he grabbed the money back.

"Well, let me see if it's Mommy's business. I'm gonna tell," I said as I walked out the door.

"No, yo, hold up! Wait," he protested and grabbed me.

"Jamie, don't tell. What you want?"

"Well, since you mentioned it, let me see. Well, first, how the hell you get all this money?"

"All right, I'll tell you if you promise not to tell. Do you promise?"

"Yeah, I promise, but I need some money too," I said as I held my hand out. My brother pulled a twenty dollar bill off the stack of money and placed it in my hands.

"Keep going," I demanded, and he pulled off another twenty

dollar bill.

"A little more."

"Well, hold up. How much I got to give you?" he asked with an attitude.

"I need at least a hundred dollars for this one! This is big!"

"Okay, here is a hundred dollars. Don't ask me for nothing else."

"Okay," I said as I counted the five twenty dollar bills in my hand. "Now, how you get this?" I asked.

"Well, you ain't gonna tell, right?"

"No, already. I got you!"

"Okay, C.B. gave it to me."

"Gave it to you for what? I ain't stupid. He's not just giving you all this money. You selling drugs, Kee?"

"No, Jamie. All I got to do is bag up the drugs. You see these little vials?" he said as he reached in another drawer.

"I put the work in these. I don't sell drugs. I just bag up, and occasionally, I drop the packages to the block."

"So, Kee, tell me what really happened about C.B. getting shot and all. I knew there had to be more to that story."

"Sit down," Kee said as he cleared his clothes off the bed, making room for me. Inside, I felt privileged. I almost never got invited to sit down in my brother's room to talk.

"All right, you know C.B. gets money, right?" Kee questioned.

"Yeah," I said as I listened intensely.

"Well, he hustles. He got two blocks. One on Springfield Boulevard, and one on Hollis Avenue. These blocks make a lot of money, so several people have been trying to kill C.B. so they can take over the block, but he ain't having it. C.B. got mad soldiers on the strip, and they be holding it down!"

"Oh my goodness. You don't be scared to go out there?"

"No, li'l sis. Your brother's about it. I ain't no punk."

"But what if they try to do something to you?"

"That's what protection is for."

"Protection? What you talking about?"

"Calm down, Jamie. I got this. I'm safe. C.B. told me what to do."

"But, Kee, even he got shot. I don't want nothing to happen to you." For the first time I thought about how sad I would be if something happened to my brother.

"Oh, so you care about me now?"

"I always care about you. It's you that treats me mean."

"Now, li'l sis, I'm going to be all right. Besides, I'm not out there like that. If something does happen to me, it's gonna be a war. Trust me! You getting ready to start junior high, so you gonna wanna stay fresh, right?"

"Yes."

"Okay, well, I'm gonna make sure you do. Okay?"

"I guess," I said as I thought about the money.

That day everything started making sense. I had noticed a change in my brother's behavior. Overnight, he changed from a little boy to a man. My brother was hard-core. He had a swagger and a walk that was worth a million bucks, and he didn't play! I've never seen him scared of anyone other than my parents.

He commanded attention, and he demanded respect. Kee became C.B.'s right-hand little man. Everything that went down, Kee knew about it. Kee worshipped the ground C.B. walked on, and C.B. kept Kee fresh. I felt protected, knowing if I had a problem, I could call my big brother. When it came to me, he had a no-tolerance policy. If there was trouble, he came and dealt with it. He chastised me in the house, but in the streets, he didn't let anybody bother me! In my own special way, I admired him.

* * *

It was July 11th, the day of my twelfth birthday. I got up and prepared for my party. After a serious amount of pleading, I finally convinced my parents to allow me to have a house party in our basement. Our basement was pretty large. My dad had a minisound system and a bar downstairs, where we had our family functions. There was also a second kitchen and a bathroom in our basement.

I helped my mom load the basement kitchen with food and beverages.

"Jamie, I hope this is enough food. I know y'all kids can eat."

"Mom, we are going to be fine."

"Okay, I just want everything to be okay. My baby is twelve years old today! You ain't my little baby no more. You are growing up, girl."

"Yup, that's right, and next year, I'm going to be a teenager."

"Okay, let's take one year at a time," Mom said as she laughed.

The basement was decorated nicely in pink and white streamers and pink and white balloons. The food was ready, wrapped up in aluminum containers on the stove. There were trays of popcorn, chips, and pretzels out on the tables, and a big glass bowl full of fruit punch stood in the middle. Everything was ready for my guests to arrive.

I went upstairs and changed into my birthday outfit. My cousin Tanya and my aunt Carolyn bought me a green and white short set from the Benetton store. I put on the outfit and a new pair of white, low-top Reeboks my mother had bought me. You couldn't tell me I wasn't fresh to death!

The doorbell rang, and my guests began to arrive. I had guests come from my school, church, and dance school, which were all mostly girls. My brother's friend, Ernesto Shaw, was my DJ. Today he is a renowned hip hop deejay, DJ Clue. He had crates and crates of records loaded up on top of each other in the bar area of the basement. Clue brought his friends, and my brother also invited his friends. The party was filled with mostly older teenagers.

The lights were dim in the basement, and the music was bumping. My mother stayed upstairs in her room as per my request, and we got our party on!

Jamaican music had just really gotten popular, and Clue kept the hottest records on repeat. The girls were whining their waists and gyrating like they do in the music videos, and the guys got up on the girls from behind, dancing. The walls were flooded with boys dancing and girls whining in front of them. Some of my friends were even on the floor with the boys, whining and shaking to the music. I loved to dance, so I was having a ball in my overpacked, hot, stuffy basement. I quickly caught on to the latest dances, and I got it in on the dance floor! The energy in the basement was incredible. Everyone was enjoying themselves. Not one person was sitting down. Clue had talent. He got on the mic and made everybody get up and dance, girls and guys!

"Girls girls every day, From London, Canada and the USA. Girls, girls, every day. King mon Shabba mon nana everyday," the girls sang out loud as Shabba Ranks "Trailer Load" song came on. I screwed up my face and started doing the tick whining dance I saw the girls do in the video.

"Go, Jamila, go, Jamila, go, Jamila," the crowd roared as they gathered around me. I began to really get into the moves as I thrived off the attention. My friend Kim brought her cousin who was from Jamaica with her to the party. As I danced, she began to challenge me, whining up on me, trying to outdo me.

As she began to dance and I realized she was coming for me, I placed my hands on the floor, and I bent down and began to dance. She copied me, trying to outdo my dance, so I had to think quick. I jumped into a full split with both of my legs straight out, and I began to whine up and down in my split. The crowd went wild, and the girl walked away.

"Go, Jamila, go, Jamila, go, Jamila," they yelled as I continued to dance on the floor, imitating the women who I had seen on the videos.

"Ah, yo, that's enough," my brother said as he leaned over and grabbed me off of the floor.

"Come on, Kee, it's my birthday."

"Yeah, I hear you, but all my friends ain't going to be watching you dance like that!"

"Okay, okay," I said as I got up and followed him. I went over to the table and got some punch. My mother had just filled up the bowl, and the juice was going like hot cakes. I poured the juice in a cup, drinking to catch my breath from all that dancing I had done. The juice tasted good, but it had a strange tang to it. After I drank the juice, I got the energy to just dance and wild out even more. I wasn't the only one either! Girls were lifting up their shirts, dancing and kissing boys in the corner. It was going down in the basement! Thank God we convinced my mother to stay upstairs.

My brother's friend Brian was standing over by the table with the punch on it.

"Yo, Brian, what the hell is in that punch?" my brother questioned.

"Oh, your father had some Smirnoff Vodka behind the bar, so we mixed it," Brian replied.

"Yo, y'all is bugging. This is my little sister's twelfth birthday. Her friends are mad young, and y'all got these little girls going crazy! Look at my sister."

I was on the dance floor dancing and laughing away.

My brother kept everything under control the best that he could. He was a kid too, but he busted up all the foul play in the basement. We all had a ball that night. I was twelve years old and finally growing up. I quickly noticed Kee didn't like the lustful stares I got from his friends. I was no longer a little girl to them; now, they were paying me attention, and I loved it. My brother's friends wanted to dance with me, but my brother kept blocking their moves. He acted more like a father than a brother who was only two-and-a-half years older than me.

My party was a success and the talk of the neighborhood. This was my first taste of teenage party life, and I enjoyed every drop of it! I couldn't wait for the next opportunity to get my dance on!

My twelfth birthday party officially put me on the map in my neighborhood! The older girls began to take notice of me, and they showed me a lot of attention. I started hanging out with them and getting into the activities they were in. I convinced my mom to allow me to go to the movies, skating rinks, and even parties with them. My mother especially liked Kim, who went to our church. She trusted me with her. I was twelve years old, and Kim was fifteen years old. I was in awe of Kim. She had it going on! Her brother, Stretch, was C.B.'s partner on the drug turfs they ran, and he made mad money! Stretch bought Kim everything. She had all the biggest door-knocker earrings and mad jewelry. My little earrings were nothing compared to Kim's truck jewelry. When we went out, she would let me put on her smaller set of door-knocker earrings. When I put them on, you couldn't tell me nothing!

Kim introduced me to all of her friends, including this girl that lived on the end of the next block from my house named Nakia. Nakia was a very tall, slender, maple-skinned girl with a large nose and chinky eyes. Nakia and I became close. She would often pick me up from my house because she lived right down the street.

Kim and all of her friends were in high school. They were all fly girls who rocked designer clothes and lots of jewelry. Most of their boyfriends were drug dealers who showered them with gifts. I quickly learned from them the strategies of how to get money out of guys.

We were all middle-class-suburban girls, but we were attracted to the hustling dudes who lived in the projects on the south side of Jamaica, Queens. We learned that in the projects the boys made way more money selling drugs than on our side of town. The project boys were driving hot cars as early as sixteen years old, wearing trunk jewelry, and balling out of control! Back then, the boys loved to spend their money on their girlfriends. It was a prize to have a girlfriend from our part of town. To them, we were "sophisticated girls" because our parents had money and owned their own houses. I watched Kim intensely. I looked up to her, and I idolized her respect in the neighborhood. I wanted to grow up and be exactly like Kim! That became my new goal.

*S*hortly after my twelfth birthday, I got up early one morning, cleaned up, and did my chores. I finished early so I could get out of the house and enjoy my day.

"Mommy, I cleaned up my room, and I did everything you told me to do. Can I please go to Kim's house to play? Please!" I begged my mother as she sipped her coffee and read the newspaper.

"Jamie, I wish you would find some friends your own age. Kim is a nice girl, but she is in high school. She's a little too old for you to hang out with."

"Mom, she's only a couple years older than me. Mommy, I'm lonely in the house by myself, and I just want to have a little fun. I do everything you tell me to do, and I get good grades in school, right?"

"Well, I guess so," she responded.

"Kim has her younger sister Carrie who is my age. I hang out with her too, Mommy. We just hang around her house and talk and stuff."

"Okay, where is Sister Walker at?"

"Mom, she's always in the house when we are there."

"All right, I guess, if Sister Walker is there. She is a good Christian woman, so I guess it's okay."

"Thank you, Mom, so much! You are the greatest!" I said as I kissed my mother. "Oh, by the way, I need a little money, just in case we decide to go somewhere."

"Oh, Jamie, you always want something," she said as she reached in her pocketbook and pulled out twenty dollars. "Don't ask me for anything else, and your butt better be back in the house by eight o'clock. When the streetlights come on, you better be home. You hear me, girl?"

"Yes, Mom, I hear you."

I quickly grabbed the money and put it in my pocket. Then I walked out of the house. I was excited about spending the day with Kim. There was always excitement happening when I was around her!

I walked down my block and crossed over Springfield

Chapter Twenty-Three

Boulevard, which was the busy street my church was on. I walked a block and a half more down to Kim's house. When I arrived at her house, I rang the doorbell.

"Who is it?" Kim's mother, Sister Walker, asked.

"It's Jamie. Is Kim home?" I said loudly so she could hear me through the large wooden door.

"Yes, baby, come on in," Sister Walker said as she opened the door.

"How is your mother, Jamie?"

"She's fine, thank you," I replied as I entered the large brick house that covered the whole corner of the block.

"Kim, Kim, come downstairs. Jamie is here to see you," Sister Walker shouted up the stairway.

"I'm coming," Kim yelled back, and I sat on the living-room couch. Kim came down the stairs slowly as if she had just got up.

"Yo, you up mad early," Kim said. Kim was a dark-skinned sort of stocky girl with beautiful white teeth and medium-length hair.

"Yeah, you told me to come through when I got up," I replied.

"I forgot you get up before the break of day. C'mon. Come upstairs with me," Kim said as she led me up the stairway to her bedroom.

As we walked up the stairs, Kim's brother Stretch's door opened.

"Yo, who is that, Kim?" Monessa, Stretch's pregnant girlfriend, said as she peeked out his room. She was a pretty, with light Mocha skin tones and long hair and a voluptuous body. Her stomach was bulging out. She was about six months pregnant.

"Oh, it's my friend Jamie," Kim replied.

"Stretch, it's just Kim's little friend," Monessa said before closing the door.

"Yo, Kim, why y'all friends coming through so early?" Stretch grumbled as if I had awakened him.

"This is my friend from church," Kim replied.

"Oh, oh, oh, my bad," Stretch responded as Monessa shut the bedroom door.

We entered Kim's room. She got back in the bed, and I watched television waiting for her to get up. I stared at all the large rap posters she had covering her bedroom walls, and I studied all the pictures she had taken of her friends. Her friends would go to this store called 60 Second Photo in Green Acres Mall, and they would all take pictures with each other. I immediately gravitated to the photos she took with her boyfriend, Minute.

I wish I had a boyfriend to take photos with, I thought to myself. The private telephone line in Kim's room rang. Kim jumped out of her sleep and answered the phone.

"Hello," she said and paused.

"What, girl? . . . Say, word? . . . Oh, I'm coming over there right now!" she said in an irritated tone as she hung up the phone. "This boy keeps playing with me! I'm so sick of his garbage. Miesha just left from Minute's crib with Minute's brother, and Minute had a girl at the house with him! I got to get over there now!" Kim shouted and quickly gathered her items to jump in the shower.

"Jamie, pick out something for me to wear," Kim instructed, and she grabbed her towel. I opened up Kim's large walk-in closet full of designer clothes. Looking up and down the shelves, I finally picked out a pair of dark denim Calvin Klein shorts and a white T-shirt. Then I went in her bottom drawer and picked out a pair of panties and a bra, and I brought them all to her in the bathroom.

"Get my Gucci bag off the dresser and pass it to me," Kim said as she took the items from me at the bathroom door.

I went to her dresser and saw the large tan and brown bag with "*Gs*" on it. It was hot. I put it on my arm and stared at how I looked in the mirror. *I want a Gucci bag too!* I said to myself as I brought Kim her bag.

Kim quickly got dressed and knocked on Stretch's door. "Stretch, Stretch, open up," she yelled.

"Yo, Kim, what's the matter, baby?" Stretch responded sympathetically hearing the urgency in her voice. Stretch was a tall, chocolate boy with a long, thin frame.

"I need you to take me to Minute's house. It's important!"

"C'mon, Kim, I ain't even got no sleep yet. I just came in this morning."

Kim began to cry, and she pleaded for her brother's help.

"Please, I got to get over there right away. Miesha said he got some girl in the crib. I want to catch him so I can break up with him for good."

"See, Kim? This is why I didn't want you messing with no boys. Didn't I tell you they were no good! I'ma get up 'cause I'ma beat the brakes off Minute. I told him if he hurts you, I would take his life. What he thinks—I'm some sort of joke? Give me a minute. I'ma throw something on. Stop crying, okay?" Stretch said at the door of his room.

I listened intensely, and I could tell by the sound of Stretch's voice it was on and poppin'!

Stretch quickly got dressed, and we followed him out of the house into his green Mazda MPV van. Kim got in the passenger seat, and I got in the backseat. Stretch got in the car and started it up. The music immediately came on. You could feel the bump in the car's system. *"Do me, baby! Do the Humpty Hump, come on and do the Humpty Hump. Do me, baby,"* the song "The Humpty Dance" blasted out of the speakers.

"Yo, let me go get my gun just in case this fool acts up," Stretch said as he left the car running and went back in the house.

My eyes opened wide! *Minute is in trouble now,* I thought to myself. Kim sat quietly in the front of the car. I could tell she was really hurt as I watched the tears flow down from her eyes.

Stretch got back in the car and turned up the music and raced off. When the Humpty song went off, he played it again. "Yo, Kim, you like this song?" he asked.

"I guess it's okay," she responded.

"Okay? This is the joint! This is my man Tupac's song. Remember the dude I told you I went to the studio with in California? He's gonna be that next hot dude, I'm telling you," Stretch said as he bopped his head to the music.

"Yo, Shorty, do you like this song?" Stretch asked me as he watched me bop my head in the backseat.

"Yeah, this is hot. I like it," I responded.

"Yeah, Shorty, you got taste," Stretch said as he looked back at me.

"Yo, why you look mad familiar?" he questioned.

"I told you, she goes to the church," Kim replied.

"Oh, that's right, you the little girl who sang at the anniversary."

"Yeah, and you know me too from my cousin C.B.," I responded.

"C.B., that's my main, man!" Stretch said as he stared at me closely.

"Yeah, that's my cousin!" I said proudly.

"Oh, shoot, you Kee's little sister."

"Yeah," I said, taken back that Stretch knew Kee.

"Okay, that's my little man. That's why you look so familiar. You and your brother got them same big eyes. What's your name?"

"My name is Jamila, but my family calls me Jamie," I responded.

"Jamie, you like my man Tupac's music, huh?" Stretch asked as he played different Tupac tracks.

"Yeah, it's hot! The tracks sound different," I responded.

"Yeah, I made these tracks with my West Coast dudes out in Cali. They on a whole other flow!" Stretch said as he bopped his head to the beat.

"Yeah, that's what's up," I responded as I moved to the music. I was happy to gain Stretch's esteem.

We pulled up in front of the Woodhull Housing project by the back building where Minute lived. Quickly changing his demeanor, Stretch parked the car to go upstairs.

"No, let me go up first, Stretch, and I'ma bring him down," Kim suggested.

"No, Kim, I'ma run up on this dude in his house," he demanded.

"Please don't, I got this!" Kim begged.

"Okay, but make sure you bring him outside!"

"C'mon, Jamie," Kim said as she opened the back door for me to go with her.

We entered the medium-sized brick building and waited for the elevator. Finally, the elevator arrived, and we stepped over the fresh urine that someone had just pissed out and pressed the button to close the door.

We got off the elevator at Minute's floor, and Kim ran to knock at the door.

"Yo, who is it?" Minute yelled out.

"It's me, open up the door!" Kim demanded. The door opened, and Minute was in his boxers and a wife beater.

"Ah, yo, what the hell you doing here?" he questioned. Minute was a medium height, chocolate tone boy who had a short Caesar haircut.

"Let me in!" Kim said as she forced her way past Minute and through the door. I followed behind her. Kim walked all through the house, looking to see who was there.

"Yo, where is that bitch at?" she yelled.

"Ain't no chick here. What you talkin' about?" Minute asked.

"Don't play with me. I'm tired of you cheating on me!"

"I don't know what you talking about."

"You think I'm stupid, right?" Kim asked furiously.

"You need to tell your little friends to mind their business. I know Miesha called you with that bullshit. I could tell by the look in her eyes when she left that she was gonna call you. Yo, that was my cousin."

"Your cousin who?"

"My cousin Angela."

"Why I don't know your cousin Angela? I know your whole family, Minute. Stop lying!"

"Now, baby, for real, that was my cousin on my father's side. You know I love you and only you, baby," Minute said as he kissed Kim's cheek. Kim shrugged him away, and he went and grabbed a shoe box.

"Look, baby, I was getting ready to call you anyway. I just got this money last night, and I want to take you shopping," Minute said as he waved around a knot of money.

"Oh, for real, baby," Kim responded as her anger quickly dispersed.

"Yeah, let me get dressed and we can go to Jamaica Avenue now."

"Oh, okay, let me tell my brother he can go ahead."

"Your brother who? Stretch?"

"Yeah, he drove me over here."

"Baby, you trying to get me killed or something?"

"No, I just asked my brother for a ride. I'ma go downstairs and tell him that everything is okay and I'm staying with you."

"Okay, yeah, tell him to go ahead."

Kim and I went back to the car. Stretch was standing outside the car with a screw face. She acted as if nothing happened.

"Stretch, I'm sorry. I made a mistake. The girl was only his cousin. Miesha didn't know what she was talking about," Kim said.

"Did you speak to the girl?" he asked.

"No, she wasn't there."

"Then how do you know it was just his cousin?"

"Minute told me."

"Kim, I didn't raise no fools. Go get that dude and tell him to come down here now!" Stretch said in a no-nonsense voice.

"Oh, okay," Kim said, clearly frightened of Stretch.

We went back upstairs and rang the doorbell, and Minute came to the door fully dressed.

"You ready, baby?" Minute asked, and he kissed Kim on the lips.

"Yeah, but my brother wants to see you."

"He want to see me for what?" Minute questioned angrily.

"'Cause I, I had, um, I told him a girl was here when Miesha called me earlier."

"See, Kim? You be doin' dumb shit. Now I got to go see this tall-behind crazy man about somethin' that's not even true."

"Well, c'mon 'cause he ain't leaving," Kim said, and Minute went to the window where he saw Stretch posted outside, leaning on his car.

"Oh, shoot, Stretch looks mad as hell. Yo, let me go get my gun."

"Your *gun*? Are you stupid? That's my brother. What you need your gun for?"

"Man, girl, you better be glad I love you," Minute said deciding to leave his gun behind.

He took his bankroll and stuffed it in the pocket of his jeans, and we went downstairs.

"Yo, what's up, Stretch?" Minute said in an upbeat tone, trying to lessen the tension. He reached to give Stretch a pound (a handshake). By this time, all the little project boys were outside posted up in front of the building.

"Man, I don't want no pound. What's up with this girl in the crib?"

"Um, nah, um, that was just my cousin. Miesha be trippin'. I knew she was gonna call Kim."

"Listen, I told you once before and never let me have to tell you again or it ain't gonna be pretty. If you hurt my sister, I'ma hurt you," Stretch said as he used his large body to push up against Minute and point at his head.

"Ah, yo, everything good over there?" one of the boys in front of the building yelled.

"Yeah, yeah, this just my brother-in-law. We having some family problems, that's all," Minute responded back.

"Oh, all right," the boy said.

"I love your sister, man. I ain't gonna do nothing to hurt her. Matter fact, I'm gonna take her shopping now on Jamaica Avenue. She been asking me to buy her some stuff." Minute had a charismatic personality. He knew just what to say to calm Stretch down. Money seemed to make everything all right.

"Oh, all right, get in. I'ma drop y'all off," Stretch said as he got back in the car.

Minute got in the front, and Kim and I jumped in the back of the MPV. The music bumped as we rode down Jamaica Avenue.

"Oh, what's this?" Minute asked.

"Oh, these the tracks I did with my man Tupac," Stretch responded.

"Yo, these are fresh to death, man."

"Yo, you like them?"

"Hell, yeah. Turn it up," Minute said as Stretch turned up the volume. Minute bopped his head as if he was really into the music, gaining Stretch's esteem.

"Yo, my man, you got talent, Stretch."

"Yeah, you think so? Listen to this next track," Stretch said as he continued playing music all the way until we got to our destination. By the time we got to the avenue, Stretch wasn't even mad anymore. Minute talked him out of his anger just like he talked Kim out of hers.

"All right, y'all. Kim, call me if you need me. I'm going back in the crib."

"Okay, Stretch," Kim said as she got out of the car and hugged him through the window.

"All right, Stretch, one love," Minute said, and he gave him a pound.

"Yo, Money, do my little sister right," Stretch said as he slapped Minute's hand.

"I got you, my man," Minute said as he got out of the car.

We went into the Coliseum, and Minute bought Kim the new Bangle earrings that had just come out, a Cuban lynx chain, and three pairs of sneakers. Kim was so happy! You could tell by the expression on her face. Money took away all her pain.

Hanging out with Kim became a normal routine. The more time I spent with her, the more I wanted to be like her. Kim didn't fit the typical description of what I was taught was pretty, but she possessed a domineering tone that let everyone know she was a "boss chick." Being Stretch's younger sister, she possessed power in our neighborhood. Nobody challenged her, because they didn't want to have to deal with the wrath of Stretch.

* * *

"Yo, Jamie, I'm thirsty. Let's stop at the store," Kim said as we got off the city bus in our neighborhood one bright afternoon.

We went into the Bodega, and Kim bought us Bon Ton Potato Chips and Pepsi. While Kim was paying for our items, I heard a loud noise.

"Boom, boom, boom!" Three shots fired. We quickly ran to the door and saw a large guy on a motorcycle fall to the ground. Blood was everywhere.

"Oh, shoot. That looks like Cory's bike," Kim screamed. We ran over to see the boy, and Kim started screaming uncontrollably. "Cory, Cory, no, no!" she yelled. Cory lay on the ground unconscious, with blood coming from everywhere!

I stared at the heavyset boy as blood poured from his body. I had so many mixed emotions. I had no clue who he was, but I imagined the pain those who loved him would experience. As I pondered those thoughts, I also cried for this man whom I did not know.

Sirens sounded, and the cops came on the scene, followed by the ambulance. Kim ran to the pay phone and called her house. "Stretch, Stretch! I'm on Hempstead and Springfield. They just shot Cory," she said frantically and paused.

"Come now. Hurry up, the cops just got here," she said and hung up the phone.

"Kim, who is Cory?" I asked reluctantly.

"He's one of my brother's good friends. He runs one of the blocks in Hollis. He's a boss."

The cops came and immediately taped off the area of the crime scene with yellow tape and moved us away from the area. Stretch came flying around the corner in his green MPV and quickly hopped out of the car. He bypassed the police and ran over to Cory.

"Cory, yo, Cory," Stretch said as he grabbed Corey's lifeless body. "Don't leave me, Cory. We got so much out here to do. Cory, wake up! Yo, wake the hell up!" Stretch yelled passionately, and he fell to his knees and cried. The officer grabbed Stretch.

"Young man, you can't be over here, sir," the cop scolded.

"Get off of me! This is like my brother, man," Stretch said as he pushed the cop away. The cop backed off. Stretch bent over Cory's body and cried profusely. Kim went over and hugged Stretch and cried with him too. I didn't know Cory, but I cried with them. It was so sad. Cory was pronounced dead on the scene! He was killed by a local drug rival who wanted his drug turf.

Left and right, bodies were dropping in retaliation for Cory's death. Overnight, our nice suburban neighborhood became very dangerous! Crack cocaine was increasing on the scene, and people were constantly getting shot over territories, blocks, and money. It was the late '80s and the street policy was kill or be killed. This was my first encounter with death up close and personal. I realized that day street life wasn't a game!

*M*y large boom box blasted the Salt-n-Pepa song, "Push It," as I played in the basement of my house! The twins and I were dancing our hearts out to the up-tempo beat preparing for the hip-hop lesson that we would receive the next day.

"Five, six, seven, eight, duhn, daa, duhn, push it good. Dun, duda, duhn, push it real good," I said, calling out the steps as we practiced to the music.

My brother walked down the stairs with his friend Brian. "What y'all doing down here?" he asked as he peeped over the basement banister.

"We minding our own business, why?" I said sarcastically as I kept performing. Renée and Michelle stopped to stare in awe of Kee and his cute friend Brian.

"Hey, Kee," the girls said.

"Yo, what's up? This is my man Brian," Kee said as he introduced Brian to the twins.

"Hey, Brian," the twins both said as their eyes sparkled.

"Look, we practicing for this show. We got things to do now," I said hastily to get the boys to leave.

"Yo, what show?" Brian asked.

"Oh, we are the new Smurfling dancers for the Shirt King's in the Coliseum Mall. They having a grand reopening, and we are dancing," Renée said proudly.

"Oh, word? That's fresh," Brian responded.

"Okay now, we got to get back to rehearsal," I said as I fanned them away.

"Yo, who you talking to like that!" Kee shouted, motioning as if he was going to lunge after me.

"I'm talking to you. You always be acting funny when you have company; now I got company so be gone!" I said with my hand on my hip.

"I should punch you in the back of the head with your smart mouth," my brother said as he climbed down the steps to approach me.

Chapter Twenty-Four

"Mommy! Mommy!" I screamed, and my brother stopped in his tracks.

"Yes, Jamie," my mother yelled from upstairs.

"Nothing, Mah, she's good!" my brother shouted back, and he went back up the steps.

"Better had," I said to my brother as he left.

"Okay, y'all, let's finish up," I said as I restarted the music. "Five, six, five, six, seven, eight," I shouted as we repeated the dance moves over and over. We danced for several hours until we got ready to go to bed.

Then we changed into our pajamas and lounged on the bed. The rest of the night we had girl talk. The twins were way more advanced with boys than I was. I sat back and listened and learned from their experience.

"Jamie, do you know how to kiss?" Renée asked as she brushed her long, wavy hair on my bed.

"No, not really," I answered reluctantly.

"Renée, you know she ain't never had a boyfriend," Michelle interjected.

"Except her fake boyfriend from down South," Renée said as they both laughed.

"I don't know why y'all laughing at me. I'm okay with myself. When the time is right I'll have a boyfriend," I said defensively.

"It's good to have a boyfriend, Jamie. You do all types of fun things with them, including kissing. You never kissed a boy before, right?"

"No," I said in embarrassment.

"Okay, go and get us three pieces of ice so I can show you how to kiss."

"Okay," I said as I dashed downstairs with excitement. I wanted to learn how to kiss! I quickly got the ice out of the freezer, put it in a cup, and came back upstairs.

"Okay, put your lips on the ice like this. Then, stick your tongue out and lick the ice while you kiss on it," Renée instructed as she demonstrated with the ice.

"Like this?" I asked as I imitated her with my lips on the ice, licking out my tongue.

"No, your tongue is too far out. You have to gently lick the ice while you kiss it," Michelle instructed as she demonstrated with the ice.

Renée spent about a half hour teaching me how to kiss. By the time I learned, my lips were frostbit!

"Yeah, that's it. Now you know how to kiss. All we have to do now is find you a boyfriend," Renée said with a smirk on her face.

"I'm going to lose my virginity this year," she said proudly.

"Wow, Renée! That's a big step," I said.

"Well, me and T'chaka have been together for four years, and I think it's time," Renée said as she braided her long ponytail.

"You not scared?" I asked.

"Nope. I'm growing up, and that's a part of life," Renée responded.

"Yup, I'm gonna lose my virginity too this year," Michelle joined in.

"Too bad you don't have a boyfriend; you could do it too!" Renée said.

"Uh-uh. I ain't trying to do all that."

"Why not?" Renée asked.

"If you had a boyfriend you wouldn't do it?" Michelle questioned.

"Nope. I gotta save myself for my husband," I said proudly.

"Your husband?" the twins both said and looked at me with disgust.

"This is not *Leave It To Beaver*! Nobody does that anymore," Renée boasted.

"Well, I do. I ain't trying to go to hell!" I responded.

"What are you talking about?" Renée interjected.

"Pastor Mixon tells us on Sunday we will go to hell if we have sex and we aren't married," I said.

"He's lying to you. Most men have sex with other women even when they are married. He probably does too," Renée said.

"Okay, you done took it too far now, girl. Don't talk about my pastor! Ain't nobody ever tell you to shut up about things you know nothing about?" I said defensively.

"Okay, I ain't trying to insult you, but my older cousin Shawna told me it feels good. So I'ma try it! I'll let you know how it was when I do."

I turned the station on the television to change the conversation. I pretended to watch TV, but I was in deep thought.

What's the matter with me? I'm twelve years old, and I've still never kissed a boy. Now the twins are ready to have sex? I felt so out of touch and out of the loop. The rest of the night we watched television and fell asleep. I dreamed about finally having a boyfriend and taking my first kiss!

* * *

"Jamie, y'all get up now," my mother shouted from the end of the steps.

"Yeah, Mom, we getting up now," I said in my morning voice.

"Okay now, you been buggin' me about taking you to Secaucus to get this stupid bag. I'm not going in a bunch of traffic so if you gonna go, you better come on," she said.

That's all I needed to hear. I wanted my Gucci bag so bad I could taste it. Every day I begged my mother to take me to the outlet, and now she was finally ready to go!

"Get up, girls." I shook the twins. "We going to Secaucus." I grabbed my stuff to jump in the shower.

"Secaucus? For what?" Renée said in a groggy voice.

"To go get my Gucci bag for school," I responded.

"Gucci bag? What is that?" Michelle asked.

"Oh, it's a designer pocketbook," I said as I walked out of my room to jump in the shower.

I sang away in the shower as I imagined my new bag on my arm. *Man, I love my mother. She plays hardball, but in the end, she always gives in.*

I got out of the shower, and the twins were up. I dried off, put on lotion and took out my clothes.

"Wow, you have no breasts at all," Renée said as I unwrapped my towel to put on my lotion.

"Why you looking at me for? And by the way, yours aren't all that big either," I retorted.

"But at least I have little nubs. You don't even have that!" Renée said back smartly.

I pretended not to hear her as I sang the "Push It" song and got dressed.

The twins got in the shower, and by the time they came out, I was already dressed. They opened up their suitcases and put on the matching outfits their mother had packed for them.

"What name brand is that?" I asked as they put on their pink and white overall jumpers.

"I don't know," Renée answered hastily.

"Where did you get them from?" I asked.

"Oh, my mother shops for us at this store called Conway in Manhattan," Michelle responded proudly.

"Oh, okay," I said, and I went down the steps and called my cousin Tanya on the phone.

"Tanya, do you know where the store Conway is in Manhattan?"

"Hello, Jamie."

"Oh, hi, Tanya."

"Yeah, why you ask?"

"Cause the twins say their mother shops at Conway for them."

"I hope they weren't bragging. That's a real cheap store where they sell a bunch of cheap stuff."

"Worse than Alexander's and Sears, Tanya?"

"Yup. The stuff is so cheap it tears up when you wash it!"

"For real?"

"Yeah, girl. Tell your friends to step their dressing game up!"

"Oh, I certainly will. Well, I got to go. My mother is taking me to get my Gucci bag today."

"Oh, you going to Secaucus?"

"Yup, and I can't wait. I'm going to call you when I get back."

"Okay, cuz. Good-bye!"

"Good-bye, Tanya," I said as I hung up the phone.

I ran back upstairs, and Renée and Michelle were almost dressed.

"Y'all look really cute," I said sarcastically.

"Oh, that's usual," Renée responded.

"Too bad your clothes are cheap," I said in a nasty voice.

"What did you say?" Renée said with her hands on her hips.

"Too bad your mom shops at that cheap discount store Conway for your clothes. See, all my clothes are designer," I said as I proudly opened my closet doors.

"See, Guess, Aeropostale, Gap, and Benetton. Fly girls wear designer clothes. Too bad y'all ain't fly," I boasted.

"You sound stupid. Life isn't all about name brands," Renée quickly rebutted.

"Yes, it is. Ask my cousin Tanya," I responded.

"What good is it to wear name brand clothes if you ugly and black with nappy hair, and can't get a boyfriend?" Renée interjected.

"Oh, you mad 'cause your clothes is cheap. Just step up your dress game, that's all," I said as I laughed away her comment.

The twins weren't too happy with my comments, but I felt good. I finally got them back for their smart comments about me not having a boyfriend.

The car was silent as my mother took us to the Gucci factory outlet. I turned on the music and watched the scenery through the passenger-seat window.

We approached the ticket booth for the New Jersey Turnpike, and my mother took a ticket from the toll-booth clerk.

"Which exit is Secaucus, sir?" my mother asked.

"It's three exits down. Exit 15E. Get off the exit and follow the signs," the tall clerk responded.

"Thank you," my mother said as she rolled up the car window. We were almost there, and I was so anxious. I pictured in my mind what kind of store it would be and what would be on the shelves.

As I stopped daydreaming, we approached the store. It was surrounded by several other outlet stores, all in a little shopping community.

"Girls, this is it," my mother said as she entered the parking lot. We quickly raced out of the car, leaving my mother behind, and entered the tall glass Gucci store doors.

The Gucci store was different from the department stores I was accustomed to. The upscale store was flooded with expensive accessories neatly arranged. We browsed through the clothing racks that were filled with high-priced clothing, even with the outlet discounts!

"Look at this ugly shirt," Renée pointed to a red shirt on the rack.

"Look at the price tag. One hundred twenty-five dollars for *this*?" Michelle said as she shook her head.

"C'mon, y'all, let's go to the pocketbooks," I said as we left the clothing section. They had all types of bags with *G*s all over them, but I didn't see a bag like Kim's.

"Jamie, do you see what you're looking for?" my mother asked as she approached us.

"No, Mom, I don't see it," I said disappointedly.

"May I help you?" a store clerk asked as she saw my mother and I browsing through the showcases.

"Yes, ma'am, my daughter is looking for a Gucci tote-style bag," my mother said.

"Wow, you're a lucky young lady," the white clerk said as she checked me out.

"Yeah, but you don't have the bag I'm looking for here in the showcase," I said in a disappointed tone.

"I have a shipment of totes that just came in. They are a very popular item, so they go out as quickly as they come on the shelves."

"Oh, yeah?" my mother replied.

"Yes, ma'am, but I have two hidden in the back. Let me go get them," the clerk said as she headed to the back of the store.

I waited patiently with anticipation. The lady brought out a smaller version of the tote bag Kim had, but it didn't have a pocket zipper compartment in the front. She brought out two colors. One was all-black with small *G*s on it, and the other was tan and brown with big *G*s on it. Both had red and green signature-striped Gucci handles.

"This is all we have left," the clerk said as she handed me the bags. I quickly grabbed the tan bag and tried it on my arm, looking at myself in the long mirror in the store. My mother tried on the black one.

"I like it, Mom," I said as I stared at myself in the mirror.

"Yeah, they are both kind of cute," my mother responded as she stared at the black one on her arm in the mirror.

"How much do you want for these, ma'am?"

"Full price, they are over two hundred dollars apiece, but discounted, they are a hundred and ten dollars apiece. That's a great price."

"Yeah, Mom, Kim paid two hundred fifty dollars for hers," I said anxiously.

"I really like this bag," my mother said as she stared at the black bag.

"Mom, let's get both, one for you and one for me," I suggested, thinking about being able to switch up with my mother.

"You think so?" she asked as she contemplated the purchase.

Michelle and Renée watched the entire transaction with envy. They rolled their eyes and acted uninterested in the items in the store.

"Yes, Mom, let's get them," I said as I hugged her shoulder.

"Oh, all right, Jamie. Ma'am, we will take both of these, please," my mother said as she handed the clerk the bags. The clerk went to the back and neatly wrapped our bags in white paper and placed them in a green Gucci box, which she placed in a large gray shopping bag that had Gucci spelled out on the front in large white letters. My mother handed the lady her credit card, and the woman handed my mother the bags.

I was so happy! I actually had my own Gucci bag! The whole way back to Queens, I smiled as I thought about rocking my bag to school! I wanted to be the flyest girl in my junior high school! In my mind, I already was.

My mom and me, at 12 years old, at Disney World
in Orlando, Florida.

"Jamie, you got to keep your hands up to block your face like this," Kim instructed me downstairs in her large open basement. "Never let anyone take the first hit; you take it always! You hear me?" Kim asked as she positioned my fists.

"Yes, Kim," I replied softly.

Kim was the one who taught me how to fight. She was always beefing with some girls, usually over Minute. Kim knew how to fight really well, and she taught me her skills.

"Now hit me," Kim said as she got up in my face.

"No, Kim, I don't want to hit you."

"Oh, okay, so you wanna be a punk."

Pow! Kim hit me hard, right in my jaw.

"Why you did that for?" I said as I grabbed my face.

Pow, Pow, Pow! Kim hit me again three times, very hard, getting me upset.

"Oh, so you mad now?" Kim asked as she danced around me like Mohammed Ali in his heyday.

"Kim, I don't want to fight you," I said as I cried.

Pow, Pow! Kim hit me again, and I just stared at her.

"And yah mother is ugly," Kim mocked me as she hit me again, dead in my chest.

"What you said?" I questioned, angry about her comment.

"Your mother is—" Kim said, and before she could get the last words out of her mouth, I hit her back hard. *Pow!*

She hit me again, and we got it in, in the middle of the basement floor!

Kim got me down on the ground. "See, Jamie, you can't let anybody put their weight on you, or you are finished. You are small, so you got to stay up on your feet and keep hitting. Duck the punches and move around. Whatever you do, don't let them pull you down to the ground! If you have to, grab their hair. Wrap it around your hand like this." Kim demonstrated with my hair. "Then start popping them in the face," Kim advised as she let me up off the ground.

"Oh, like this?" I said, and I grabbed Kim's hair and started punching her in the face.

Chapter Twenty-Five

Kim got aggressive and fought me back. I had flashbacks in my mind about being laughed at after I got beat up by this jealous girl named Shavon at school. My first month of junior high was a disaster after that. I didn't know how to fight, but I was determined to learn. I could not stand to get beat up anymore by anyone, not even Kim. I fought Kim like my life depended on it, and she fought me back like I was one of those girls who was messing with Minute.

I cried as I fought Kim. Tears were streaming down my face, but that day I learned how to fight. We fought in Kim's basement nonstop for what seemed like hours! After we finished, my hair was sprouted wildly on top of my head. I had bruises and scratches, yet I gained my respect!

"Jamie, you can fight! Don't let nobody tell you any differently," Kim said as she hugged me.

"Oh, so you not mad at me?" I asked.

"No, girl. This is the same way Stretch taught me how to fight. You ain't nobody's sucker. If somebody says they wanna get it in with you, you beat them to the punch. Okay?" Kim advised.

"Yes, Kim. If they want to fight, I'm going to be the one to get it off first," I said proudly.

"That's my girl! Jamie, you gonna be all right," Kim said as she hugged me again and helped me fix my hair.

That day in the basement with Kim changed my whole being. I was no longer a punk. I felt I had the courage of a lion. I couldn't wait to seize the moment to practice my new skills on my first victim!

* * *

"Nakia, tell me more about Phil," I asked on a cold November day headed to school.

"He goes to some vocational school in South Jamaica. He hustles with Lite, and he got a job, too. He's kind of cute, and he lives right off of Linden Boulevard."

Nakia was telling me about Phil when we bumped into Nakia's friends, Debbie and Glynnis.

"What's up, Nakia?" Debbie said as we all approached the Q27 bus stop. Debbie was a very pretty light-skinned girl with long hair. Her stomach protruded, and she seemed to be in her last trimester.

"I'm chillin'. What's up, y'all?" Nakia responded back.

"Nothing. This baby is kicking my butt! I was so sick this morning, I almost didn't make it to school," Debbie said as she rubbed her large pregnant belly.

"Oh my goodness, you are getting so big!" Nakia said as she rubbed Debbie's stomach too.

"Yeah, I can't wait for this to be over already," Debbie complained as the Q27 bus approached.

"What's up with your baby's father?" Nakia asked.

"Oh, he's chillin'. He been out of town a lot lately. He's trying to get his money up for the baby. You know I got my learner's permit, so I'ma try to get him to buy me a car," Debbie said as we loaded on the bus.

"He gets money like that?" Nakia asked.

"You know them South Jamaica boys get real money. And now he's going out of state too! Me and my baby gonna be real right!" Debbie said as we rode along on the bus.

Nakia was fascinated by Debbie and her pregnancy. The whole ride to Hillside Avenue she asked Debbie a bunch of questions about her pregnancy and her boyfriend.

All of Nakia and Debbie's friends had boyfriends. The more money your boyfriend had, the flyer you would seem to them. They each competed among themselves about who could get their boyfriend to buy them the most stuff. I felt disconnected because I didn't have a boyfriend.

We approached Hillside Avenue and Springfield Boulevard, and all got off the bus in front of McDonald's.

"Hey, baby girl. Hey, baby love. Hey, love, hey, love," the caramel-skinned, stocky bum sang his heart out as he solicited money from the store patrons.

"Hey, baby love. Hey, love. Hey, love," we all sang and laughed, imitating him. This bum was faithful. We knew we would see him every morning without fail. We began to enjoy seeing him. He was our early-morning joke.

We went into McDonald's and stood in line to order breakfast. "Yo, I got y'all," Debbie said as she pulled out a knot of money. It was clear Debbie's boyfriend was taking good care of her!

We ate our breakfast, and I walked the girls to the doors of Martin Van Buren High School. I wished I was in high school so I could enter the school that appeared as big as a castle to me. Unfortunately, my age denied me access, so I waited for the bus at the bus stop in front of their school to get to my junior high.

As my bus approached, a black Suburban pulled up, blocking the bus. Four older boys jumped out of the vehicle, an older black male, followed by two small Puerto Rican-and-black mixed kids who went to my school, also exited the vehicle. The little boys' father was with them, and he ran up on the bus. He was a middle-aged, dark-skinned black man with a bald head.

"Ah, yo, bus driver, don't move," the man shouted as the four boys ran up on the bus. The boys barricaded the bus so no one could get on or off!

"Ronald, which one of these dudes took your chain? Point them out!" the angry father shouted as the timid, light-skinned children looked around for the high school bullies who robbed them.

"Him, him, and him, Daddy. They took it," Ronald said, pointing out the boys, and his father and his crew pulled the boys off the bus and beat them down badly.

"Oh, you want to bully little children and rob them? You messed with the wrong man's kids this time!" the father said as he beat the brakes off the boys who robbed his children. One of them broke loose and ran. The father ran after him and caught him, and beat him down in the middle of the street.

"Oh, y'all robbers," the father said. "Take all their money, and I want their sneakers," the father demanded to his crew who quickly followed his orders. One of the boys they were beating began to cry. "Oh, you should have thought about that before you played the role of a robber," he said, and he stripped the boys of their shoes. "I'm serving all you little dudes notice. These two here are not to be messed with! They're mine, and Big Dre don't play!"

It all happened in a matter of minutes! Then the whole crew loaded back up in the Suburban and pulled off. After the action, I got on the bus, and all of the kids going to my school were in a frenzy talking about the fight we had witnessed. The bus driver pulled off and acted normal, as if these types of occurrences happened frequently on his New York City bus route.

"Yup, that's right. Them big-ass high school dudes shouldn't have robbed Ronald. His father is a big hustler from Hollis. Yo, he don't play!" Harold said. Harold was a cute Jamaican and Chinese boy with chinky eyes.

"That's right, them Van dudes always think they can take advantage of us," Little Jeff said.

Jeff was a cute, short, brown-skinned boy from Hollis with curly hair. Today, he is better known as "Ja Rule," the rapper.

"Yup, they got what they deserved," Harold agreed.

The energy on the bus was crazy. Everybody was doing their own reenactments of the fight. Fabiola and Karen were on the bus together. They were best friends. Fabiola was a pretty, jet-black girl with long hair, and Karen was a Mocha-colored girl with medium-length hair. They were both from Ozone Park. Gina and Nicole were also on the bus. They were best friends. Gina was a dark-skinned, skinny girl who wore a short Jheri curl-hairstyle, and Nicole was a pretty chocolate-toned girl who was sort of thick. She wore a long Jheri curl-hairstyle.

Harold and Gina were supposed to be a couple, but Harold started liking Fabiola. Harold was talking to Fabiola on the bus about the fight when Gina stepped in Fabiola's face.

"Ah, yo, I'm not gonna keep playing with you! Let's fight," Nicole said in an angry voice, clearly charged from the recent incident.

"Yo, chill, Nicole. We ain't even together no more," Harold said as he pushed Nicole back.

"I don't care. She ain't gonna be with you," Nicole said as she positioned herself to fight.

"Yo, Nicole, I don't want to fight you. Me and Harold is just friends," Fabiola pleaded.

"No, bitch, don't cop no plea now. Let's do this!" Nicole said as she took off her coat, and Gina tried to hold her back.

I watched from the sidelines as I sat next to my friend Ieshia. Ieshia had café-au-lait skin and wavy black hair. She looked Spanish and black. Her cousin Sheryl, who went to Martin Van Buren High School, was good friends with Kim and Nakia, so we hung out and became cool.

"Why she keep messin' with Fabiola? Fabiola don't want no problems with her," Ieshia said.

"Well, you know Nicole and Harold been together since like fourth grade. She's mad 'cause they broke up," I interjected.

"So what? He don't want her no more, and that's that!" Ieshia snapped. Ieshia was friends with Fabiola, and she didn't like what was happening.

"I know they ain't gonna try to jump her. It ain't going down like that," Ieshia said as we moved closer to Fabiola.

"Well, you know what we got to do if they do," I said as I clicked my earrings off and slid them in the pocket of my Gucci bag.

"Hey, pretty girl," Little Jeff said to Ieshia.

"Hey, Jeff," Ieshia replied, cracking a smile.

"Pretty girls don't fight, Miss Lady. You too fly for that," Little Jeff said as he backed Ieshia away. Jeffrey and Ieshia moved to the middle of the bus where they began to laugh and talk. There was something about their relationship that made me know it would stand the test of time. Today, Ieshia is Jeff's wife.

Everybody seemed to have a boyfriend except for me! I was in the seventh grade, and I never had a boyfriend. I never even kissed a boy! I felt so pitiful. I was behind in times compared to all the rest of the girls I was around.

We got off the bus, and I waited as everyone got their rolls and bagels from the corner deli. Then we all started to walk down the long hill to our school, JHS 172.

"Freak that. I want to fight her now!" Nicole demanded as she broke loose from Gina's arms. Fabiola was standing next to Ieshia and me.

"Oh, God! I don't want to fight her," Fabiola yelled as she saw Nicole charging toward her. Nicole was bigger than Fabiola, and she had a lot of heart.

"Listen, girl, whatever you do, don't let her get the first hit. If you let her beat you up, everyone is gonna laugh at you. Fight her like your life depends on it," I coached, thinking about my embarrassment after losing a fight.

Gina came running behind Nicole. "Get off me. You get off me," Nicole said as she broke loose and got in Fabiola's face.

"Yo, I said I don't want to fight you," Fabiola said abruptly as Nicole leaned forward. Out of nowhere Fabiola caught Nicole in her mouth with her fist! *Boom! Boom! Boom!* The girls began to fight! From the very first hit, Fabiola was getting the best of Nicole!

"Didn't I tell you I didn't want to fight you? You keep on messing with me, right?" Fabiola said as she pounded on Nicole with her fist.

"Oh, okay now, I'ma show you," Fabiola shouted beating Nicole down to the ground. As Nicole was lying flat on her back, Fabiola picked up a tin garbage can that was in front of one of the houses on the block of the school and pushed Nicole inside the garbage can and rolled her down the hill.

"Ah, ah, help me!" Nicole screamed as the crowd laughed and Gina ran after the can. Nicole was so embarrassed! She talked all that trash, and she got beat up! Fabiola broke her fear of fighting, and I did too! I learned the bigger they are, the harder they fall!

Throughout my junior high school years there was always constant fighting around me. I learned to keep my hands up, always be ready, and under no circumstances let anyone get the first hit!

"Let's skip school today. C'mon, we gonna have fun!" Nakia said as we walked to the bus stop one morning.

"I don't know. I never skipped school before. What if my mother finds out?" I said in a scared voice.

"Listen, I got this. I'ma call your school and act like your mother. I'll give you a letter and sign it so you can take it to school tomorrow. I'll say you had a doctor's appointment."

"Oh, man, Nakia, I don't know," I said reluctantly.

"Listen, don't be chicken. You want a boyfriend, right?"

"Yeah, I guess so."

"Well, here's your shot!" Nakia said as she made her proposal while we walked down the street.

"Oh, all right," I said, giving into Nakia's intense peer pressure.

We walked to Nakia's boyfriend, Lite's, house on Murdock instead of to the bus stop. Lite lived a couple houses down from DJ Clue on the same side of the block.

My heart raced as I thought about seeing Phil and possibly kissing him! I was scared to death, but I couldn't show Nakia my feelings. I pretended to be okay, but deep down inside, I had butter-flies in my stomach that were trying to overtake me!

We reached Lite's house, a two-story attached brick cape. I could never remember his exact house, because all the houses on the block looked exactly the same. They were all attached to each other in a row. Nakia rang the bell as I nervously stood to the side. Lite answered the door. He was a medium height, slim, light-skinned black boy with wavy hair. He looked Spanish, but he was black.

"Yo, what's up? Y'all come in," Lite said, letting us in the door. We walked into the living room, and Phil was sitting on the couch. My heart pounded as he turned around and made eye contact with me.

Phil was a walnut-complexioned, medium-height, stocky boy with a low Caesar. He was sort of cute.

"Hey, Jamila, so you finally came to check me out," Phil said.

"Yeah, I guess so," I said as I grinned nervously.

Lite and Nakia went upstairs to Lite's room and left me alone

Chapter Twenty-Six

with Phil. It was like a dream. I couldn't believe I was sitting in Lite's living room next to Phil—alone! I was so nervous I couldn't say much. We sat and watched television as I acted as if I was really into the program.

"So what's up with you, Jamila?" Phil asked me as I watched the morning show intensely.

"Nothing, I'm just chillin'," I said as my heart raced.

"So I finally get to meet you face-to-face," he said as he put his arm around my shoulder.

"Yeah, yeah, I guess so," I said as I jumped in reaction to his arm around me.

"Relax. I'm not going to bite you," he said as he grabbed my shoulder.

"No, um, I just . . . Well, you caught me off guard," I responded hesitantly.

"Look, Jamila, I just want to get to know you better, that's all," Phil said as we sat on the couch watching *Good Morning, America.*

After talking to Phil for a while I began to relax. He was actually funny and very charismatic. He was sixteen years old and more advanced than me. I told him I was only twelve, but my age didn't seem to matter to him.

After about an hour of watching television, Phil decided to make his move. He grabbed my chin and turned my face into his, then he leaned over to kiss me. My heart raced as his lips touched mine. I quickly remembered the techniques Renée had taught me with the ice. I leaned forward and kissed Phil back, just as Renée had instructed me. Phil's tongue met mine, and I followed his lead.

I kissed Phil, and he began to touch my body. I could tell by his gestures and his passion that he wanted to take this further than I would allow. I quickly grabbed his hands and pushed him back.

"Listen, I don't want to lead you on. You are cool and all that, but I don't get down like that," I said in a no-nonsense tone.

"What you saying?"

"I'm not no easy chick. I don't know what you heard, but I'm a virgin, and I'm not giving nothing up," I said in a feisty tone.

"No, no, I'm not trying to go there. I just want to get to know you. For real," he said as he grabbed my hand and kissed me again.

I kissed him back simply to practice my technique. This kissing thing wasn't so difficult after all, like I thought it would be! Phil proceeded to kiss my neck, then he sucked it hard, leaving two big hickeys.

We finally stopped kissing and spent the rest of the morning and afternoon talking and chilling. Lite and Nakia eventually came downstairs, and we all became like one big happy family. We ordered Chinese food and watched videos all afternoon.

Three o'clock approached, and we got up to leave. Nakia kissed Lite good-bye, and I kissed Phil good-bye, then we left.

"Oh my goodness, girl. You finally had your first kiss!" Nakia said as we walked down Murdock Avenue.

"Yeah, I guess so," I responded.

"You guess so? What's up? You not feeling Phil?" she asked.

"No, um, he's all right, I guess."

"Okay, so you really not feeling him?"

"No, it's just not what I imagined. Ain't his head kind of big?" I questioned.

"Girl, you buggin'? Phil is all right!"

"He's okay, I guess. I don't know. It's just not what I pictured."

"Oh my God, look at your neck. You got two big hickeys!"

"You can see them?"

"Yeah, girl, they are huge!"

"Oh, man. Yo, my mother's gonna kill me!" I said as I panicked.

"Just stay away from her for a couple a days. They gonna go away," Nakia said as we walked home.

Nakia walked me to my house, and I went straight to my bedroom. I felt so dirty! I kissed this boy I didn't even know. I got two hickeys, and I cut school! I was very disappointed with myself. *Why didn't I just tell Nakia no?* I thought to myself as tears rolled down from my eyes. I stared at the two large hickeys in the mirror in my room. *What have I gotten myself into?* I questioned myself.

I managed to avoid my mother as I went out to school that next morning. Nakia picked me up as usual, but I wasn't feeling her. Worse, when we met up with our friends, everyone knew about what happened with me and Phil.

"Girl, let us see your hickeys," the girls asked.

"Oh, you growing up, Jamila," were some of the comments I got. I guess I should have felt proud 'cause this is what I thought I wanted.

The truth is, I felt like a slut! This wasn't the romantic encounter I pictured in my mind. I wanted to share my affection with someone who I truly loved.

I came home from school and locked myself in my room again. About half an hour later I heard a loud knock on my door.

"Yo, open up!" my brother demanded furiously. "Yo, open up the door *now*!" he yelled.

"What? What?" I said with an attitude.

"Ah, yo, you messing with the kid Phil?" my brother asked aggressively.

"Wha . . . what?" I said, taken off guard by his comment.

"You cutting school and hanging out with boys!" Kee shouted as he approached me full of rage. "Ah, yo, don't play with me!" He grabbed my neck.

"Ow!" I yelped in pain as he touched my sore neck.

"And you letting this boy put hickeys on you? Yo, I'm gonna kill Lite, Phil, and Nakia! Yo, you're a whore," my brother said as he smacked me in the face hard. Normally I would have reacted, but inside, I felt convicted. I knew what I had done was wrong.

"And you know I'm telling Mommy," he yelled as he raced out of the room.

"Yo, Mommy," Kee yelled as he went downstairs. I knew at that moment it was over!

Shortly after, my mother ran up the stairs. "Open this damn door, Jamie," she shouted as she banged hard on my locked door.

"No, Mommy," I said as I cried.

"Jamie, you open this door now!" she yelled at the top of her lungs.

"No, Mommy, I'm scared," I replied frantically.

"After all I do for you, *how* could you do this to me?" she said furiously. "Open up now, Jamie!" she continued to yell and bang on the door intensely.

"No, Mommy!"

"Why? Jamie, why would you do this to me?" my mother asked as she fell down and cried at the bottom of my closed door. I was taken off guard. I never saw my mother cry like that before. Her cries stabbed me in the middle of my heart.

"I love you so much. I do all I can for you, and you do this to me. Why, Jamie? Why?" she asked as she cried intensely. "Why!" she shouted loudly and wept.

"Mommy, mommy, please don't cry," I said as I opened my door and fell in her arms.

"Mommy, I'm sorry. I didn't do nothing with him. We just kissed, and I really didn't even like it. I'm just, well, I was just trying to fit in. Everyone has a boyfriend except for me. I felt left out, but after I kissed him, I felt nasty. I promise, Mommy, I'll never do it again. Please forgive me, please! I'm so sorry," I said as I collapsed and threw my arms around my mother, who was lying in a fetal position on the floor, and we both cried.

*A*fter the incident with Phil, my mother cut off my mixing with the high school girls. She no longer trusted anything I said. She put me on a strict schedule, and she started monitoring my whereabouts. She also forced me to hang out with girls my own age, so I became good friends with April. Her older brother was a good friend of my brother. April went to my junior high school, but she was a grade higher than me. She lived on 108th Avenue, four blocks down from me. That was the same block Nakia's friend Glynnis lived on.

April was a dark-skinned, heavyset girl who wore a bob-style haircut. She had a very pleasant personality, and she sang very well. Just like me, April didn't have a boyfriend, so there was no pressure in our relationship. I was free to be myself, and so was she! April's father was a scientist, and her mother was a doctor. Like my parents, they kept April busy in extracurricular activities.

* * *

April convinced me to join the Top Teens of America. This was a junior sorority-style organization for ritzy black kids. They had pageants, conferences, and all types of activities with different chapters across the nation. We would often take trips with the group, and we learned a lot about our African American heritage; at the same time, we had a bunch of fun!

April and I became very close, and so did our parents. April's father would drive us to school every morning, and my mother would come and pick us up when school was over. Every Wednesday night we had Top Teen of America meetings, and our parents would alternate picking us up and dropping us off.

After several months, I finally landed back the trust of my mother, who felt if I continued to hang out with wholesome girls like April I would be all right. For the most part, she was right.

My seventh-grade year started off rocky, but it ended smoothly. I enjoyed myself, even though I was banned to only hanging out with junior high school students.

Chapter Twenty-Seven

April and I were like white on rice. Whatever we did, we did it together. We enjoyed each other's friendship, and it was genuine. I loved April for her, and she loved me for me!

April got accepted to Fiorello LaGuardia High School of Performing Arts as a vocal major, so she decided to graduate as an eighth grader to attend the school. I was happy for her, but I was disappointed I would be all alone next year. I had no clue what my next year in junior high would consist of! All I knew is I would be separated from my true friend!

* * *

School was out, and everybody was outside in the neighborhood! The local hustlers would shine up their cars and cruise through with their music bumping.

I admired the hustlers in the neighborhood. They had three major qualities that I wanted: money, power, and respect! I quickly learned the more money you had, the more respect you got from others, and the respect gave you power! I couldn't wait till I was old enough to get my own money. I knew in my heart one day it would be my chance to shine!

For my thirteenth birthday, I convinced my mother to give me a party at Astroland Park in Coney Island, the home of the Cyclone roller coaster. I loved amusement parks! It gave me a rush to climb up to the top of the hill in a roller coaster, and then to come racing down.

I invited my friends from school, church, and dance school. Even my brother and some of his friends came to the party. We all had a ball! We stayed in the park until midnight, riding the rides, playing the games, eating and watching the fireworks. I won a bunch of teddy bears and other prizes in the park! It felt good to be thirteen. I was finally a teenager, a certified young adult.

* * *

I got my first real job at age thirteen. Mrs. King had a summer camp program for children at the Laurelton Theatre of Performing Arts. She hired me to become the dance teacher for the children in her summer camp program. I worked Monday through Friday from 8 a.m. to 12 p.m., making eight dollars an hour. You couldn't tell me anything! I was a workingwoman, and I was in charge! The children looked up to me just as I did my dance teachers, and I loved it!

"All right, ladies, let's go! I'm ready to begin class," I said as I pranced in front of the large dance studio room, which was covered with glass mirrors. "Today, we are going to start on a routine for our show in the Flushing Meadows Park for Queen's Day. There are gonna be a lot of performers out there, and we got to represent, ladies! I want you to watch me. Watch my feet closely and get the steps first, then you can work on the hands. Do you guys understand?" I said as I stood in front of the dance class. The class had about thirty little girls in it, from ages five to ten years old.

"Yes, Jamila," they said loudly.

"No, that is, 'Yes, Miss Jamila,'" I said sharply.

"Yes, Miss Jamila," they said in unison.

"That's better," I responded, and I popped in my Janet Jackson *Control* tape into the tape cassette deck of the studio's sound system.

Janet Jackson's song "Control" blasted on the sound system, and I began to teach the steps of the dance routine as I stared at myself intensely in the mirror.

"And one, and two, and three, and four, five, and six, seven, and eight. One and two and up, down. Step hit, step kick, step hit, and step kick," I said as I demonstrated the steps. "Okay, ladies, I'ma show you one more time, and then it's your turn," I said as I rewound the tape and showed them the steps again.

"Okay, y'all ready? It's your turn. Here we go! Five, six, seven, eight!" I shouted loudly as the small children attempted to duplicate my steps. They were all over the place. Some were spinning to the right, others to the left. Some were kicking while others were stepping. Frustrated, I put my hand over my head, and tried to figure out how we would possibly be ready for this show that was in just four weeks! I had no clue how difficult it would be to teach a bunch of kids who lacked any formal dance school training! I was in for a rough journey.

My cousin Tanya and my aunt Carolyn
on Easter Sunday.

*A*s the summer went by, my father's oldest sister, Aunt Carolyn, who was my favorite aunt, grew sick, and my father suggested that his mother to come up and take care of her. I was able to get my cousin Kanika to fill in for me at the Laurelton Theatre, while I went down South with my parents to pick up my grandmother.

My brother was in summer school making up the classes he had failed during the school year, so he couldn't go with us. My parents left my brother behind with strict orders not to let anyone in our house while they were out of town. My mother, my father, and I loaded into my father's customized van, "Brown Sugar," and we headed to Kinston, North Carolina. As usual, I slept in the bed in the back of the van most of the ride, listening to my father's '70s mixed tapes over and over until we finally arrived in Kinston.

When I got there, I immediately hooked up with my cousin Donnell's girlfriend, Monique, who planned to take me to a club.

She took me to these cheap little stores in the mall that were packed with girls. She picked out a black short shirt set with silver trimmings for me. It was cheap, but I have to admit, it was cute! I tried on the outfit and loved it, so I bought it. Then Monique took me to pick out some sandals to match.

"Jamie, look at these; they're cute," Monique said as she picked up a strappy pair of black sandals with heels.

"Yeah, they are nice, but Monique, I never wore high heels before."

"Girl, they ain't even no real high heels. It's a small heel on these. Try them on," Monique said as she instructed the salesman to bring me out the shoes. As we were sitting on the chair in the crowded store waiting for my shoes, I heard someone call my name. At first, I thought he was talking to someone else 'cause I didn't know many people down South, but the person continued to shout my name louder and louder.

"Jamie, Jamie," a strong country male voice shouted.

I looked around to see who it was. I turned my head and saw a nicely built boy with a white wife beater T-shirt on, some shorts, and Nike flip-flops.

"Jamie," he shouted as I stared. "It's me, Dino!"

Immediately, my heart began to race! I hadn't seen him since the day my mother sent him away from my grandmother's house, when I was ten years old. I stood and stared in awe. Dino's skin was a smooth chocolate complexion, and his muscles bulged out of his wife beater. Dino had really grown up, and he looked so good!

"Hey, Dino," I said as I stared him up and down.

"When did you get down here? Fishkell didn't tell me you was coming in town!"

"I just got here, but we are only staying until Tuesday. My aunt Carolyn is sick, so we came to pick up my grandmother so she can take care of her."

"Oh, wow. I'm sorry to hear that. Yo, you looking good. You are all grown-up now," Dino said as he checked me out.

"You, too," I responded with a smile as the store rep came back with my shoes.

"Here you go, miss," he said as he handed me the box. I grabbed it and put on the high-heeled sandals.

"Oh, okay. Those are nice," Dino said as I put on the heels and stood up. I was too scared to walk. I didn't want to embarrass myself in front of him, so I quickly stretched my foot out and looked down at my feet.

"Yeah, I guess they're okay," I said.

"Yeah, they go good with your outfit," Monique responded.

"Where you going?" Dino asked.

"Oh, I'm going to the club with my cousins," I responded.

"The club? Yo, you doing a lot. Solo know you going to the club?" Dino asked.

"Look, I ain't no little girl anymore I'm a boss lady now," I said with confidence.

"Oh, yeah, well, we gonna see about that. If you a boss lady, you gonna be my little boss lady," Dino said as he put his arm around my shoulders and walked me to the store counter.

"Well, that's gonna cost you," I laughed.

"A'ight, and I can pay, but that's gonna cost *you!*" he said as he pulled out a large knot of money from his pocket and paid for my shoes. Monique watched us from the sideline of the store.

I grabbed the bag, and Dino and I walked. "So I guess I'ma see you at the club," he said.

"I guess so, if you gonna be there," I said back in a sassy tone, and Dino laughed.

"Girl, I love your New York accent. You sound sexy as hell with your feisty self," he said, and I laughed.

"Be there or be square," I responded.

"Oh, I'ma be there. So you better not do nothing I ain't gonna like," he said as I continued to laugh. His dominance and his charm had me mesmerized. I was on cloud nine. My true love was back!

Monique and I left the mall and headed to her car. "Jamie, you better be careful," Monique said as she opened the car doors.

"Be careful for what?" I questioned.

"Girl, Dino is a trip. You know he just came home from the juvenile detention home."

"No, I didn't know that."

"Yes, girl, him and his brothers get money, but Dino is wild, honey. I can't believe you got him spending money. The girls say he is cheap as hell!"

"For real?"

"Yeah, Jamie, and he is possessive. If you mess with him, he ain't gonna let you be around nobody else, girl."

"Yeah?" I questioned. Monique had no clue that what she said just excited me even more. I couldn't wait to get back to the house so I could get ready for the club. Wait till Dino sees me in my new outfit. *Look out, Kinston, 'cause here I come!*

* * *

I put on my pajamas, got in the bed, and waited for my parents to go to sleep. My mother checked in on me, and I pretended to be fast asleep. My parents went up to the guest bedroom of my grandmother's house, which was upstairs.

When everyone in the house was asleep, my cousin Elaine, who was five years older than I, helped me get ready. I put on my new outfit, curled my hair, and Elaine fixed me up with her makeup.

I stood in the mirror and admired my reflection. I looked amazing! I definitely did not look like a thirteen-year-old. I looked more like eighteen. My cousins Vicki, Elaine, and I tiptoed out of the house. We met Elaine's friend, Sweetycake, who was parked out front, and we drove to the club.

When we arrived at Club Phase, which was downtown Kinston, the street was packed with cars. The club doors were roped off, and people were waiting to get inside. My heart raced with anxiety. I couldn't wait to get inside the club! We quickly found a parking space and rushed to get in line. I had to take it easy. I hadn't yet mastered how to walk in my new high heels. I strolled behind my cousins, trying to play off my inexperience in walking in high heels.

We got to the door of the club, and Elaine called for a bouncer named Mike. Mike came out and escorted us in. We bypassed the people waiting in line, and we didn't even have to pay! The girls standing in the line rolled their eyes as Mike pushed them back to let us through. I felt so important. I couldn't believe I was actually about to step inside a club!

I walked in the doors of Club Phase and felt like I made it in to paradise! There were mirrors all over the walls, and disco balls spinning different colors in the air. There was a huge bar on the left side of the club and a small stage in the middle surrounded by a large dance floor. The club was packed with guys and girls. Everyone had drinks in their hand, and several people were dancing on the dance floor.

My cousins found a table in the back. We sat down and watched the people dance on the dance floor. The music was bumping, the sound system was loud, and the DJ was hyping up the crowd. I was enjoying the vibe. I couldn't believe I was really inside a club!

"What's up, y'all? C'mon, let's dance," I said anxiously as I tapped my cousin Elaine.

"No, girl, not yet. Wait 'til the club gets packed," she responded. Elaine was a pretty, caramel-complexioned, bright-eyed girl with medium-length hair.

"Why? There's more room for us to dance like it is," I said in disappointment.

"Look, girl, we ain't trying to look pressed. Ain't nobody really on the floor yet. We got to wait," Vickie said in a nasty tone. My cousin Vickie was reluctant to take me out with them. She felt I was too immature. Vickie had just turned twenty years old. She was a tall, brown-skinned girl with small, narrow eyes.

"Oh, all right then!" I responded back, agitated. I intensely watched the people dancing on the dance floor. I couldn't wait to get out there to show off my skills. *New York is in the house, and you gonna know it!* I said to myself as I studied the corny dance moves of the Southerners.

A waiter approached our table.

"Would you gals like to order a drink?" he said in a strong country accent.

"Yes, give me orange juice and vodka," Vickie ordered.

"Oh, I want Pepsi and Bacardi," Elaine said.

"Give me orange juice and vodka too," Elaine's friend Sweetycake added. Sweety-cake was a jet-black, petite girl with a beautiful bright smile.

"And you, young lady?" the waiter said as he stared at me.

"Oh, um, uh, I'll just take an orange juice," I replied.

"Okay, ladies, I'll be right back with your drinks," the waiter said, and he went to fill our order.

While we were waiting for our drinks, Donnell came through the door with his best friend, Billy, which was Dino's brother. Donnell had on his black shades, a dark denim jean suit, and a fresh pair of sneakers. Billy was also dressed to impress. When they came through the doors, they caught everybody's attention, especially the ladies!

"Oh, girl, there goes Solo," a girl at the bar shouted.

"Yeah, girl, he looks fine as hell," whispered another girl who was sitting at the table next to us.

My cousin was the man in Kinston! Everybody respected him. Donnell and Billy ran the drug trade in the hood. Everything moving through the city moved through them!

I slouched down in my chair, hoping Donnell wouldn't spot me. I prayed he wouldn't embarrass me at the club.

The waiter came back with our drinks, and I began to nervously sip on my orange juice, hoping to avoid Donnell. It was hot in the club, and I was thirsty. I guzzled down my orange juice, and my throat began to burn.

"Elaine, this orange juice tastes strange," I said after I took a large gulp.

"Let me see," Elaine said, and she tasted my drink.

"Jamie, this is orange juice and vodka!" Elaine shouted.

"See what I told you? Now Aunt Liddie gonna kill us, Elaine!" Vickie said nervously.

"Nah, I'm okay, y'all. I'm all right," I said as I intensely listened to the music. The DJ came on the mic.

"Listen, y'all, I'ma switch up the tunes. Shout-outs to all my Jamaican crews," the DJ said as he began to blast Reggae music.

I couldn't take it any longer! That was my cue. I hopped out my seat and ran to the dance floor. I began to whine away to the Jamaican music. I kicked off the high heels that began to hurt my feet, and I let loose on the dance floor. The liquor had me twisted! I forgot about the people around me. I even forgot I was hiding from Donnell. I danced in the middle of the dance floor like my life depended on it.

The next thing I knew, I had a circle of people around me cheering me on. The attention took me up another notch, and I got it in! I was doing all the new Jamaican dances I learned in Brooklyn. The crowd went wild as I got on the floor and gyrated to the music. People even stood up on chairs to watch me dance. I was enjoying myself! I felt like I was on *Soul Train!* A boy got behind me, and I started dancing with him. Just as we were getting into the song, I felt a strong push!

"Ah, yo, get your hands off my old lady," Dino yelled as he came out of nowhere.

"And you get over here," Dino demanded as he grabbed me off the dance floor.

"Hold up, let me get my shoes," I said, breaking loose to get my feet back into the high heels. I was so embarrassed as the whole club watched and stared. Before I could make it off the dance floor, Donnell and Billy approached me.

"What the hell you doing out of the house?" Donnell scolded.

"Well, um, I was, um . . . I just . . .," I said as I stumbled for words.

"Oh, you doing way too much. Carry your butt back to the crib," Donnell demanded. "Who you here with anyway?"

"Vickie and Elaine," I responded in a low voice.

"Where they at, yo?" he questioned.

"Oh, they over there," I said as I pointed to the table where my cousins were seated. Donnell walked off to go to the table, and Dino jumped in my face.

"I don't know what type of dudes you use to dealing with in New York, but my chick ain't gonna be dancing all over no dudes! You gonna mess around and make me do something to that boy," Dino said in his strong Southern accent.

"What?" I questioned as I looked at him and screwed up my face.

"Oh, you think I'm playing with you? Okay, watch this," Dino said, and he went back on the dance floor and swung at the dude I was dancing with, and they started fighting. Billy jumped in, and so did Donnell. Everybody stormed out of the club as the fighting got more intense. My cousins rushed me outside, and we jumped into the car. The police came and everything! It was absolutely crazy! The fighting caused them to shut down the club early that night.

As Dino came out of the club he spotted me. "Ah, yo, why you out here 'causing trouble?" he said as he wiped the sweat off his face.

"I, um, I wasn't trying to cause no problems," I said nervously, trying to digest all that happened.

"Nah, you all right, but for real, I don't want you up in no clubs. Go back to your grandmother's house and call me at this number when you get up," Dino said, and he wrote his number down on a piece of paper while he leaned against Sweetycake's car.

"Oh, okay," I replied attentively as I grabbed the number, and we pulled off.

We arrived back at my grandmother's house, and I tiptoed through the doors. I pulled off my clothes and jumped in the bed. I had a pounding headache that just wouldn't quit. All I could think about was Dino. *Man, he must really like me,* I said to myself as I thought about the events of the evening. I guess I finally have a real boyfriend, and my boyfriend ain't no punk!

* * *

The next morning I got up late, and my head was still pounding. I looked in the bathroom mirror and wiped the smeared makeup off of my face. Everything seemed so surreal. I couldn't believe I was actually inside a club! And now I have a boyfriend! I washed my face, brushed my teeth, and ran to the phone to call Dino.

I unfolded the little paper he had given me and dialed the number on my grandmother's old rotary phone.

"Hello, may I speak to Dino, please," I asked the older woman who answered the phone.

"Hold on, baby, let me see if he is up. Dino! Dino!" the woman yelled as her voice crackled.

"Hello," Dino said in a low voice as if he just woke up.

"Hey, Dino, this is Jamie."

"Oh, what's up, little mamma?"

"Nothing. I just got up."

"You know I want to see you, but I ain't coming to your grandmother's house. You know what happened the last time."

"Yeah, I know."

"Can you get out of the house?"

"Yeah, I guess. But where you want me to go?"

"Go to your cousin Yvonne's house, and I'ma meet you over there in the projects."

"Oh, all right. I guess I can pull that off."

"Call me when you get to Yvonne's house."

"Okay, Dino. Give me like an hour," I said and hung up the phone.

My head was still hurting, but I was excited about seeing Dino. I jumped in the shower and got dressed. My cousin Donnell was still sleeping, thank God! I was able to convince my parents that I wanted to spend time with my cousin Yvonne. My dad dropped me at the Mitchell Wooden Housing project where Yvonne lived. The housing project down South weren't like New York's housing projects. They were two-level brick apartment houses all attached together, surrounded by open grass. Clotheslines stretched along the back side of the housing project where clothes were hung out to dry.

As we approached, kids were outside playing and riding bikes. All the neighbors were out on the porches sitting on lawn chairs. The housing project reminded me of a park full of people on the grounds. I quickly got out of the car and knocked on the door.

"Who is it?" my cousin Yvonne's daughter, LaRetha, shouted through the door.

"It's me, Jamie," I said as she hurried and opened the door.

"Hey, Jamie," LaRetha joyfully shouted as she hugged me. LaRetha was seven years old. She was a cute, plump, heavyset brown-skinned girl who had medium-length coarse hair.

"Hey, baby. You are getting so big," I said as I walked into the house.

"Jamie, Jamie, it's Jamie," Latoya, LaRetha's little sister, shouted. She was a cute, petite, light-skinned little girl who was five years old.

As I sat on the couch, my cousin Yvonne came down the stairs. She was only twenty years old and pregnant again! She already had two children and was now work-ing on her third! "Hey, Jamie, what you doing over here with your crazy self?"

"Nothing, cuz. I just came to check on y'all, that's all. Can I use your phone?"

"Yeah, but you can't call no New York. I ain't got no long distance."

"No, it's a local call."

"Oh, okay then," Yvonne said, and she directed me to the phone.

I called Dino and told him I was at my cousin Yvonne's house. He told me to chill out, and he was on his way. As I sat on the couch talking to Yvonne, I watched the roaches run back and forth on the walls and even on the furniture. It creeped me out. I wasn't used to any roaches!

My cousin was very poor, and her lifestyle reflected it. The kids ran wild through the house in dingy clothes, and there was junk all over the place. As I waited for Dino, I grew hungry. I went into the kitchen and found a box of Fruit Loops. I took a bowl out of the cabinet, rinsed it off, and poured the cereal into the bowl and put some milk in it. As I dipped my spoon into the Fruit Loops a small roach floated to the top of the bowl. I screamed at the top of my lungs and dropped the bowl into the sink.

"What are you screaming about?" Yvonne said as she wobbled her petite pregnant frame into the kitchen.

"Girl, there was a roach in my cereal," I said frantically.

"Oh, please, girl, a roach ain't never hurt nobody. Child, please," Yvonne said as she brushed me off. I was starving, but I refused to eat anything there.

Soon, there was a knock on the door, and Yvonne went to answer. "Who is it?" she asked.

"Yo, it's Dino," Dino said in a loud, aggressive voice.

"Dino? Who you looking for, boy?"

"Yo, open up, Yvonne, I'm here for Jamie."

"Oh, okay, I see why you came over here. You ain't slick, girl," Yvonne said to me as she opened the door for Dino.

Dino came in the house, and Yvonne's kids jumped on him.

"Hey, Dino, can you give us some money to go to the store?" LaRetha asked as she pulled on Dino's shirt.

"Oh, that's all I'm good for?" Dino asked, reaching in his pocket. He gave the kids money.

"Yo, Jamie, let's go," Dino said.

"Let's go? Where you think she's going?" Yvonne responded in a feisty tone.

"Yo, she's going with me. Stop playing, girl," Dino rebutted.

"Uh-uh! My uncle Nelson ain't gonna kill me," she shouted.

"Come on, Yvonne, we ain't going far. I got you. I'ma bring y'all back some groceries."

Yvonne stopped and thought for a moment. "Boy, you better not get my little cousin in no trouble."

"Yvonne, I got this. We gonna be right back."

"Right back?"

"Yes, Yvonne, I promise."

"Well, okay, but y'all better be careful!"

I grabbed my Gucci bag and left with Dino. We walked down to the Front, which was the area Dino hustled in where I first met him. We stopped at the store, and I bought something to eat while he picked up money from the block.

"Dino, yo, who's that?" Dino's friend, who was on a dirt bike in front of the store, asked.

"This is my old lady, why?" Dino said proudly.

"Oh, 'cause she sure doesn't look like she from here. Yo, where you from?" the boy asked me.

"I'm from New York," I responded.

"Oh, man. You even got a New York accent. Talk for me again," he said as I laughed.

"What you want me to say?" I asked.

"Man, I love them New York accents. My cousin Derrick lives in New York, and he got a sister named Frankie. Do you know him?" the boy asked.

"New York is so big. There are thousands of Derricks. What part of New York is he from?" I asked.

"Um, I, well, maybe Brooklyn."

"Nah, I don't know Derrick. I'm from Queens."

"Wow, ain't that where Run-D.M.C. and LL Cool J is from?"

"Yes, that's right."

"Man, I wish I could go to Queens," the boy said as he daydreamed on his bike.

"Jamie, c'mon," Dino said as he busted up the conversation, and we walked away.

"Listen, I don't want you out here talking to no boys. You my old lady. They ain't got no business hollering at you," Dino said as we walked to the playground and sat down on the bench. Dino proudly put his arm around my shoulder, and I felt like a million bucks!

"So, I finally get to see you again. Yo, I always be asking Fishkell about you. He be telling you?"

"Well, I really don't speak to Eric when I'm in New York."

"What you be doing in New York?"

"I don't know what you mean."

"Like, what you do for fun?"

"Nothing much. I just be chilling."

"So you got a boyfriend in New York?" Dino asked in a serious tone as he stared me in the eyes.

"No, Dino, I don't have a boyfriend."

"You ain't lying to me? I can find out for real," he responded back aggressively.

"No, Dino. For real. I ain't got no boyfriend."

"All right, so it's official; you my lady."

"Yeah, I guess so," I said as I stared back at him. Dino looked me in my eyes, grabbed my hand, and leaned over to kiss me. My heart raced as I kissed him back passionately.

Dino and I stayed in the park most of the day just talking and laughing. I felt feelings for Dino that I never felt for anyone else before. When I was with him I felt special, protected, and loved. All his friends who saw us admired us. Dino was the man to them, and now he had a girlfriend from New York! We chilled in the park till it got dark, then Dino stopped at the store and got groceries for Yvonne. After that, he took me back to her house.

Not too long after I got back to her house, my father came to get me, and I went back to my grandmother's house. I was on cloud nine. I actually had a boyfriend! I sat on the couch watching television as I processed all that happened.

"Jamie," my dad called.

"Yes, Dad."

"Listen, your aunt Carolyn's not doing well. They just rushed her to the hospital."

"Oh, no, Daddy," I said in a frantic voice.

"Baby, it's gonna be okay. We're gonna leave here in the morning so we can get to the hospital to see her. Pack your luggage. We gonna leave early in the morning," he said as he kissed my forehead.

I didn't know how to feel. I was upset about my aunt being sick, but I really didn't want to leave. I wanted to stay behind with Dino. I called Dino, but he wasn't home. Tears streamed down my face as I realized I was about to leave my newfound love. I cried myself to sleep, not knowing when I would see Dino again. I was heartbroken!

* * *

The next morning we got up early. My grandmother loaded in the van with us, and we headed back to New York. I pressed my face against the window of the van as I watched us leave Kinston. My tears kept rolling as I experienced the pain of leaving my first love.

My dad drove us straight back to Brooklyn. We arrived in the late afternoon and pulled up to Brookdale Hospital where Aunt Carolyn was hospitalized.

We all got out of the car quickly, anxious to see how she was doing. The nurses wouldn't let me up because I was too young to go into the Intensive Care Unit, so I had to wait in the waiting room. After about an hour, I remembered how Kee and I snuck up to see C.B., so I made my way up to the Intensive Care Unit where Aunt Carolyn was housed.

As I found the room, I saw her lying on the bed with multiple tubes running out of her. Her skin was pale, and her body was weak. My grandmother stood over Aunt Carolyn, rubbing her forehead, and my dad was on the other side, holding her hand.

As I entered the room, I heard my grandmother pray, *"Lord God, we call on You in the name of Jesus. Lord God, You told us in Your Word if two or more call on Your name that You will be in their midst. Father God, we need You today. I ask You to please come in and help my daughter! Strengthen her, Lord, and please, my God, don't let nothing happen to my baby."* My grandmother's voice cracked, and she began to cry.

"Lord, You have always been faithful to our family. There was nights I didn't know how I would feed my children, yet You provided. Lord, I know we ain't always live life the way You require, but today, God, I ask that You forgive us, Lord. Have mercy, Lord. Please. Please, God, save my baby," my grandmother prayed passionately as she wept.

Tears began to flow down my cheeks, and they just wouldn't stop! At that moment, I realized how sick Aunt Carolyn really was. I ran over to my grandmother and collapsed in her arms. We all cried as my aunt lay unconscious in her bed. She had breast cancer, and the cancer had spread all through her body.

We stayed at the hospital for several hours, and then my parents and I left to go back to Queens. My grandmother refused to leave my aunt's side, so she stayed back at the hospital.

* * *

It was approximately nine o'clock in the evening when we made it back to Queens. As we pulled up to the house, my mother noticed that her car was moved into the driveway.

"Nelson, I didn't leave my car there!" my mother angrily said. My parents quickly jumped out of the car to get in the house when they noticed the front end of my mother's car was smashed in.

"Oh, no, Nelson! Nelson, Kee done crashed my car," she shouted at the top of her lungs.

"I'm gonna kill that boy," my father responded angrily. He quickly put his key in the door, and we walked into the house. The music was booming, and Kee had several of his friends dancing in the living room. The house was a mess. Empty liquor bottles were everywhere!

"Kee! Kee! Where are you at?" my mother yelled as everyone looked around in astonishment. Kee wasn't expecting us back until Tuesday night, so we caught him off guard.

"Y'all boys get out of my house now!!!" my father bellowed in a loud voice. Kids came out of everywhere! They were in the den, in the basement, upstairs, and even in my parents' room. My mom caught some girls lying in her bed in her bedroom, and boy, was she outraged!

My brother was so embarrassed as my parents came through the house hollering.

"You fast-behind hussies. Get out of my house," my mother demanded as she picked up a frying pan to wave the girls out.

Next, she noticed my brother's twin friends, Chris and Matt, who she passionately hated, were in the house too. "I *know* you don't got them twins in my house! Chris and Matt, get out of here and don't ever come back!" my mother demanded as she began swinging her pan at them, and they ran out the front door.

I looked around in astonishment. I couldn't believe my brother had a house party and crashed my parents' car! It was crazy!

My brother stayed on punishment a long time behind that party. Come to find out, DJ Clue crashed my mother's car. Kee couldn't drive a stick shift, and Clue said he could. Clue ended up crashing the car into the pole when the gears got stuck and wouldn't shift. Walking in that house and seeing the expression on my brother's face is a sight I'll never ever forget. Kee was caught red-handed!

* * *

My aunt slowly began to recover as my grandmother prayed over her daily. She was discharged from the hospital about a month later, and my grandmother took care of her at home.

I spent a lot of time in Brooklyn when my grandmother was in New York. My parents took turns checking on my grandmother and my aunt, so we went to Brooklyn often. I became very attached to my grandmother. She taught me a lot. My grandmother would often pull out her Bible and read me passages. I loved the stories she told me about God rescuing His children.

"Baby, let me tell you, if you ever run into any problem in life, I want you to know you have a Friend who will never leave you or forsake you. His name is Jesus. All you got to do, baby, is call on Him. If you don't know what to say, just open your mouth and say 'Jesus!' As you say His name, He will come and help you. You understand, baby?" my grandmother instructed as I lay down on her lap.

"Yes, Grandma. All I got to say is Jesus!" I said repeating her same tone.

"That's right, baby, and He will come and help you."

"Grandma, do you think He's gonna help Aunt Carolyn get better?"

"Yes, baby."

"If God is a good God, why would He let Aunt Carolyn get sick?" I questioned.

"Baby, we can't never question God. He is bigger and greater than what we can ever imagine. Everything always happens in God's plan for a good reason. You may not understand it now, but you'll understand it better by-and-by," Grandmother said as she rubbed my hair and began to sing "Amazing Grace" in her sweet Southern voice. I fell asleep in her lap as I listened to her sing.

That day, my grandmother interjected her faith into me. I felt safe hearing her say no matter where I was, or what troubles I encountered, I could call on Jesus. I heard the pastor say it, but when my grandmother said it, it took on a whole new meaning. That day, I became proud to have Jesus as my Protector and as my Friend!

My friend Kim at her house in Queens
Village with rapper Tupac.

*T*he school year had just begun. I had spent all the money I made at my summer job at the Laurelton Theatre on clothes. I officially became a label princess. Everything I owned had a name brand. I felt empowered by the attention I got from the clothes I wore. Overnight, I became an official "fly girl."

It was an early-fall morning, and I was headed to the bus stop where I met Nakia and Kim.

"Hello, Jamie," Kim said.

"Good morning," Nakia added. Kim began to cough loudly.

"You okay, Kim?" I asked.

"Yeah, I'm all right. I just feel a little sick," she said as she looked at me. I immediately noticed her face looked slightly pale.

"You don't look okay," I interjected.

"I don't know. For the last couple of mornings I've been feeling sick, but by the afternoon I'm okay," Kim said as she finished eating her White Castle's breakfast sandwich.

"Oh, maybe you coming down with the flu or something," Nakia suggested.

"I hope not. I hate being sick," Kim said as she threw her empty White Castle's bag in the garbage. She stood stiff by the garbage and leaned over.

"Yo, you all right?" Nakia questioned, and Kim immediately vomitted her morning breakfast into the garbage can.

"Oh my goodness, Kim. Yo, you are really sick," I said and pulled some tissue out of my bag and gave it to her.

"Girl, did you get your period?" Nakia asked.

"Well, um, no," Kim said as she wiped her mouth.

"You are probably pregnant!" Nakia said.

"Oh my goodness, girl! Stretch will kill me. My period isn't that late. Maybe it will come this week," Kim said as she began to look nervous.

"Why don't you just take a pregnancy test to be sure?" Nakia suggested.

"A pregnancy test?" Kim questioned.

Chapter Twenty-Nine

"Yeah, a pregnancy test. I missed my period before, and I thought I was pregnant. I got a pregnancy test, peed on the stick, and it came back negative. You need to take one so you can know for sure."

"Okay, but where can I get one?" she asked.

"C'mon, let's go across the street to Cason's Pharmacy," Nakia said as we crossed the street and went to the pharmacy.

We opened the large glass door and entered the small neighborhood pharmacy. The shelves were packed with medicine and medical products. The old man, Mr. Cason, who owned the store, stood behind the counter.

"Where are the pregnancy tests at?" Kim whispered to Nakia.

"Oh, they're behind the counter," she responded.

"Oh, so we have to ask Mr. Cason for it?" Kim asked in a nervous voice.

"Yeah!"

"Uh-uh, girl. He knows my mother. I can't ask for that," Kim said.

"Whatever, girl. Mr. Cason ain't thinking about us," Nakia responded.

"Well, you ask him then," Kim interjected.

"All right, shoot. He ain't my daddy," Nakia said as she broke away from us and approached the counter. "Can I see your pregnancy tests, please?" Nakia asked as Mr. Cason put his head down and looked over his glasses at her.

"One minute please," he said, and then he went to the back and pulled out three boxes.

"This one is twelve dollars, this one is ten dollars, and this one has a double applicator, so it's sixteen dollars." Nakia looked over the products as she tapped Kim under the counter.

"What's the difference?" Kim asked whispering in a low voice.

"They are all the same," Nakia told her.

"Get the cheapest one then," Kim said quietly.

"Okay, I'll take the ten-dollar one," Nakia said, and Kim took out the money and passed it to Nakia. Nakia paid for the pregnancy test, and we got ready to leave the store.

"Listen, girls, I don't mean to be in your business, but if you gonna do adult things, use condoms. I done seen you all grow up into fine girls. Don't mess your lives up early with no kids now," Mr. Cason said as we headed for the door.

"Yes, Mr. Cason," Kim said as we walked out of the store.

"Oh my goodness, girl! I'm so embarrassed," Kim said as we headed back across the street. Our bus had already left, and it was clear we were all gonna be late for school.

"Girl, please, Mr. Cason is a regular man. He be getting it in too! Don't let his old face fool you," Nakia said as we all laughed. "C'mon, let's go in White Castle. Go to the bathroom and pee on the stick," Nakia instructed, as she busted open the pregnancy kit.

"Oh, okay," Kim agreed.

Nakia showed her what to do, then she and I sat at one of the booths and anxiously waited for Kim to come back.

What if she is pregnant? I thought to myself. *Man, that will be crazy!* I bounced my leg in anticipation waiting for her to come through the door.

About ten minutes later, Kim came out of the bathroom shaking her head.

"What, girl? What is it?" Nakia asked anxiously.

By the look in Kim's eyes, I already knew the answer.

"Girl, I'm pregnant," Kim said, as tears streamed out of her eyes.

"Oh, man!" I said as I passionately hugged Kim and cried too.

"Why y'all crying for! It's a blessing to have a baby. You can dress him up all cute in Baby Gap clothes. And you know you got to get an Aprica stroller. We gonna go to the mall and take pictures at Sears, and oh, if it's a girl, I'll take her to get her ears pierced. And we—"

"Hold up," Kim interrupted. "Who's to say I'm having this baby?"

"Well, I know you ain't getting no abortion. That's killing, Kim. That's wrong," Nakia said as we walked out of White Castle.

"I don't know what I'ma do. I got to tell Minute," Kim said.

At that moment, I knew life for us was going to be different. I wasn't even having sex yet, and Kim was pregnant! I knew I didn't want to be there when Stretch found out!

The twins, Renee and Michelle, and me in the middle (at 13 years old), dressed for a Sweet Sixteen party.

*I*t was a fall evening, and I was doing research for a school project at the public library . . . until the lights went out.

"Miss, we are closing. Please bring the books to the counter that you want to check out," the short gray-haired librarian instructed.

"Jamie, come on now, the library is closing," my mother said as she stood over me.

I loved the library! I often got caught up in time as I would get lost in the books. There was so much to learn and so much wisdom to obtain. From a young age, my mother treated my brother and me to trips to the library. For me, the library was just as good as going to the movies!

"Okay, Mom. I guess I'm going to have to check out all of these," I said as I grabbed the large stack of books.

"Jamie, no! Pick out a few of them quickly and leave the rest. If you still need to read them later, I'll bring you back," my mother said as the librarian watched me select the books and go to the front counter.

I checked out my books, then my mother and I left the library.

"Come on, Jamie, we're going to be late picking up Kee," Mom said as she glanced at her watch. We quickly rushed to the car, and my mother drove to Jamaica High School where my brother attended night school to make up for the classes that he had failed.

As we pulled up to the school, the classes had already let out. We were late! There was a big commotion outside the school. A bunch of boys were lined up in front of the school. All I could see was a big circle around these boys, and I stared to see what was happening.

"Oh-oh, look, Mommy, look," I said as I stared out of the window to see the fight.

"Mind your business, child! That ain't got nothing to do with us," my mother said as we waited for my brother to approach the car.

My eyes were glued to the window. I wanted to see the fight.

"Mommy, mommy, that's Kee in the middle of the circle," I yelled as I noticed my brother, and I quickly unlocked the door to get out.

Chapter Thirty

"Oh, my Lord," my mother screamed. She reached in the backseat to get the club she used to lock the steering wheel of the car. Mama ran like a wild woman, and I followed her!

We pushed our way around the large crowd. My brother was fighting three of the Springfield Boulevard boys.

"Get the hell off my damn child," my mother yelled as she swung her red club in the air. Her voice scared the boys, and they backed off of Kee, who was holding his own.

"You damn hoodlums. You want to fight somebody's kid? Fight me! You got the right one now, baby," my mother said as she swung her club.

"Listen, we don't want no problems with you, Momma," one of the boys said, and he let go of Kee.

"Boy, I ain't your damn momma, and the way you look, you ain't got no damn momma, you peezy hair ugly Gremlin," my mother shouted in rage as the kids in the crowd laughed.

"Mom, come on," Kee said as he grabbed her hand.

"No, these boys want to jump you! Oh, I'll show them what jump is," she shouted in rage. I had never quite seen her so angry before!

My brother and I managed to get her back to the car. We drove home, and my mother examined my brother for bruises. Kee had a big knot on the top of his forehead and a couple of small bruises. He looked okay to have been jumped by so many boys.

"Look at my baby. I can't believe they did this to you," my mother said as she put Band-Aids on my brother's cuts.

"Mom, I'm okay," Kee said as he attempted to calm her down.

"Oh, Kee, them big ole boys tried to take your life. What if I wasn't there?" she said as she began to cry.

"Mom, don't cry, I'm okay," he said.

"But what if they come back?"

"Mom, after all you did out there, they ain't coming back. Plus, it's over. I beat up one of the boys, and they jumped me. It's over now," my brother said convincingly.

"Well, I pray so! You stay home tomorrow, and hopefully, this thing will die down! If not, I'm going to call the police!"

Kee stayed home for the rest of the week. I constantly checked on him as he locked himself in his room.

"Look at my face, Jamie," Kee said as I sat down on his bed.

"Kee, it's not that bad," I answered.

"Yo, these dudes trying to mess up my face, man," he said in an angry tone I had rarely ever heard.

"Kee, it's okay! It's gonna heal!" I said as I leaned over and hugged him.

"Somebody got to pay for this! I ain't going out like this, Jamie, for real."

"Kee, chill out. You know them boys are dangerous!"

"I don't care what they are! They are gonna respect me! Since they don't want to give me my respect, I guess I have to take it!"

*   *   *

As my brother grew older, his ways began to quickly change. He was no longer mild spoken and polite. He turned into a full-blown rebel who took no shorts!

It was a late-October afternoon after the Springfield boys jumped Kee at night school when my brother came running through the doors as I was sitting at the kitchen table eating a snack.

"Yo, Kee, what happened? What happened?" I asked frantically.

Kee was sweating bullets. He opened up his jacket and pulled out a black 9 mm gun. "Oh my God!" I said loudly as my brother put his hands over my mouth. "What have you done?" I asked as I lowered my voice.

"Jamie, I couldn't take it no more. Them suckers still keep coming for me. So I had to handle my business."

"Handle your business? How?"

"I, um, I just shot the block up."

"Shot the block up!" I yelled in a loud voice.

"Shhh, you gonna get me in trouble."

"Look, boy, are you crazy? You about to get yourself in trouble. Did you kill somebody?"

"Naw, Jamie, I just let them dudes know I ain't no punk."

"Oh, man, Kee, they gonna kill you now for real," I said as I began to cry.

"So what? You want your big brother to be a sucker?"

"No, but I don't want you dead either," I said as I cried in my brother's arms.

I just knew the Springfield boys was gonna get Kee, but I was absolutely wrong! When the boys saw Kee had the heart to shoot up the block, they began to like him! They even asked him to be down with their crew. Kee turned down their offer, but they still respected him. Every now and then, Kee would have beefs, but things got much better for him in our neighborhood. Kee's stunt on Springfield made him a ghetto superstar!

I was proud to have Kee as my brother. I knew he had my back, and no one in my neighborhood would disrespect me. This security caused me to look up to my brother. In my eyes, he was that dude!

My grandmother, Retha Davis, and my grandfather,
Hosea Davis, in the early 80s.

*A*s the school year progressed, Aunt Carolyn grew sicker and sicker. After church on Sundays we would all go to Brooklyn and spend time with her, Tanya, and my grandmother. I loved spending time with my grandmother. She was full of wisdom! She always seemed to give me the correct advice just at the right time!

We pulled up at my father's apartment building in Brooklyn. Tanya was sitting out on the stoops as we approached. My father strongly believed in providing for his family, even his sisters. So, when my aunt had a tough time finding an affordable apartment, my dad decided to invest in a four-family house in East Flatbush, Brooklyn.

"Hey, Aunt Liddie. Hey, Uncle Nelson," Tanya said with excitement as my parents walked up the steps of the building.

"Hey, baby," my mother said as she kissed Tanya.

"Hey, love," my father said as he hugged my cousin.

"What's up, Kee and Jamie?" Tanya said as she greeted us.

"Hello, Tanya," my brother and I responded as we walked into the hallway of the building and proceeded up the tall flight of stairs.

We rang my aunt's doorbell, and my grandmother came to the door. "Look a-here. Here comes my favorite little family," my grandmother said, and she let us into the apartment. As we entered, I could smell my grandmother's good Southern food.

"Um-um, it smells good in here," I said as my grandmother hugged us all.

"Yeah, Grandma fixed something good for her babies to eat," Grandmother said as she hugged me tightly. I pushed my way into the house and proceeded to Aunt Carolyn's room. As I pushed back the door, I noticed her pale, skinny body lying in the bed.

"Aunt Carolyn," I said as she opened up her eyes and smiled. I quickly rushed to the bed and threw my arms around her.

"Hey, baby," she responded in a weak voice.

"Aunt Carolyn, I missed you so much. I couldn't wait to come see you!" I said as I sat on the edge of her bed and held her hand.

"I miss you, too," Auntie replied as she squeezed my hand

tightly.

No matter how bad my aunt Carolyn felt, she always picked up her spirit when I came around. I would sit on the side of her bed and talk to her about everything that was going on in my life, and she paid attention. She actually looked forward to my visits with her.

Nobody on this planet could cook like my grandmother! Her meals were fantastic. I hated that my aunt was sick, but I loved being able to see my grandmother every weekend.

"Grandma, you know I'm running for Vice President at school?" I said as we all sat around the kitchen table eating.

"Yes, baby, I heard. Your daddy told me. I told them, baby, you are very special. You Grandma's little angel. One day you gonna do some big things, you watch and see," she said as she served the baked chicken and collard greens she had made.

"Yeah, Grandma?" I questioned.

"That's right, baby. All you got to do is stay with the Lord. He got a special assignment just for you."

"Yes, Grandma, I will."

"Baby, you still singing at church?" Grandma asked as we ate our meal.

"Yes, Grandma. I sing lead next Sunday."

"Nelson, I sure would like to go to the church and hear my baby sing," my grandmother said as she looked at my father.

"Well, uh, I guess we can come and get you," Dad replied as he chewed away on the neck bone in his collard greens.

"Yeah, Nelson, I'll like that. I ain't been to no church since I've been up here," my grandmother said.

"Ma Retha, I'll pick you up on Sunday morning and drop you back off," my mother interjected.

"Oh, yes, Liddie. Thank you. I can't wait to hear my little angel sing!"

It was official. My grandmother was coming to church with us on Sunday. I was a little nervous about her seeing me sing. *What if I mess up?* I thought to myself. *Oh, I'm being foolish! I can't wait to show my grandmother what her little angel is working with!*

* * *

It was Sunday morning, and I was up early with my mother so we could pick up my grandmother from Brooklyn.

Not long afterward, we arrived in front of my father's building, and my mother blew the horn. Grandma Retha opened the door of the building. She was dressed to impress! My grandmother had on a beautiful pink silk suit, with a pink and white large hat that had a pink flower in the middle. She started walking toward the car as she caught the attention of the neighbors. "Wow, miss, you look very nice," the man next door said as she came down the steps.

"Oh, thank you, baby," my grandmother responded, and she gave him her million-dollar smile.

I loved to see my grandmother dressed up! It's like she transformed into a whole different person. When she wore her church clothes, my grandmother had a swagger that was out of this world!

She got in the car, and we headed back to my house. My mother and I still had to get dressed.

"Kee, hurry up, boy. We almost ready to leave for church," Mama said as she fixed her hair in the bathroom mirror.

Grandma sat on the living-room couch, waiting patiently.

"Hello, Mom," my dad said as he came out of his room in his T-shirt and shorts.

"Good morning, Hosea, why aren't you dressed for church?" she questioned.

"Well, uh, Mom, uh, you see, I work all week and um—" he stuttered, and my grandmother interrupted him.

"Young man, now I *know* I raised you better than that! Sunday is the Lord's Day and as for me and my house, boy, we gonna *always* serve the Lord!" she scolded.

"Well, I do serve the Lord. I just—"

Grandma quickly interrupted. "Well, that settles it! Go get dressed so we can go," she said as she leaned back on the couch with her feet up in the air.

"Yes, ma'am." Obediently, Dad went back in his room to get dressed.

I was so shocked! In all these years, I never saw my dad go to church with us in New York! Ms. Retha didn't play any games. She meant business when it came to her Lord! The whole family got dressed, and we all headed out of the house to Maranatha Baptist Church, including my father!

I left my family and went downstairs to the church basement with the other choir members. My dad, my mother, my grandmother, and Kee waited for the usher to seat them.

Sundays at Maranatha Baptist Church were serious business. Like my grandmother, the women loved to get dressed up for church. Oftentimes, it was the only place they went where they could show off their stylish fashions, especially the older women. Sunday mornings was a fashion show. Everyone was dressed to impress.

All the choir members wore long choir robes. We marched in unison inside of the church doors, up into our seats on the pulpit. Like clockwork, each Sunday, we sang two hymns from our burgundy standard church hymnbook. Then we sang a regular selection before the church announcements.

It was time for our selection, and my turn to sing the lead. I nervously glanced over at my family, who were seated in the third row. My grandmother and my mother were hyped up and into the service, while my father and my brother struggled to stay awake.

Marvetta, the choir director, signaled the choir to stand up. We all stood up in unison. She pointed at me, and I came down from the choir stand and grabbed the mic. As I came down, I could hear the church members say, "That's all right now!" "You better sing, Jamie!"

The church members loved to hear me sing. They would shout and applaud before I opened my mouth. I untwisted the raveled up mic cord and took the mic off the stand.

"Yeah, Grandbaby, sing for Grandma. Let the Lord use you, baby!" my grandmother said loudly as the church members all took notice. I was so embarrassed, but I was definitely going to take her advice.

The music on the church organ began to play, and the choir members began to move from side to side as I held the mic and studied my audience. I knew just where everyone was sitting and what they were doing.

"Sometimes this way seems so very hard. But Jesus said that this wouldn't be. Yes, He did. Yes, He did. But if I can hold on and stand the storm, Jesus said that He would give me the victory, yes!" I sang passionately in my deep adult alto voice, and the church cheered me on!

Before I could finish the first verse, the members stood up on their feet, clapping their hands, getting into the song. My grandmother stood up first. She began to clap her hands and do her little old-school rock. Others quickly followed, including my mother.

As we got to the bridge of the song, I thought about my aunt Carolyn and all of her struggles. Even though she lay sick in her bed, she refused to let go of God. I thought about how my grandmother said, "Regardless of what we go through, God will always have our back." As my appreciation and admiration for God stirred from the bottom pit of my soul, I began to sing in another key!

"Nothing, nothing, nothing, nothing. Friends may come, friends may go, but I'm determined to hold on. He'll be my lawyer in the courtroom and my doctor in the sick-room," I sang passionately as the Holy Spirit entered the building. My dad even stood up and was clapping, getting into the song, when all of a sudden my grandmother got out of the aisle and ran up right next to me in front of the pulpit and began to catch the Holy Ghost! It was over after that! The whole building went into a frenzy. I couldn't even finish the song. Grandma grabbed my hand, and we shouted together in the front of the

church.

I had never caught the Holy Ghost before, but as my grandmother grabbed my hand, it was like fire shot up my spine. We began to dance together, and the rest of the church followed.

My dad was majorly embarrassed. He told my brother his stomach was hurting, so he'd be waiting for us in the car, and he slipped out of the spirit-filled service.

Whatever my grandmother brought with her into that service, it was powerful. Don't get me wrong. We always had a good time in church, and people always caught the Holy Ghost, but not like that! Even the little kids in the choir stand were shouting! It took like an hour for everyone to calm down, and the pastor hadn't even preached.

My dad waited for us out in the car. We came out of the crowded service and headed over to him.

"Hosea, what happened to you, baby?" Grandma questioned as she got into the front seat of the car.

"Oh, nothing, Ma, my stomach was bothering me, but I'm okay now," my father respectfully responded as my mother rolled her eyes and screwed up her face in the backseat. I silently laughed to myself.

"Well, Hosea, that little girl you got there is very special! God is gonna use her in a major way. You watch out for her!" she said as she turned around and smiled at me.

Maybe God does have a plan for me, I said to myself as I daydreamed in the backseat of the car. I don't think I ever experienced another church service quite like that one!

My brother and me, at 13 years old, posing on my
Aunt Carolyn's couch on Christmas morning

C hristmas approached as the holiday spirit filled the air! My neighborhood was lit up with houses decorated for the holidays. Christmas lights, sleighs with Santa Claus and his reindeer, and snowmen were sighted on our lawns. It became a silent contest of whose house would be decorated the best. Every year we could count on our neighbor's big corner house to win! He had lights draped on every part of his house. It was like a museum. People would come from all over to admire the nativity decorations he had uniquely set up on his large property.

I loved the Christmas season. I liked going to the mall and viewing all the wonderful decorations. I also liked shopping for gifts. In some strange way, the packed malls and long lines in the store excited me. I had to join in and be a part of the shopping celebration!

All season long I begged my mother for these red, high Gucci boots I had seen in a music video. When my mother found out they were two hundred dollars, she flipped out! "Hell no! I ain't buying no two hundred dollar boots, Jamie! You can forget it!" she would say as I constantly nagged her. I wanted these boots so bad I could taste them! I saw myself in my mind with them on. I knew just what I would wear with them. I had a fetish for these boots that just wouldn't quit.

Mama and I went Christmas shopping. We bought gifts for all my family members in New York. We were all having a big celebration at Aunt Carolyn's house. This was the first Christmas we had ever spent with my grandmother in New York, so it was highly anticipated. My father's two brothers, Thomas and Johnnie, would be there with their families, and we'd all get to enjoy my grandmother's holiday cooking.

It was Christmas morning, and I awoke abruptly to see what was in store for me under the tree. It was a family tradition to get up early and unwrap our gifts together. My brother, my mother, my father, and I unwrapped all our gifts. I was happy about the designer clothes my mother and father bought for me, but I was a little disappointed that I didn't get the Gucci boots I wanted. I couldn't wait to grow up so I could buy my own things.

My mother was up early cooking sweet potato pies for our

Chapter Thirty-Two

Christmas dinner. We all got dressed and loaded in the car and headed to Aunt Carolyn's house.

When we arrived, I was surprised to see Aunt Carolyn out of the bed and helping out in the kitchen! She almost looked like her old self. I quickly jumped in her arms and hugged her with excitement.

"Look at you, Aunt Carolyn, you look good," I said as I checked out her new wig. The chemo treatments had taken out most of her beautiful hair.

"Look at my baby. You look good too, sugar," she said as she hugged me back.

Aunt Carolyn's apartment quickly got packed. Uncle Thomas came with his wife Mary and his son George. Uncle Johnnie came with his wife Yvonne and his two daughters, Ebony and Kanika. My grandmother was overjoyed to have her children together on Christmas. She cooked a meal that was fit for a king! We had turkey, fried chicken, chitlins, ham, chicken and dumplings, collard greens, candied yams, cranberry sauce, macaroni and cheese, stuffing, rice, and a slew of cakes and pies. My grandmother made a triple-stacked pineapple upside-down cake to die for!

There was always tension at our family functions, especially if Uncle Thomas and Aunt Mary were there. My mother couldn't stand my aunt Mary! She would always refer to her as "the ugly black witch." They had an extensive history of bitter wars. Dad dated Aunt Mary back in the day, and he cheated on my mother with her. Mary was a psycho, stalker-type who was accused of only getting with my father's brother, Uncle Thomas, as a get-back. Time moved on, but the tension never ended.

"Liddie," Aunt Mary said as she greeted my mother when she walked in the door. "Mary," my mother imitated her greeting in a bougie voice.

"Oh, Mother Retha, it's so good to see you. I miss you so much," Aunt Mary said as she grabbed onto my grandmother in a phony fashion. My mother rolled her eyes, watching the grand slam performance Mary was putting on.

"Oh, Hosea, it's so good to see you," Aunt Mary said as she ran over to hug my dad. He started to hug her back . . . until he caught my mother's sharp eye contact.

"Oh, uh, hi, Mary," he said as he reached out to shake her hand instead. As Aunt Mary came in the house, everybody's energy changed.

"Oh, look a-here at the beautiful children. Hello, Kee, and hi, Ms. Jamie," she said as she hugged my brother and squeezed my cheek. Nobody had squeezed my cheeks in years! *I'm not a little kid, you crazy lady,* I thought to myself. I quickly took up my mother's feelings and walked away.

We all exchanged Christmas gifts. I helped my mother pick out everyone's gifts, and they all loved them, especially my grandmother. We bought her a 14 karat gold, #1 Grandmother charm with a beautiful rope necklace. Grandmother was into jewelry, so she immediately put it on and showed it off to everyone.

Aunt Mary stood up and passed each of us boxes with our gifts in it. I could tell by her fabulous presentation that our gifts were going to be good. I quickly opened up my nicely wrapped box to discover a plain, cheap looking, sweatshirt that had a price tag marked half off. I was outraged as I pulled the flimsy, irregular shirt out of the box. She had gotten my cousin Tanya and my cousin Kanika the same shirt in different colors. We went in Tanya's room and laughed about how cheap Aunt Mary was.

"Look at this shirt, girl," Tanya said as she pulled out her pink shirt Aunt Mary got her.

"Aw! I'ma rock this to the club tomorrow night," Tanya joked as she pranced in front of the mirror, and we laughed.

"Yeah, girl, I'ma rock this with my new sneakers the first day back to school," I said as we all laughed again.

"Look, y'all. She left the price tag on my shirt," Kanika said as we quickly came over to see it.

"Two dollars and ninety-nine cents. Wow, y'all, we were worth a whole two dollars and ninety-nine cents," Kanika exclaimed as we stared at the price tag in disbelief.

"She probably didn't even pay that for it. She probably got a discount since she bought three," I said as we laughed and clowned. My brother walked in and showed us his gift from Aunt Mary. He got two pairs of tube socks.

"Look at these cheap socks Aunt Mary bought me," he said as he held up his present.

"Well, at least you can make use of them. What the hell we going do with these cheap-behind sweatshirts? You wash them once, and they finished," Tanya said as we compared our cheap gifts.

It was finally dinner time! We had an adult table and a kids table. We all sat silently and enjoyed my grandmother's awesome cooking. Aunt Carolyn sat and ate with a sparkle in her eyes. It seemed like her family, all together, brought joy to her eyes.

After we finished eating, Aunt Carolyn called me to her room. "Jamie, come here. I need you to help me with something," she shouted.

"Yes, ma'am," I said as I quickly went after her.

"Baby, come sit down on my bed."

"Yes, Aunt Carolyn."

"I want you to know I love you very much."

"I know, Aunt Carolyn. I love you, too!"

"Yeah, baby, I know you do. Your aunt Carolyn doesn't know how much time I'll be around for. This cancer done really took a toll on me."

"No, Aunt Carolyn, you gonna be okay. God ain't gonna let nothing bad happen to you. He's a good God, Aunt Carolyn."

"Yes, Jamie, He is. That's why He sometimes allows things to happen that we don't understand. I don't want you to be worried. When I die, I'm going to a better place."

"Oh, uh-uh, you ain't going nowhere. We need you right here on earth, Aunt Carolyn," I interjected sharply.

"Listen, baby, never ever doubt God, no matter how things seem to be. Will you remember that?"

"Yes, Aunt Carolyn," I said in a sad voice, trying to figure out what she was trying to tell me.

"Baby, reach under my bed. I got something down there for you," Aunt Carolyn instructed, and I quickly jumped up and grabbed the large box from under the bed.

"This is for me?" I asked with excitement.

"It certainly is," she said with a large smile as I eagerly unwrapped the box. I opened it to discover the red Gucci boots I wanted so badly.

"Oh my goodness," I said as I quickly tried on the boots.

"Quiet down now. I couldn't afford to buy all your cousins this type of gift," she told me as she quickly shut the door. I was so happy!

"Your mother said all you've been talking about is these boots, so I sent Tanya to the store to get them."

"Oh, thank you so much, Aunt Carolyn," I said as I wrapped my arms around her. "You are my favorite aunt, forever!"

We all had a good time that Christmas. My father enjoyed playing cards with his brothers and watching the game. Aunt Carolyn and all the women sat around the kitchen table talking and remembering old times. Aunt Carolyn kept the tension down between Aunt Mary and my mother. She was an excellent host. All the children played in Tanya's room. We pulled out the Monopoly board and spent hours playing the game. It was good to see the Davis family all on one accord. It was a Christmas that I'll never forget!

* * *

The holiday season brought more surprises and changes. Kim decided to keep her baby and finally got the nerve up to tell Stretch. Of course, he went bonkers, but his baby's mother, Monessa, was able to calm him down. He sat down and had a long talk with both Kim and Minute about their responsibilities as a parent. Then he took Minute for a drive around the neighborhood alone. God only knows what Stretch said to him on that ride.

Kim was often sick in the morning, but she was determined to get her high school diploma. "Girl, I ain't dropping out of school. I got to be able to take care of my daughter!" Kim would say when people asked her what she was gonna do.

After Kim got pregnant, it was like she started a trend. It seemed like all of her friends, one by one, were getting pregnant, except for Nakia. They began to brag about their pregnancies and how they would raise their children.

"Girl, you know my baby gonna stay fly. I'ma buy all the hot little baby sneakers that come out!" the girls would brag as they admired and praised each other.

I felt so out of the loop! I guess it would be fun to have a baby around, but I don't even have a boyfriend! Inside I was lonely and confused. I seemed to be the only single one in the bunch. I wanted desperately to make my own mark and gain acceptance. I just had to figure out a way!

My cousin Kanika and me, at 14 years old.

The spring approached, and April convinced me to try out for LaGuardia High School of Performing Arts, better known as the "*Fame*" school. Since I was a little girl, I watched *Fame,* the show, on television and always imagined myself attending the school. I wanted to be a dance major and be in Debbie Allen, the actress's class. *I would love to dance with Leroy!* I used to think to myself as a child. Now I was all grown-up and finally had my chance to make it happen.

I knew how to dance, sing, and act, so it was difficult for me to choose a major, but I decided to pursue acting. I filled out the application and got a letter back to come and audition.

It was my audition date for the "*Fame*" school, in Manhattan, and I was nervous. I really wanted to get into the school, but what if they didn't pick me? My worst fear was failure.

My mother got up early with me, and we drove to the subway, where we got on the train and headed to the high school. I observed the scenery on the crowded train. The hustle and bustle of the New Yorkers I watched gave me a rush! I wanted to be a part of the city's fast-paced life.

"Jamie, are you sure you want to take all these trains to get to school every morning?" my mother asked as she clinched her pocketbook tightly on the train.

"Yeah, Mom, ain't it fun?" I said as I looked around at all the people in the train, including the bums.

"Well, all right, Jamie," she said, but I could clearly tell she didn't feel the same way.

We took three subway trains until we arrived at LaGuardia High School of Performing Arts. I stood and stared at the large white building that stood eight stories high! I could tell by my first look, this wasn't your typical high school. We entered the building and went down to the auditorium, where the principal welcomed us and allowed us all to go on a tour of the school. This school was amazing! It had real dance studios with mirrors and bars, two large grand auditoriums, two big lunchrooms, art studios, and state-of-the-art music studios. They even had drama theatre rooms. Escalators

Chapter Thirty-Three

took us up to each floor, like the ones in a mall. I admired all the beautiful artwork that surrounded the school. There were all types of murals and paintings! This place was awesome. As I toured the school, my desire to attend increased.

It was my turn to audition. I took a deep breath as they called my name. Gracefully, I walked into the large Drama Theatre and introduced myself to the five panelists. I immediately noticed Mr. Moody, who was a well-known actor and instructor, at the school.

"Jamila, tell us why you want to come to this school," the first panelist asked.

"Well, since I was a little girl, I watched *Fame* on television, so it has indeed been my dream to attend your prestigious school, sir," I said as I tried to properly enunciate my words.

"Okay, well, how do you think you can be an asset?" the second panelist asked.

"Well, I'm a hard worker, and I'm very ambitious. I believe as I develop my talent, it would spark an energy within me that would shine brightly to my peers. I'm a team player, and I can't wait to work with your wonderful team," I said passionately.

"Great, enough said. Let's see what you got," the third panelist said.

I did one of my monologues from *Mahalia Lives*. I had played this role so frequently that the words became one with me. I cried as I performed, then I began to passionately sing, *Sometimes I Feel Like A Motherless Child*. As I performed, the panelists were intrigued. You could hear a pin drop in the room. I held their attention until I sang my very last note.

"Very good, very good!"

"Bravo!" the panelists began to shout as I wiped my tears.

"Good work, Jamila. We will be in touch with you," one of the panelists said as he escorted me out of the room where my mother stood to greet me.

"How did you do, Jamie?" my mother eagerly asked.

"Mom, I think I did good. I certainly got their attention. Especially when I sang. I don't think they expected me to sing," I said as we left the school.

"Jamie, I am so proud of you. I was a drama major in college and, baby, you doing things yah momma has never got to do. Something tells me all my dreams going to come to pass through you. I always wanted to be a famous actress, but I could never sing like you. Don't take your gifts and opportunities for granted. I grew up in a small country town, but you, baby, you live in the great Big Apple! You can become whatever you desire, Jamie. Whatever you do, don't give up!" my mother said as we walked down the busy Manhattan street.

The energy of the city and the subway charged me! I couldn't wait to get the results back from my audition. My new passion was to take New York City by storm!

* * *

The spring approached and Aunt Carolyn grew very sick and was hospitalized. The family was all told to rush to the hospital. The doctor said she had a very short time to live. The cancer had spread and eaten up her liver. Everybody was an emotional wreck as we huddled over the hospital bed. A pastor who was friends with my grandmother was present, as well as all my aunt's brothers from New York. The pastor preached, and Aunt Carolyn caught the Holy Spirit.

"Thank You, Jesus, thank You, Lord. Thank You!" she yelled in her weak voice. Aunt Carolyn had become so shriveled up. Her head was completely bald, and her body appeared almost lifeless.

My grandmother held on to my aunt's hands as my aunt began to praise the Lord in her hospital bed. Everybody was in tears, including my father and my brother, who often showed no emotions. My grandmother began to sing "Precious Lord" as she wiped Aunt Carolyn's forehead, then she prayed passionately. *"Lord, I don't understand You all of the time. But, Lord, I say thank You anyhow. I never expected to see my children sick, but I know, God, Your purpose is greater than me, so I say thank You anyhow. Lord, You know the pain I feel deep down in the pit of my soul, but I say to You, Lord, thank You anyhow. Keep us, Lord, we need You. I don't trust the doctors, Lord, but I trust You. God, You are great and merciful, and You can do anything. So I say, God, I thank You. God, I thank You! I'm hurting, Lord, but I thank You! Take my baby out of her misery and let her see Your wonderful kingdom."* We all sang church hymns and sat beside my aunt's bed until visiting hours were over.

As soon as we entered the house, the phone rang. Aunt Carolyn had passed away! We all huddled together as a family and all began to weep!

* * *

I couldn't believe my aunt Carolyn was gone. It all seemed to happen so quickly. At first I was angry with God. I didn't understand why He didn't just heal her. But as I saw how my grandmother handled her death, it strengthened me to do the same.

We had a large funeral for Aunt Carolyn in Kinston, North Carolina. Everyone from everywhere came. It was packed! Aunt Carolyn had so many flowers that they almost didn't fit in the building.

My grandmother taught me the words to "Amazing Grace," and I sang it at the funeral. There wasn't a dry eye left in the building. I sang that song in honor of my aunt who I greatly missed. I sang from the bowels of my soul. I wanted Aunt Carolyn to be proud of me.

As the preacher announced the last viewing of the body, lines began to assemble around the church for the viewing. My aunt and my cousin passed out, and other relatives were holding on to the casket as if they refused to let her go. Uncle Tit even tried to get in the casket. It was crazy! We never had anyone in our family so close to us die. Nobody handled Aunt Carolyn's death well. She was greatly loved.

When I went down to Kinston, I found out Dino had gotten locked back up for selling drugs. No wonder I hadn't heard from him! All our family from near and far came to pay their respect to our family for our loss. For the first time in a while, the Davises were all on one accord. We had to be strong and keep things together for my grandmother.

* * *

I came back home to discover a letter addressed to me from LaGuardia. I had bubbles in my stomach when my mother passed it to me. I quickly opened it up to discover I was accepted! Great joy came over me that was so well needed at the time. I couldn't wait for next year to arrive. *"Fame, I'm gonna live forever. I'm going to learn how to fly,"* I sang passionately as I announced my great victory. I anxiously anticipated my new school. Look out, world, here I come!

* * *

*I*t was the summer of 1991, and I had just turned fourteen years old. My training bra was filling out, and you couldn't tell me I wasn't grown! Time was flying by, and I was on my way to high school. In my mind, I wasn't a little girl anymore. I was a young adult, and I wanted my young adult privileges! I was able to convince my mother to loosen her tight reins around me, and I was given new privileges. I was allowed to hang out with the older girls. I could go to parties, to the movies, and to the mall all by myself. My mom even let me start traveling to Brooklyn to see my cousin on the subway train, by myself. I took pride in my newfound privileges, and I felt good about growing up!

Kim had a baby girl. I would often go by her house to see the baby. Back to back, all our friends began to give birth. Everybody seemed to have a baby daddy! Having a baby was highly glorified during this era and became the "in thing" to do. I couldn't wait to have my chance at motherhood. I wanted a baby daddy too, but first I had to find a boyfriend.

The summer came to a close. I saved up my checks from working as a dance instructor at the Laurelton Theatre and couldn't wait to go shopping with Tanya.

I packed my overnight bag and headed on the train to meet Tanya. When I finally got to Brooklyn, she was waiting for me on the stoop with her best friend Yolie. Tanya was super-duper fly! She had gotten a large settlement check from my aunt Carolyn's insurance company and Tanya went bonkers. She lived in the mall, for real! Tanya would wear an outfit once and toss it, and I would come and collect all her designer hand-me-downs.

"What's up, little cuz? What took you so long?" Tanya asked as she stood up impatiently.

"Tanya, that train ride is mad long. I got to travel from Queens to Manhattan, and then to Brooklyn. It's three trains I got to catch," I responded.

"Well, you better get used to it! That's what you gonna have to do from now on going to school."

"Yeah, I know."

Chapter Thirty-Four

"All right, go put your bags upstairs. We getting ready to go to the Apollo."

"The Apollo?" I said excitedly.

"Yeah, girl. I got us tickets to a taping of *Showtime at the Apollo*. Father MC is performing, girl, so hurry up," Tanya said as she rushed me.

"Oh my God! We probably gonna get to see the black lady with the Jheri curl that always sits in the front of the show," I said zealously as I hurried into the house to drop off my overnight bag. I opened Tanya's door, and I felt creeped out. The apartment seemed so strange without Aunt Carolyn around. I didn't like to be in the apartment by myself. I was scared I would see a ghost or something. I quickly dropped my bag and headed back out the door.

Tanya, Yolie, and I got on the number 3 train at Sutter Avenue and took it straight uptown to 125th Street. This was the first time I had ever been to Harlem, and I was excited. I intensely studied the African American Mecca. There were street vendors on every block. People were outside selling all types of things from books to tapes, to incense, to shirts, and all kinds of other trinkets. You name it, they had it spread out on the ground! The street peddlers were making their sales pitches as we walked down the block.

"I got shirts, two for five dollars. You can't beat my price anywhere. Hey, you sexy ladies, come check out my shirts," the panhandler shouted as we walked down 125th Street. I was mesmerized by all the action that took place on this block.

"Oh, oh, look, there's the Apollo," I said as I looked up and recognized the landmark building I had only seen on television.

"Oh, shoot, there goes Tupac," Tanya said as we passed the large picture back-drops that were hanging up on the side of the walls of the Apollo Theatre.

"Yeah, and he looks so sexy!" I said as I admired Tupac Shakur, a well-known actor/rapper, who was by himself on 125th Street.

"Oh, Tanya, I'm going to ask him to take a picture with me," I said anxiously.

"Girl, you not scared?" Tanya questioned.

"I'm sure not!" I said, and I broke away from Tanya and Yolie to approach Tupac.

"Hey, Tupac," I said as if he was a close friend.

"Hey, Shorty, what's up?" he replied.

"Nothing, I just want to take a picture with you, that's all," I said as I gave him my puppy dog face.

"Oh, all right. Pick out the backdrop."

I quickly picked out the backdrop I wanted, and the photographer took our picture together.

"Yeah, Pac, I think you know my peoples," I said as I waited for the photographer to give me the Polaroid picture.

"Who's your peoples?" Pac questioned.

"Stretch, from Queens."

"Yeah, that's my man! He's one of my producers. How do you know Stretch, Shorty?"

"Oh, he's from my neighborhood, and I'm friends with his sister Kim."

"Oh, shoot, Kim, that's my girl!" Tupac said zealously.

"Yeah? She just had a baby girl," I interjected.

"Yeah, I know. Her brother almost killed her too. I know the whole story!"

Tanya and Yolie stood in amazement as they watched me hold a conversation with Tupac. Fans caught on to the fact that it was Tupac, and they began to swarm us. I had Tupac sign my picture, then we hurried to get in the crowded line for the *Showtime at the Apollo* taping.

We waited in line and finally entered. When we got inside, the theatre was surprisingly small. It looked so much larger on television. Just as I suspected, the lady with the Jheri curl who appeared in every episode was sitting right in the front row. We sat like ten rows behind her.

I enjoyed the show thoroughly, especially Father MC's performance! *"Treat her like she wanna be treated. You should treat her right,"* his song played loudly on the theatre's state-of-the-art sound system.

The curtain came up and Father MC began to perform. The crowd went crazy! We all stood up in our seats, dancing to his popular up-tempo R&B song. I loved his stage performance. He had two dancers dancing with him, and their energy was crazy! They rocked the crowd!

I left the Apollo that night feeling like I had finally arrived! I was experiencing life like I never had before. I met Tupac Shakur, and I got to see Father MC! In my own little mind I felt like I too was headed for stardom!

The next day, Tanya took me school shopping. I didn't even have to spend my own money! She took me to Fifth Avenue in Manhattan and introduced me to all types of new designer stores. She bought me a yellow Fendi clutch bag with *F*s all over it to match my yellow high-top Reeboks. Tommy Hilfiger was real popular at the time; Polo and Guess also. Tanya got me laced for school! I had never bought so many clothes at one time! We couldn't even take the train home! We had too many bags, so we caught a Yellow Cab instead. It was clear Tanya had a lot of money now, and I enjoyed helping her spend it!

Me, at 14 years old, posing on my living room
couch, rocking my door knocker earrings.

*T*he first day of school finally arrived, and I was so excited. I put on my red and yellow-striped Tommy Hilfiger shirt and my dark denim Tommy Hilfiger jeans. I unwrapped the white tissue paper off of my yellow high-top Reeboks and put my books inside my yellow Fendi clutch bag. I had a fresh French roll with crunch curls in the front that Lorna, the Jamaican hairdresser, in Brooklyn did for me. I stared in the mirror, and my reflection told me I had it going on!

I ate my breakfast, then April's dad blew the horn out front. "Mommy, Daddy, I'm leaving," I said as I grabbed my lunch money off of their dresser.

"Good luck at school," Mama replied as she turned over in the bed.

Going to school in Manhattan meant I had to be out of the house by 6:30 a.m. in order to get to school on time. I often left before anyone in my house even got up.

I got into April's dad's, Mr. Martindale, car, and he took us to the Parsons and Archer subway station, where we arrived at approximately 6:45 a.m. The subway station was busy. Many adults going to work and children going to school congregated there.

We went through the turnstile, entered the large major subway station, and walked down the steep stairs to the subway platform where everyone stood awaiting the next train to arrive. Parsons and Archer was the last stop on the E train line in Queens. We lived in a two-fare zone, which meant most people who lived in Jamaica, Queens, had to take a bus after they got off the train.

"Oh my goodness, Jamila, I can't believe my best friend is going to school with me this year! We are going to have so much fun!" April said as we waited for the train to arrive.

"Yeah, girl, I'm so nervous. This is all new to me. I can't believe I'm taking the subway to school," I said as I observed all the people reading their newspapers, waiting for the train. I felt so mature!

"Hey, April," a group of children said as they walked up to us.

"What's up, y'all? This is my best friend Jamila. She's going to LaGuardia this year," April said, and the group greeted me.

Chapter Thirty-Five

"Hold up. Is that Shalon?" I asked as I recognized the tall, skinny, light-skinned girl from Bernice Johnson's Dance Studio.

"Jamila?" she responded in an excited voice.

"Yeah, girl, what's up?" I said as we gave each other a hug.

"I haven't seen you in years, ever since you and the twins stopped going to Bernice Johnson's," Shalon said.

"Yeah, girl, it has been a while. Do you still go to B.J.'s?" I asked.

"No, you didn't hear? Most of the dance school split up. Carolyn started her own dance school, and so did Lorna," Shalon responded. "Why did y'all drop out anyway?" she asked.

"Well, my mother felt like they was showing extreme favoritism, and she ended up getting into a crazy argument with Debbie, the dance instructor, so she pulled me out and the twins' mother pulled them out too."

"So what's up with the twins?" Shalon asked.

"Oh, they chillin'. They both going to Springfield High School this year."

"Oh, okay, so you gonna be a dance major, right?" Shalon asked.

"No, I'm going to be a drama major," I responded, and she giggled.

"Wow, I'm not a dance major either. I'm a vocal major. All that money our parents spent on dance school and we're not even going to school for it," Shalon said as we both laughed.

"Oh, look, there goes Ebony. Do you remember her from Bernice Johnson's?" Shalon asked me as a heavyset, fair-skinned girl walked up.

"Oh, yeah. She was in the 7-10 class," I said as Ebony came over.

Shalon spoke up, by way of introduction. "Ebony, this is Jamila, April's best friend. She's going to LaGuardia this year. Do you remember her from Bernice Johnson's?" she asked as we waited on the platform for the train to arrive.

"Oh, shoot. You was always hanging out with Renée and Michelle. Yeah, I remember you," Ebony responded.

"Are you a dance major?" I asked.

"No, I'm a music major, but there are a few dance majors at LaGuardia from Bernice Johnson's, Roger and Karen," Ebony said.

"Oh, Roger goes to LaGuardia too?"

"Yeah, and there are a few others," she said as April stared on, intrigued.

"I can't believe y'all all know each other," April said as she listened to the conversation. By the time the train arrived, there was a whole crew of us gathered to go to LaGuardia.

The train ride was fun. Everyone told jokes, performed, and even imitated the homeless people on the train. There wasn't a dull moment. Everybody on the train knew we were the kids from LaGuardia by our talent. Our crew wasn't shy at all. No one minded showing off their skills.

We took the E train to the D train to the #1 train, where we got off at Sixty-sixth Street and walked through this long tunnel underneath Lincoln Center. My school was directly across the street from Lincoln Center and right next door to Martin Luther King, Jr., High School.

As we came out of the tunnel, we bumped into a lot of children who went to King next door. Our school and their school were like apples and oranges. LaGuardia students were very talented, reserved children from all across the city. King students were more rowdy and ghetto. I quickly took notice of a group of guys dressed in all Polo who went to King.

"Yo, April, what's up with them?" I said as I checked the boys out.

"Oh, girl, they are the 'Low Lifes' from Brooklyn," April said.

"The Low Life Crew?" I questioned.

"Yeah, girl, they are a part of this gang from Brooklyn. All they wear is Polo, Ralph Lauren clothes," she said.

"Word? Every day?" I asked.

"Yeah, girl. They stay fresh!" April said.

"Well, how can they afford to all dress like that every day? Polo is expensive as hell!" I asked.

"Girl, they from Brooklyn. You know them Brooklyn boys stay boosting their clothes. They are known for running up in stores and taking out the whole rack," April said as we laughed.

I hadn't even gotten to school yet, but I was loving my journey! As we stood outside of the big, tall white school building, I observed the students who looked way different from the teens I was accustomed to seeing in Queens. There were all different types of children from all kinds of backgrounds. From punk rockers to thugs, we all stood outside waiting patiently for the school doors to open. I took notice of all the different fashion trends. Each borough of New York City had its own style. You could literally tell which borough we were from just by the way that we were dressed. By socializing and talking to different students, I was able to distinguish the different trends.

LaGuardia students had an aura about them! Everybody seemed very confident about themselves. You had to be the top in your major in all of New York City to get accepted into the school. Getting accepted was a major accomplishment! Unlike the children I was accustomed to being around, LaGuardia students walked about embracing their own unique personalities with pride and confidence. I was immediately attracted to the positive energy, which motivated me to bring out my best!

By the time the school doors opened, I was bursting with anticipation to get in. I couldn't believe I was finally in high school, and a student at the prestigious High School of Performing Arts, at that!

All the freshmen were advised to go to the auditorium for orientation. We piled inside the school's state-of-the-art theatre and watched the well put together orientation film introducing us to The School of the Arts. Our orientation was designed to make us feel as though we had all hit the jackpot. We were now a part of this distinguished club and had the privilege to utilize the school's resources to develop our skills.

Afterward, we left the auditorium and went to our separate departments. I walked down the stairs into the drama department, where all the freshmen awaited to begin our day. As I sat down in the small theatre and waited for my drama class to begin, a short, pretty, brown-skinned girl sat next to me.

"Excuse me, do you mind if I sit here?" she asked in a high-pitched voice.

"No, sit down," I said as I moved my belongings off the chair.

"My name is Qiana. What's your name?"

"Oh, hello, my name is Jamila," I said, and I shook her hand.

"Oh, okay, that's a pretty name."

"Thank you," I said as the teacher started the class.

"Children, settle down, settle down," Mr. Moody said as he stood up in front of us in the small theatre. Mr. Moody was a medium-height black man with a large bald spot in the back of his head. He was in several popular movies at the time, including *The Last Dragon*, so his face was very recognizable to us.

"Welcome to the Freshmen Drama Workshop, class. My name is Mr. Moody, and I'll be your teacher this semester. I know many of you have experience in drama. In this class, we are going to brush up on your technique. I'll be teaching you guys different exercises to help you get into character. We will also do a lot of skits and monologues. It is my goal by the end of this semester to have you prepared to do a small theatre production," he said as he handed orientation packages to each of us.

"Here at the School of the Arts, your major concentration will be drama. That's not to say your academic classes aren't important, because they are, but most of your day will be spent right here in the drama department.

"Take a look at your program schedules. Freshman drama classes will begin each morning at 8:30 and end at 11:00. Then you guys will go to lunch and after lunch, the rest of your academic classes will begin. I expect you to be in my class on time each morning and dressed in all-black. You can wear leotards and tights, sweatshirt and sweatpants. It doesn't matter, but you must be dressed comfortably. You cannot wear jeans to my class. Again, I'll repeat, no jeans. I advise you to get in here no later than 8:15 every morning so you have time to change in the dressing room," Mr. Moody said as he paced back and forth in front of the class.

"There is no talking, no playing, and no eating or chewing gum in my class. If you come to play or waste my time, there's the door—you are free to go! This experience will be whatever you make it. The choice is up to you. My hope is that we'll have a good time together, and you will learn a lot.

"Okay, let's get to know each other. We are going to start here in the front. When I point to you, tell me your name, what borough you are from, and your experience in drama," Mr. Moody said as he pointed at a white girl with freckles sitting in the front row.

"Hi, everyone, my name is Alician Moore. I'm from Staten Island, and I've been acting ever since I could remember. I've starred in commercials since I was three years old. I've played in *Annie* on Broadway. I've been in over a dozen movies, and most recently, I appeared on *The Cosby Show*," she said as Qiana and I looked at each other.

One by one, all the children talked about their many accomplishments, including the talent agencies they belonged to. I felt so out of place. For the first time in my life, I really was up against serious competition! For the most part, I was an underdog.

It was my turn, and Mr. Moody pointed to me. "Well, um, my name is Jamila Davis. I am from Queens, New York. I've been acting since I was like ten. I played the role of Mahalia Jackson in the off-Broadway play *Mahalia Lives*, and I'm a part of the Laurelton Theatre group in Queens, New York, run by Ms. Cloretta King," I said nervously, feeling rather inferior about my accomplishments.

"Oh, I know Ms. King and her group. Tell her Mr. Moody says hello," Mr. Moody said putting a smile back on my face.

"And you, young lady," Mr. Moody said as he pointed to Qiana.

"Hello, everyone. My name is Qiana Flynn, and I'm from Uptown Manhattan. Yeah, Harlem in the house!" Qiana said in an upbeat tone, and the class began to chuckle, breaking the ice in the room.

"Well, I've been acting since I was eleven. I graduated from the School of the Arts Junior High School, here in Manhattan, where I was in a ton of school plays. I don't have any other professional experience under my belt, but I'm up for the challenge this year. And, Mr. Moody, I loved your performance in the *Last Dragon*. I'm so excited about being in your class," Qiana said as Mr. Moody smiled. Qiana had a personality to die for! She was definitely ghetto, but she was very charismatic and kept everyone laughing.

Our morning drama classes ended, and we headed up to the fifth-floor lunchroom.

"So you from Harlem?" I said to Qiana as we walked up the stairs and got on the escalator.

"Yeah, that's right, I'm a Harlem girl," she replied.

"I just went to Harlem like a couple of weeks ago to the Apollo," I said proudly.

"Oh, yeah? I go to the Apollo all the time. They always giving out free tickets."

"Yeah? That was my first time going, but I loved it up there."

"Your first time?" Qiana questioned.

"Yeah, girl, I'm from Queens," I said as we rode the escalator.

"Oh, okay. I've never been to Queens."

"Oh, boy, you got to come check out the Coliseum."

"Yeah, that's that mall the rappers be talking about. I think it's like the Mart on 125th Street."

"The Mart?" I questioned.

"Yeah, the Mart! You got to check it out. They got mad stuff in there!"

"For real? I want to go there," I said eagerly.

"Okay, how about we go one day after school. You take me to the Coliseum, and I'll take you to the Mart," Qiana suggested.

"Okay, you got a deal," I said as we got off the escalator at the fifth floor and headed for the cafeteria.

"Man, this school is big! They got two cafeterias in here," Qiana said as we looked for the cafeteria.

"Oh, look here at the sign pointing to the cafeteria; so I guess it's this way," I said as we made our way down the hall.

We entered the large cafeteria that was packed with freshmen and sophomores. Soon we found a seat and got in the long lunch line.

"Jamila, is that you?" a voice said as I stood in line, and I turned to see who it was.

"Robin! Oh my God! I didn't know you was coming here," I said as we hugged.

"Yeah, girl. I haven't seen you since the recital at Lincoln Center," she said.

"Yeah, girl. You still go to Bernice Johnson's?" I asked.

"No, I'm an instructor now at Carolyn Devour's studio."

"Oh, I heard she has her own dance school now."

"Yeah, it's right in Rochdale Village where I live."

"Oh, okay. How are the classes?" I asked.

"Oh, they are off the hook. You should come check it out!" Robin said as she joined me in the line.

"Oh, Qiana, this is my friend Robin. She's from Queens too," I said as I introduced them.

"Hi, Robin, I'm Qiana."

"Hi, Qiana," Robin responded.

We got our food, and Robin sat down with us. She caught me up on everything that had happened ever since my mother decided to pull me out of Bernice Johnson's. It felt like old times. I was really happy to see her familiar face.

As we ate our food, we watched children perform. The lunchroom was the place kids loved to go to in order to show off their talent! Kids were singing opera and gospel. A couple of children even busted out their dance moves! It was clear at that point these children weren't shy. Everyone had the same dream: to one day make it and be famous!

Lunch ended, and we all went our separate ways. The school was so large I got lost several times trying to find my academic classes. I saw April and two of her friends walking down the hall.

"Hey, April," I called out.

"So far how was your first day?" she asked.

"It was okay, but I keep getting lost."

"Oh, we all did the same thing. You gonna get it soon. Look, there are two sets of escalators, the front and the back ones. You need to write down what escalator is closer to each class. That way, you'll know how to get back there," April explained.

"Oh, Jamila, this is my friend, Talia, and you already know Ebony."

"Oh, yeah. Hi, Talia, your hairstyle is really nice. I've never seen those types of curls before," I said to the light-skinned girl with medium-length hair that April introduced as Talia.

"Yeah, yeah. I hope you don't copy my style. I like being original," Talia responded in a nasty tone as she rolled her eyes.

My mouth just dropped. I couldn't believe how rude she was!

"Oh, Jamila, never mind her," April said as she tried to change the subject.

"Nah, for real. You know how everybody be jocking me. People don't know how to just be themselves," Talia said as she interrupted April.

"Look, miss, I don't know you nor do I care about your hairstyle—or you, for that matter. You're April's friend so I was just being nice. But on that note, April, I'm out. I'll meet you after school," I said as I rolled my eyes at Talia in disgust and walked away. I couldn't believe that girl! She was really feeling herself!

I went to all my academic classes and really enjoyed the setup. My school was designed like a college. Our academic classes were also given in a college type of setting. Not only were the drama teachers experts in their field, so were the academic teachers. I could tell by the looks of things I was really going to enjoy my stay at LaGuardia.

School ended, and I met April and Robin out front. There was a whole crew of us from Queens who met up in front of the school, and we all went home together on the train.

The train ride was amusing as the children showed off their versatility and talent. The train was our showboat, and everyone loved to perform. It was like karaoke, but just on the train.

We arrived back at the Parsons and Archer train station, and Robin, April, and I went to McDonald's. As we were leaving, this cute brown-skinned boy tapped me on my shoulder.

"Excuse me, beautiful, could I speak to you for a second?" he asked as I turned around and smiled. "What's your name, beautiful?" he said as he held the door of McDonald's open for me.

"That's it," I said as I smiled back.

"Your name is 'That's It'?" he questioned, thinking I was trying to be smart.

"No, my name is Beautiful," I said as I smiled back at him.

"Stop playing. Your name is Beautiful for real?"

"Yeah. My name is Jamila. It means Beautiful in Arabic," I said as I checked him out from head to toe.

"Oh, okay, Jamila, or Beautiful. Can I have your number?"

"Um, I don't know," I said as April tapped me.

"Girl, he is cute; pass him the number," she whispered in my ear.

"What? You got a boyfriend or something?" he questioned.

"Look, I don't even know your name," I said as we stood outside of McDonald's.

"Well, my name Captain, and I came to save you today. You look a little down, like you might need a little me in your life," he said with charm, and I laughed.

"No, what's your name for real?"

"My name is Craig, but they all call me Bozo."

"You from around here?" I asked.

"Yeah, I'm from 40."

"40?" I questioned.

"Yeah, 40 Projects, down the block."

"Oh, oh, okay."

"Where you from?"

"I'm from Queens Village."

"Oh, so you one of them bougie chicks?"

"I ain't bougie!"

"What school you go to?"

"I go to LaGuardia High School of Performing Arts in Manhattan," I replied.

"Oh, yeah, you bougie, for sure, but it's okay. I need a bougie girl in my life. Here's a pen, let me get your number."

"Oh, you insult me, and you want my number?"

"Look, I didn't mean to insult you. I actually gave you a compliment. I've had enough ghetto girls for a lifetime. Maybe you can teach me something. I want to come see you in Queens Village. Maybe we can do something proper together," Craig said, as he laughed and pushed a paper and pen into my hand.

I took a breath and stared at him again, then wrote down my phone number as he smiled away.

"Okay, here's my number too," he said as he wrote down his number on my McDonald's bag.

"Okay, so I'ma call you tonight. Until then, think about me," he said. I smiled, and we walked to the Q83 bus stop.

"Wow, Jamila, he's cute," April said as we waited for the bus.

"Yeah, he's all right, but girl, he's from the projects," I replied.

"Yeah, girl, he's probably a bad boy. You know what they say about them bad boys."

"No, what?" I questioned.

"They're the most fun!" April said, and we both laughed. I ripped the number off of my McDonald's bag and headed home on the bus.

As I stared out the window, I thought about Craig and what he was all about. *Will he really call me?* I wondered as I thought about the opportunity of finally having a boyfriend—and a bad boy at that!

I couldn't wait to get home to recap my whole day to my mother. I could tell by the looks of things life for me was getting ready to be really fun!

My mother, my brother Kee, my dad and me (at 14 years old), at
a family function in Kinston, North Carolina.

I did my homework and was picking out my clothes for school when my house phone rang. "Hello," I said as I answered the phone.

"Hello, may I speak to Beautiful?" Craig asked as I quickly recognized his voice.

"This is she," I said as I smiled to myself, and my heart began to race.

"Well, Beautiful, this is your Captain, and I'm ready to save you," Craig said, and I laughed.

We stayed on the phone for hours laughing and talking until my mother finally made me hang up.

"So, Craig, I'm sorry, I got to go. That's my mother," I said.

"Oh, all right. Tell Mom Dukes to calm down. So you gonna meet me tomorrow?" he asked.

"Tomorrow?" I questioned.

"Yeah, tomorrow, same time, same place. We gonna celebrate our one-day anniversary. The meal's on me," he said as I paused to think about his request.

"Okay, Captain. I'll see you tomorrow, same time, same place," I said.

"Good night, Beautiful."

"Good night, Captain," I replied, and I hung up the phone.

I was on cloud nine! I was really feeling Craig. I couldn't wait to go back to school and to top it off, I was gonna see my new boo, Craig!

* * *

It was the second day of school, and I was up early getting dressed. I wanted to look my best for Craig! I put on my purple Guess shirt and my black Guess jeans. I unwrapped the new paper off my purple high-top Reeboks and put them on my feet. Then I stared at myself and smiled in the mirror. I was really anxious to get this day started.

Mr. Martindale picked me up, and April and I headed for the

subway. I had learned the routine. I headed through the turnstile, down to the platform, where we met up with all the other kids from our school.

"April, Captain called me."

"Captain? Who is that?" April asked as we waited on the platform.

"Craig, the cute boy we met in McDonald's."

"Oh, okay, girl. So you got yourself a boyfriend?" she asked.

"No, girl, not yet. I just met him. He wants to link up with me after school today."

"Oh, okay. So y'all going on a date?"

"To McDonald's. I don't think that's a date," I said as we laughed.

"You know I need you to come with me."

"Oh? You scared?"

"No, but I don't know him, girl. You don't want anything to happen to your best friend, right?"

"Oh, I don't know."

"Come on, April, please. Pretty please," I begged.

"Oh, okay, but you know I got to be home before my curfew."

"Me too. So we'll make it quick."

"Oh, okay then," she said as the train pulled up, and we loaded inside.

I sat on the train and daydreamed, thinking about my new love. I wished it was the end of the day so I could see him already.

We arrived at school, and I headed downstairs to the drama department, went into the dressing room, and got ready for Mr. Moody's class.

The school bell rang, and Mr. Moody promptly closed his door and began his class.

"Good morning, students. I'm glad to see you all followed my instructions. You all look nice in black. Today, we are going to begin," Mr. Moody said as he was interrupted by Qiana who came into the class late.

"Oh-oh, I'm sorry I'm late, Mr. Moody. I got my 'little friend,'" Qiana said as she cupped her hand and whispered, "period," to Mr. Moody.

"All right, young lady, but don't let it happen again," he said as Qiana put her stuff down and made her way over to me. "So where were we? Today, I'm going to show you guys techniques for getting into character. First, we will begin this class by stretching. I want you to all loosen up so you'll be ready to get into character," Mr. Moody said as he led us into stretching exercises.

We did our stretching, then Mr. Moody started his drill.

"Okay, I want each of you to begin acting like a dog. I want you to walk like a dog, bark like a dog, and feel yourself actually being a dog," he said as Qiana and I gave each other a strong sister-girl look.

"Girl, no, he didn't," Qiana said as she crossed her arms.

"Yes, he did!" I said as I watched the children hit the ground acting like a dog.

"Ladies," Mr. Moody said as he looked at us seriously, and Qiana and I immediately got on the floor. I felt crazy barking on the floor like a dog, but Qiana made a game of it, growling and grabbing on my leg.

"And what are you two doing?" Mr. Moody questioned as he observed us having fun.

"Oh, we are dog fighting, Mr. Moody. Just like the dogs do out in the park by my building in the Grant Projects. You said to be a dog. I'm being the dogs I see in my neighborhood. I'm not no poodle, Mr. Moody. I'm a pit bull," Qiana said as she growled at Mr. Moody, and the class laughed, including Mr. Moody.

"That's right, class, I want you to be the animals you recognize. Good job, Qiana. Keep up the good work!" he said as he walked away.

Qiana had such charm; she could get away with anything! She worked her audience, including Mr. Moody. I enjoyed her company. She always managed to keep me laughing!

It was lunchtime, and Robin, Qiana, and I sat at the table talking.

"So, Robin, Craig called me back last night," I said as we sat and ate our lunch.

"Oh, for real, girl? He's cute. That's a good look," Robin commented.

"Yeah, I know. We're supposed to meet today after school," I said.

"Wow, he ain't wasting no time," she said.

"Nope, girl. He's on it," I responded proudly.

"Who y'all talking about?" Qiana asked.

"Oh, her boyfriend," Robin commented back.

"No, he's just a friend," I interrupted.

"Oh, so you got a boyfriend?" Qiana asked.

"No. I'm single. What about you?" I questioned.

"Yeah, I have a boyfriend. His name is Jason, and he's from Brooklyn. That's my boo, and he's fine, girl. We've been together for like six months now, and I think we are going to be together forever. He's such a great lover," Qiana said as we finished up our food.

"A great lover? So y'all are having sex?" I inquired.

"Of course, we are. Nobody is still a virgin these days. Oh, my bad, are you a virgin?" Qiana asked as bubbles arose in my stomach. I was stuck. I didn't want Qiana to think I was lame.

"Of course not," I quickly commented, lying, of course.

Qiana finished telling us all about Jason, and I stood silent thinking about how cursed I was to be a virgin in the ninth grade. I didn't want the title of a virgin anymore! I desperately wanted to peel away my reproach!

It was the end of the day, and I met Robin in front of the school. April walked up with that obnoxious girl Talia.

"Oh, her hair is cute," Robin said to me as she pointed to Talia. "That's them new pineapple waves. They take your hair and gel it down, put a hairnet on it, then pull up the curls though the hairnet."

I interrupted. "Whatever you do, don't give that girl a compliment. She is so conceited," I said as April and her friends approached.

"Jamila, you dress so nice," April's friend Keisha commented.

"She dresses all right, but it's nothing special," Talia interjected.

"Whoa, what's your deal?" I asked.

"I don't have a deal. I'm just straight-up, that's all. Your outfit is okay, but it's not like you dress better than me. I'm the original Brooklyn 'Guess Princess.' Nobody has more Guess stuff than me," Talia said as I took notice of her clothes.

"See, I have on my Guess shirt, my Guess jeans, my Guess book bag, my Guess socks, and look, even my underwear is Guess," Talia said, bragging.

"Okay, well, check this out! We gonna have a Guess-a-thon! Let's see which one of us can rock the most Guess clothes without repeating an outfit," I suggested.

"Okay, bet. But you don't know what you're getting into, little freshman. I already told you I'm Talia, the 'Guess Princess,'" she said as she sashayed off.

I couldn't stand this chick! I was determined to show her that she wasn't as fly as me! She couldn't be serious. I was up for the challenge and determined to win the Guess-a-thon!

After school, we arrived at Parsons and Archer train station, and Robin and April went with me to meet Craig at McDonald's.

My heart raced as I opened the door, highly anticipating my Prince Charming. I looked all around, but I didn't see him. We sat down in one of the booths and waited about fifteen minutes for Craig to arrive.

"Girl, do you really think he's coming?" April said as she sipped on her Coca-Cola.

"Yeah, April. He said, 'same time, same place,'" I responded.

"Well, maybe he got busy or something," Robin interjected.

"No, I think he's coming. Please let's wait a few more minutes. If he doesn't show up, then we can leave," I said as I quickly changed the subject to turn Robin and April's attention away from the fact that Craig hadn't shown up. Deep down inside, I was disappointed. Was I kidding myself? *I'll probably never have a boyfriend,* I thought to myself just as Craig opened the door and walked into McDonald's.

My heart paced quickly as I saw him approaching us. "Oh, hello, Craig," I said nonchalantly as I continued to laugh with April and Robin.

"Okay, so you coming with me, right?" Craig asked.

"Going where?" I said nervously.

"It's our anniversary, right?" Craig said as I laughed.

"Yeah," I responded.

"Okay, so I get to pick where I'm taking you, and it's not McDonald's," he said, and I stared at April for guidance.

"Come on. I'ma drop your friends off, and we're going to go out to eat," he said as I stood in shock.

"Follow me, y'all," Craig instructed as he walked us out to his car.

"Whoa, this car is nice," April said as she admired the black Jetta with stylish rims on it.

"How old are you, Craig?" Robin questioned.

"I'm sixteen, why?"

"And this is your car?" she questioned.

"Yeah," Craig said nonchalantly as he opened up the front passenger seat for me to get in. I hopped in the car, and April and Robin hopped in the backseat. Craig turned on the car ignition as Mary J. Blige's "Real Love" blasted on the car stereo.

"Oh, that's my joint; turn that up," April said as she began to sing.

"Oh, oh, oh, I'm searching for the real love. Someone to set my heart free. Real love," April sang each note perfectly in her soprano voice.

"So you gonna be my real love?" Craig asked as he reached over and grabbed my hand. My insides felt like they were about to burst. I stared back at Craig and answered, "Yes." From that very moment, life as I knew it before had changed! My heart was all into Craig. I found me a cute boyfriend, and he had money! What a double pleasure!

* * *

Craig dropped April and Robin off at their houses, then he took me to his apartment in the 40 Housing Projects, in South Jamaica, Queens.

When we pulled up on South Road, the main block of the projects, it was packed with people. There were young boys hanging out on the corner, children playing, and old people just talking and sitting outside. I was mesmerized by the lifestyle of the projects. It was fast paced and busy, unlike the sort of quiet suburban life I was accustomed to. My eyes opened wide as I observed the environment.

As we pulled up on the block, a cute light-skinned boy with a nice smile came up to the car. "Yo, what up, Bozo?" the boy said as Craig rolled down the window.

"Nothing much. What's the block doing?" he asked.

"It's blazin' out here. The workers are almost done. I need some more work. I've been paging you like crazy. Now I see what you was up to," the boy said as he stared at me.

"Yeah, Mook, this is my new wife. Jamila, this is Mookie; Mookie, this is Jamila," Craig introduced us, and I greeted Mookie.

"Yeah, Jamila is a sophisticated broad, Mook. She goes to LaGuardia High School of Performing Arts, and she lives in Queens Village," Craig said as he bragged to Mookie.

"Oh, okay. So you got you a bougie broad. I see what you working with," Mookie said as he slapped Craig five.

"So, Jamila, you got a friend for me?" Mook asked.

"Yeah, I got friends," I said as I smiled.

"We'll see about all the hookup stuff later. Yo, let me go get this work," Craig said as he rolled up the window and pulled off.

We parked around the corner on the other side of the projects and went into one of the many small buildings, got on the elevator, and approached an apartment door. Craig stuck in his key and opened the apartment door where a lady sat on the couch.

"Yo, what up, Ella?" Craig said to the woman as we entered.

"Hey, Bozo, I was waiting for you to come back. Bozo, I need a hit," the lady pleaded as her eyes bulged out of her head.

"All right, give me a minute," he said as he used his key to unlock the bedroom door and we entered the small project room.

"Shut the door and lock it," Craig said to me, and I got a little nervous. Craig paid me no mind as he reached under the bed and pulled out a large box. "Yo, Jamila, just give me a second. I got to get some work to my workers on the block," he said as he pulled out the small crack vials I had seen my brother with before and counted them.

I stared intensely as I watched Craig pull out a white plate and a razor and began cutting up crack cocaine and putting it into small vials. "Yo, Jamila, count these for me," he said as I reluctantly began counting the vials. "Put them in separate piles of fifty each," Craig instructed as he continued to bag up.

At first I felt crazy, but then I got a rush, especially after Craig pulled out another shoe box filled with money. *This is what I always wanted, right? My own boyfriend who had a lot of money like C.B. and Donnell,* I thought as I observed the new environment. Before I could get through counting, there was a knock on the door.

"Yeah, what?" Craig said as the knock on the door got louder.

"Craig, Craig, I need a hit!" the woman yelled impatiently.

"Yo, wait a minute, I'm coming out," Craig yelled back in a frustrated tone.

"Yo, what is she, a crackhead?" I asked, and Craig laughed.

"Yeah, but she holds me down. Ella is my girl," Craig responded as he put his money away and took the packs and put them in his jacket.

"Look, Jamila, I'ma be right back. Let me drop this off on the block and pick up my money," Craig said, and he left.

I stayed in the small room looking out the window at all the action that was taking place in the projects. The projects looked fun and exciting. I wanted to go outside and take part in all the action! As I glanced out the window I heard a knock on the door. "Yes?" I said in a loud voice.

"It's me, Ella, open up," Ella shouted. I contemplated for a minute, then I unlocked the door and let her in. Ella was a short, brown-skinned lady with short matted hair and missing teeth.

"Hey, baby, what's your name?" she asked in a sweet voice.

"Jamila," I answered.

"Oh, that's a nice name. You know you are a pretty girl," Ella said as she cased out the room.

"Why, thank you," I said.

"Listen, Jamila, I said it right?" she asked.

"Yes," I replied.

"Oh, baby, I need a hit. Can you give me one of those crack vials right there, baby, please?"

"Oh, Ella, this is not mine, and I don't want—" I said as Ella interrupted me.

"Listen, baby, Bozo told me to get it from you," Ella said as she stuck her hand out.

"Uh, well, um, okay," I said reluctantly and handed it to her.

About fifteen minutes later, Craig still hadn't returned. Ella knocked again, and I opened the door.

"Uh, uh, Jamila," Ella said as she rocked back and forth. "I'm gonna need another hit."

"Look, I told you this isn't my stuff," I said in a frustrated tone.

"I know. Bozo said it's okay, baby, I swear. Just one more, and that's it. I promise," Ella begged like a baby. At first I told her no, but her persistence got the best of me.

"Look, this is it. Take it," I said as I wanted to get rid of her quickly.

I looked at the clock. It was going on 5:30. I was already late, and Craig still hadn't gotten back yet. *What am I gonna tell my mother?* I contemplated to myself as I paced the room. A few minutes later there was another knock on the door. I thought it was Ella so I didn't even bother to answer.

"Yo, Jamila, open up," Craig said and I got up and opened the door.

"Yo, you just left me for dead, huh?" I said as I grabbed my things to go home.

"No, baby. I'm sorry, I had to pick up my money, and these dudes were playing," Craig said as he pulled a wad of money out of his pocket. I calmed down as I observed the large amount of money.

"Yo, let me count this real quick and we can leave," Craig said and he spread the money out on the bed.

Craig was only sixteen years old, but he was doing big things! His best friend and partner was Mookie aka Mook Diamond, whose uncle Calle ran the entire project's drug trade. In turn, Mookie and Craig were getting more money than most of the older boys. Craig's lifestyle drew me to him. I liked the bad-boy image he portrayed and the fact that he showed me love and affection.

Craig counted the money, put it up, and drove me home. "Listen, Jamila, I'm sorry I spent so much time on the block today. I really wanted to get to know you better," Craig said as I instructed him to stop at my corner because I didn't want anybody to see me.

"Well, it's cool. We can get up another day," I said, as I unlocked the Jetta doors.

"What about tomorrow?" he suggested.

"Look, call me later on. I really have to go," I said as I leaned to open the door.

"Can I get a kiss?" Craig asked as he leaned over. We kissed. Craig's kiss sealed the deal. He instantly had me open!

I kissed Craig and raced out of the car. He pulled off, and I ran to my house. As I put my key in the door, my mother opened it.

"Jamie, where have you been? You had me worried half to death!" she said.

"Oh, Mom, I tried to call home from the pay phone, but the line was busy. I had theatre group, and I had to stay late after school," I said as I looked away.

"Oh, okay, baby. Please, you got to let me know what's going on. I worry about my baby being in Manhattan. You call me until you get through next time," she said as she kissed me on my forehead. She was clearly happy that I was safe.

I felt so bad about lying to my mother. I quickly went upstairs and started my homework. I took a deep breath as I sat on my bed. What a close call!

*M*y ninth-grade year took off like a rocket! Overnight, I became a shining star. Craig and I began to see each other on a regular basis. It seemed like every day I was in the projects, hanging out with Craig. He began to shower me with money and gifts, just like the older girls' boyfriends, and I loved it. I even had him take me to Kim's house, and I introduced her to Craig. Kim told me I landed a good one, so I knew I was on to something!

I got so caught up into Craig that I deserted April. All I cared about was sneaking away and spending time with him. I even learned how to skip out of school early without getting caught so I could spend more time with him. I never knew love before, but I felt I finally found it in Craig. He became that Captain he told me he would be to me! I was glad that he saved me.

Eventually, I couldn't hide Craig anymore from my mother, so I told her about him and she allowed him over because she wanted to meet him.

* * *

I sat nervously by my front door waiting for Craig to arrive. I told him to park around the corner and walk up to my door. My mother was sitting at the kitchen table, and my brother stood arguing with her about me.

"Mommy, she ain't old enough to have no boyfriend," he shouted as my mother sipped on her soda.

"Listen, Kee, you are not her father. Her father and I said it's okay, so it's okay," my mother replied.

"You don't know what y'all about to allow her to get into," my brother pleaded.

"Why don't you mind your own business? You're not my father," I yelled from the living room.

"See? That's the problem. You too fast for your own good," my brother yelled back.

"You remember what happened with her the last time with that boy Phil," Kee said to my mother.

"She was much younger back then," my mother said in my defense.

"Okay, well, when I kill this little dude, don't say nothing," my brother said, and he stormed off.

"Calm down, Kee. It's not that serious," my mother said as she continued to skim the newspaper.

I sat on the living-room couch, praying that my brother wouldn't embarrass me in front of Craig. The doorbell rang, and I got up to open it. Kee shot past me and opened the door.

"Yo, what up?" Kee said with an attitude as he stood there.

"Oh, I'm here for Jamila," Craig said nervously as he observed my brother's demeanor.

"I'm right here. Come in, Craig," I said as I pushed Kee out of the way.

"Craig, this is my mother, Ms. Davis," I said.

"Ah, um, hello, Mrs. Davis," Craig said nervously as Kee stared him up and down.

"Oh, Craig, this is my brother, Kee," I said as Kee ice-grilled Craig.

"What up, Kee?" Craig said as he reached his hand out to give him a pound. My brother said nothing and walked away. I grabbed Craig's hand as it was left hanging out and brought him downstairs with me into the basement.

"Whoa, Jamila, your house is nice," Craig said as he checked out my father's bar and music equipment in the basement. "You live like the Huxtables on *The Cosby Show*," he said as he laughed.

"No, we don't. We're just a regular family. My mom is a schoolteacher, and my father is a supervisor for Transit. They ain't no doctors or lawyers, like the Huxtables," I said as I sat down on the couch. "So, Craig, what about your family?"

"What about them?"

"Where are they, and what do they do?"

"Well, my mom is a single parent. She has three kids, and she's a nurse. And, my dad, well, let's just say he's a ladies' man," Craig said as he laughed and sat next to me.

"A ladies' man? What's that?" I asked.

"He's a pimp, Jamila."

"A pimp? Stop playing." I shook my head in disbelief.

"No, seriously." Craig got serious.

"Oh my goodness. So why don't you live with your parents?" I asked.

"I've been on my own since I was twelve years old. My life is crazy! From as early as I could remember I've been in and out of juvenile detention homes and group homes. My mother got tired of it and kicked me out, so I went to live with my dad, and that didn't work out. So I had to do what I had to do," Craig said as my heart melted. I felt so bad for him.

"Don't worry, Craig. Things are gonna work out for you," I said as I leaned my head on his shoulder, and he put his arms around my shoulders.

Just as we were getting comfortable, my brother came downstairs whistling, acting as if he was about to do his laundry. There was a washer and a dryer in the basement. Kee looked at me, then he looked at Craig and ice-grilled him again.

"Yo, Jamila, for real, I'm not feeling your brother. He's acting like I'm a sucker or something," Craig said as he got serious and caught an attitude.

"Craig, please pay him no attention," I said as I rubbed his knee.

"Man, this dude is something else! He acts like somebody is sweet," Craig said in a frustrated tone.

"No, baby, he just loves his sister. Do you have any sisters?" I asked.

"Yes, I have two."

"Okay, how would you feel if your little sister was dating a guy like you?"

"All right, I get your point, but I ain't no sucker."

"I know what you are, and that's all that matters," I said as I gazed into Craig's eyes and rubbed the side of his face.

Kee dropped off his laundry, then he kept finding excuses to come downstairs.

"Look, I really got to go," Craig said, sick of my brother's interruptions.

"Yeah, leave then!" Kee said from the laundry room.

"Ah, yo, homie, I don't think you want it with me," Craig said, as he jumped off the couch.

"What, my man?" Kee said as he flew into the room.

"Oh, hell, no," I said as I jumped in front of them. "Kee, leave him alone. I'm gonna tell Mommy," I said as I grabbed Craig's hand and pulled him upstairs.

"Listen, Jamila, I'm leaving. Don't tell your mother, but I'ma deal with your brother," Craig said as he walked out the door.

"Craig, I'm really sorry," I said.

"Don't be. I'ma see you after school tomorrow," Craig said as he walked out of my house. We saw Kee's two friends sitting on the porch, eye screwing Craig to intimidate him even more.

"Jamila, I'm out," Craig said as he grilled the boys back and took off.

I was so embarrassed! I yelled and screamed at Kee and complained to my mother. Then I went into my bedroom and cried. *I hope Craig still likes me,* I thought to myself as I sat on my bed.

Just as I was about to doze off I heard a loud knock on my door. "What?" I said in a disgruntled voice.

"Yo, open up!" my brother said in a serious tone.

"Yo, what now?" I said as I jerked open the door.

"Yo, what's up with that dude? Yo, where is he from?" my brother shouted in a hostile voice.

"Why? It's none of your business," I said in a sassy voice.

"Yo, for real, Jamie. I was just down the block and him and his homeboy pulled up in a Jetta, and they pulled out on me," Kee said in a rage.

"Pulled out on you?"

"Yeah, the dude's friend pulled out a gun."

"Oh my God," I said as I had to process all that Kee said.

"Yo, I'ma have to see your dude," Kee stated.

"Kee, please leave it alone. I really, really like him! He's really nice. He's from 40 Projects and—" I began as Kee interrupted me.

"He's from 40?"

"Yeah, but he's mad cool."

"Oh, man, Jamie. Them 40 dudes are crazy," my brother said as he backed down his rage a notch.

"Yeah, but I'm telling you, he's cool people," I said as Kee calmed down.

"Oh, all right, tell dude my bad. I want to speak to him," Kee said as he walked out of the room.

"Okay. I'll hook it up."

Kee and Craig hooked up and became cool with each other. I guess my brother liked the fact that Craig had heart. Craig even jumped into some of my brother's local beefs. The 40 Project's boys were notorious, and the boys from my side of town didn't want any problems with them. When the people in my neighborhood found out I was with Craig, they gave me my props!

"She done bagged herself one of them young get-money dudes from 40. Leave Shorty alone. We don't want no problems with them," was one of the comments I heard when I walked through my neighborhood.

Craig's status made me feel good and protected. As time went on, I caught the eyes of envy from the girls I used to look up to. Nobody's boyfriend had a car or was buying them more things than Craig bought me. It was funny how the tables in life turned!

*G*oing to school at LaGuardia, I quickly began to mature. I became good friends with Talia after I won the Guess-a-thon. She gave me a run for my money! She wore all Guess clothes, not repeating an outfit for a little over two weeks. I had to go to Tanya's house and borrow several Guess outfits to win. After I won, Talia gave me my props, and I began to really like her.

I started going home with Talia after school. She lived in Bed-Stuy, Brooklyn. I loved Brooklyn, so Talia's house became my second home. Craig would pick me up from her place and bring me home.

When I wasn't at Talia's, I was Uptown in Grant Projects with Qiana. Craig and Qiana made me fall in love with project life. I found the projects to be so much fun and fascinating. I almost never spent time in my neighborhood anymore. Compared to the projects and Bed-Stuy, my neighborhood became corny in my eyes. I lost respect for my hood, so I started repping Brooklyn.

I got away with spending time with Craig by saying I was going to Tanya's house. Tanya liked Craig, so she covered for me. My mother had no clue I was all around New York City! She thought I was active in an after-school theatre group that didn't even exist.

As time passed, Craig began to pressure me more and more about sex. I wanted to do it, but I was scared. Craig threatened to start seeing other girls if I wouldn't give in. I was nervous, but I did it. At first, I really didn't like it, as I found it rather uncomfortable, but as time went on, sex with Craig became pleasurable to me. It was so enjoyable that he no longer had to ask for it; instead, I started asking him. The more I had sex with Craig, the more I fell in love with him. I was head over heels in love. Nothing meant more to me than Craig!

* * *

It was a winter afternoon, and I was on the subway coming home from school with all the students from Queens. Everyone was laughing and talking, but my mind was on Craig. I couldn't wait for

Chapter Thirty-Eight

the train to arrive at Parsons and Archer. I really wanted to see him.

"What's up, Jamila?" April asked me.

"Nothing much. I'm chillin'," I said in a nonchalant tone.

"Jamila, you're changing. You're not the same person," she said.

"What you mean by that?" I questioned.

"I don't know about you anymore. Since you got a boyfriend you switched up," April said.

"Switched up? Girl, you trippin'. I may be a little bit more mature, but I ain't switching up," I said back in a feisty tone.

"Yes, you are. We hardly ever hang out anymore. Everything is all about Craig. You done forgot where you came from," April said adamantly as she checked me.

"Listen, are you mad, April, 'cause you don't have a boyfriend? Is that what this is really about?"

"I don't care about no boyfriend. I care about you! But you don't got to worry about me no more. When Craig is a thing of the past, don't try to be my friend anymore."

"Well, that's okay with me. Maybe you'll use this time to lose some weight and find a boyfriend," I said maliciously.

"You know what? Don't you ever speak to me again, you idiot," April said in a rage as the train doors opened and she took off! I didn't even bother to chase behind her. I was too concerned about being on time for Craig.

I walked up the stairs, and Craig was parked out in front. I quickly jumped in his car, gave him a kiss, and we rode straight to the projects. That was our normal routine. I would help Craig count his packs of drugs and his money, and we would chill in the house watching television. I just enjoyed being in his presence. I couldn't get enough of him!

It was getting late so Craig dropped me back off at my house. I went upstairs to my room and started my homework when my mother knocked on the door and came in.

"Jamie, Jamie," my mother shouted.

"What, Ma?" I said in a rude tone.

"What's the matter with you, girl?" she said back angrily.

"Nothing, Ma. I'm trying to do my homework."

"I don't care what you trying to do. You treat me with respect."

"Well, you just barged in my room. What about *my* privacy?"

"Privacy? You don't pay no bills in this house; there is no privacy!"

"See, that's what I'm talking about. Y'all always throwin' up what y'all do for us! That's your responsibility. We didn't ask to come here."

"What, girl!!! Oh, you going to school in Manhattan so you think you grown?"

"Why it got to be all that? I just want my privacy, that's all!"

"Well, okay, fine, but I'm here to tell you, I don't like your new stink attitude," my mother said as she pointed at me.

"And so what? I don't like a lot of things about you either," I said in a nasty tone and stared at her. Before I could finish my words, my mother smacked me hard across my face.

"I'm your mother, and you gonna respect me or get the hell out of my house!" she shouted, and then she slammed the door to my room.

Tears streamed down my face. I quickly began to resent my mother and her authority over me. I desperately wanted to be grown so I could be on my own.

That was the turning point in my relationship with my mother. We were no longer close with each other. We became very distant. I viewed her as "the enemy." My mother began to despise me, and I also despised her. We could never seem to get along anymore. Everything was always a problem. As the days went by, the tension increased!

* * *

Kee ended up hooking up with his friend, Chris, the twin, who encouraged my brother to start selling crack in the Baisley Housing project for the notorious Supreme Team Gang. The second day on the job, Kee got caught by the police in Baisley Projects with 99 vials of crack cocaine, and he was arrested. My parents were devastated! Instead of blaming Kee for his actions, my mother blamed me. Her good friend, Ms. Sonja, convinced my mother that she spent too much time with me and not enough with my brother. Ms. Sonja said the lack of attention caused him to sell drugs, which was the furthest thing from the truth! Selling drugs was the "in thing" to do, so Kee did it. After my brother got locked up, things grew steadily worse with my mother and me.

"You know what, little girl? I can't stand you! You turned into a fast-behind hussy! All you do is chase that damn boy. You are going to end up screwing up your whole damn life. I wish you and your brother was never born," my mother would scream at me in anger. Her words hurt. They cut through me just like a knife. Our relationship was sabotaged, and there was no way for me to fix it. Just me being in my mother's sight disgusted her!

The more intense my problems got at home, the more I searched for a way to escape. I started skipping school and spending my days shopping in the stores in Manhattan with Talia.

Talia and I could really relate. She had a boyfriend who sold drugs just like me. We would compete with each other about how much money we could get out of them to go shopping. Talia was just like my cousin Tanya. She was a label queen. She put me up on all the hot shopping spots. She even introduced me to the Albee Square Mall in Brooklyn, which was like the Coliseum. The indoor flea market had all the latest street fashions and jewelry.

Talia and I would meet up at the school doors and about-face to go and spend the money we had acquired. Cutting school became a regular routine. We shared all types of secrets with each other. Talia was more experienced than me. She even taught me how to become a better lover in the bedroom! I soaked up all Talia's advice, and the two of us became inseparable!

* * *

One day I came home from school super late and my mother stood at the door to greet me.

"What the hell did I tell you about coming home late, you fast-behind hussy!" my mother scolded.

"Why are you always talking to me like that?" I questioned.

"I can talk to you however I feel. This is my damn house. If you don't like it, get out!" she said in rage.

"You know what? That sounds good. I'ma get out!" I said as I ran upstairs and started packing all my things. My mother followed me upstairs into my room.

"You need help packing? Take all your stuff and go. I'm tired of your butt. Get out and go sleep in the street for all I care," she said as tears started streaming from my eyes.

I beeped Craig. He called me right back, and I told him to come and get me.

Craig pulled up as I loaded five big black garbage bags onto my porch. He helped me load the bags in his car and I left! My mother didn't even put up a fight. It appeared that she hated me and was happy to see me go. I was fourteen years old, and I chose to do things my way. I was out on my own!

*I*n a short matter of time, my life became similar to a roller-coaster ride. I was all over the place! I was fourteen years old and a runaway. I moved into the projects with Craig and decided to make a life with him. It felt good to remove myself from all the tension in my home. Craig was also happy to have me around. I felt like an adult, and I started to live my life as one. I continued to go to school and function in my normal routine. The only difference was I was playing house. Craig was no longer just my boyfriend—he became my sole provider!

Craig and I were living together, and it felt good. I got so caught up into him that I forgot all about my family. I was free to do whatever I wanted, whenever I wanted to do it! Nobody was there to put me down or complain.

I became the envy of all my friends. Nobody was living on their own. I took pride in my new project apartment and felt fortunate to have Craig's love and support. It made me feel special. That inner void I always had within seemed to be fulfilled.

* * *

Craig and I had been living together for approximately three weeks, and I had no contact with my family, nor did I want any. I was caught up in playing a good wife to my new husband.

One morning I woke up late, so I decided to skip my morning drama classes. I left Craig in the bed and went into the small bathroom in our apartment and got ready for school. The project heat was booming, so I opened up a few windows to get some air.

I went back into the bedroom and opened our closet door. The closet was jam-packed with my clothes and Craig's. Craig liked to shop just as much as me. As the drug money came in, we made our second home the mall. I picked out one of my many new outfits, popped the tags, and put it on. When Craig rolled over to grab me, he noticed I was no longer in the bed.

"Yo, Jamila, what time is it?" he asked in his half-awake voice.

"It's almost 10 o'clock. I'm so late for school! I have a math test, so I'm going to my afternoon classes," I said as I fixed my hair in the mirror.

"Yo, one thing I got to give you your props for is you are into your schoolwork," he said proudly as he sat up in the bed.

"Yeah, I got to be. I want to go to college and maybe one day, law school," I said as I packed my bag with books.

"That's right. I got me a sophisticated lady. Come here, baby, let me get a kiss," Craig said as I approached him and gave him a quick kiss on his lips.

"Oh, so that's all I get?" he asked.

"Yeah, boy, you still got morning breath," I said as I laughed.

"Oh, so you won't love me if I have stink breath?" Craig asked.

"No, I'm always gonna love you, but I would just have to carry around Tic Tacs for you," I said as we both laughed.

"Boo, I need some money to get to school. I'm already late, so I want to hop in a cab and take the Long Island Railroad," I said as I put my jacket on.

"Yo, bring me my jeans," Craig said, and I reached on the floor and picked up the jeans he had worn the night before. Craig took out a large knot of money and peeled me off a hundred dollars in single and five dollar bills. I got accustomed to spending small bills, as that was what Craig typically collected from his customers.

I thanked him with another kiss, took the money, and quickly left the apartment. It was early, but the projects never slept! There was always someone outside, including the hustlers who hugged the blocks twenty-four hours a day. Dope fiends and crack-heads ran rampant throughout the projects.

I learned to love the first of the month. That's when everyone got their Social Security, disability and welfare checks, and Craig made the most money. I would hardly get to see Craig from the first to the third of the month, but it was well worth it! I could count on getting lavish gifts when the large amounts of money rolled in.

My face became familiar in the projects. "Oh, that's Bozo's wife," they would say as I walked by.

Craig had respect in his hood, so no one dared to mess with me. Old and young people would always speak and greet me. I started to get cool with a few of the project girls, but Craig busted up those friendships quickly.

"I don't want you hanging out with these chicks over here. They are ghetto as hell, and most of them are hoes. You got your own square little friends. Keep them," Craig would say as he interrupted my conversations with the project girls. I followed Craig's lead because I would never want to make him unhappy. My goal was to please him and satisfy him in any way I could. I was determined to be his "ride-or-die" chick.

I walked to the corner and caught a cab to the Long Island Railroad. I bought my ticket for the train and headed into Manhattan, where I transferred to the subway station and took the train to school.

I arrived at school at about 11:30 a.m. I put my ID card into the machine and entered the building when I was detained by the school security officer.

"Excuse me, you're Jamila Davis, right?" Solomon, a skinny, tall black officer who wore glasses, said.

"Yes, Mr. Solomon. What's up?" I asked bewildered.

"Listen, I'm going to need you to come with me," he said as he got on his walkie-talkie.

"We have the fugitive here. I'm bringing her up now," Solomon shouted loudly over the walkie-talkie as if I was under arrest.

"Where are you taking me?" I asked.

"You're wanted in the principal's office. You have a brother, right?"

"Yeah, but what does that have to do with anything?"

"Well, he came to the school this morning with a crew of guys looking for you. He stated you ran away from home and your parents are concerned about you," Solomon said as my head dropped in disbelief.

Kee, out of all people, came to LaGuardia to get me? I thought to myself as the guard escorted me into the principal's office.

The principal ended up calling my father who was advised he had to come to the school and get me or the police would be notified. My dad came to the school and picked me up at the principal's office. I was so embarrassed! I thought that he would yell and scream, but instead, he grabbed me and hugged me tightly.

"Jamie, I was so worried about you. I missed you so much," my dad said as he showed me affection.

"Well, um, I, um," I said as I was lost for words.

"Baby, I don't care, I just love you for you, whoever you are, no matter what you do. You and your mother have to work things out. We can't live like this anymore!" my father said passionately as he held my hand tightly and we walked out of the building.

All the students watched me and my father hold hands, walking. My brother had made a big spectacle at the school. The students said he was looking for Craig to beat him up for helping me run away!

I was happy to see my dad, but I really didn't want to leave Craig. I had no choice, however. My dad drove me straight to Craig's apartment and had me get all my things. I went upstairs and cried in Craig's arms and tears also rolled down his face. We loved each other and enjoyed each other's company. I really didn't want to leave, but I had no choice. I had to go!

* * *

Surprisingly, when I arrived back at home my mother was happy to see me too. She came into my room, and we talked for hours. She explained to me how she felt and how she was frightened by my change in behavior.

"Jamie, I love you with all my heart. I only want the best for you. I didn't mean to call you names. I just wanted to get your attention. You can be whatever you desire in this world, but if you go down the wrong route, you can ruin your whole life," she said as she sat on my bed.

"Yeah, Mom, I understand. I'm sorry for the way I acted too. I am growing up, and I just want my privacy and respect."

"I understand that, but you have to show me you can handle it, and I'll give it to you. Is that fair?"

"Yes, that's fair!" I said as I gave my mother a big hug.

Things began to work out in my house, but my relationship with Craig got very shaky. We continued to see each other, but Craig missed me staying with him. Now our time was limited. We had to rush and sneak around, and Craig hated it! When we spent time together I felt as though Craig and I were disconnecting. He was there, but his heart wasn't really there!

* * *

Things were back to normal. April and I made up. I apologized to her for the way I treated her. I regained my focus after the wake-up call I got from my mother, and I began to excel. I aced all of my classes and got active in school activities. I continued my relationship with Craig, but it was on my terms. I kept school as my first priority and saw him when I could. Craig noticed my change, and he didn't like it. "So you all brand-new on me now. You act like you don't even want to be with me," Craig would often say.

Despite our limited contact, we were fine until one day I got a call from Nakia that rocked our whole relationship!

"Jamila, the dude you mess with that drives the Jetta—his name is Craig, right?" Nakia asked me over the phone.

"Yeah, why?" I questioned.

"Girl, hold up. What's Craig's beeper number?" Nakia asked.

"It's 468-9608—why?" I responded, becoming annoyed.

"Oh my goodness. It's the same Craig! Jamila, come down the block real quick; hurry up," Nakia said and she hung up on me.

I put on my sneakers and my jacket and ran down the block. Nakia was on her stoop with this brown-skinned, sort of thick, older girl. Nakia introduced her as Lynette.

"Yo, you mess with Craig?" the girl said in a feisty tone.

"Yeah, why?" I asked.

"That's *my* man," the girl said in a sharp tone.

"That's *your* man? How can that be when he is with me every day?" I questioned with an attitude.

"Well, he's with me every *night*," Lynette shouted.

"Every night?" I questioned.

"Yeah, he was just with me last night."

"What?"

"Yeah, he came to my house at about 6 o'clock last night, and he left around nine," Lynette said.

I thought about what she said. Craig had dropped me off at about 5:30, and I paged him several times, but he didn't call me back until after nine. What Lynette was saying made a lot of sense.

"Okay, I just got one question for you. Are y'all having sex?" I asked, reluctant to hear the answer.

"We sure are, and he *never* uses a condom!" Lynette bragged. I was sick to my stomach. My whole body became numb.

"Listen, it don't make sense for y'all two to be beefing. Y'all need to step to Craig. Why don't y'all set his cheating behind up?" Nakia suggested.

"Okay, but how?" I asked.

"Get him to meet you both somewhere and don't tell him y'all know about each other."

We took Nakia's advice, and I paged Craig from her house. He called back. I told him to meet me at his apartment. I hopped in a cab and went over to Craig's house. Nakia and Lynette came with me.

We walked up the stairway to Craig's apartment. I knocked on the door as Nakia and Lynette hid on the other side of the door.

"What's up, baby?" Craig said as he opened the door.

"You got something you want to tell me?" I asked as I stood at the door with my hands on my hips.

"What, Boo? What you talking about?"

"Who you been cheating on me with?" I asked.

"Oh, you trippin', girl. I ain't cheating on you," Craig said as he tried to get me to enter the apartment.

"Oh word? So who am I, Craig?" Lynette said as she came from behind the door and surprised him.

"Who am I, Craig?" Lynette repeated as she jumped in his face. I just stood there and stared in disbelief as Craig's face displayed his guilt.

"Ah, yo. What are you doing here?" Craig yelled at her.

"You tell me, Craig. I thought you didn't have a girl!" Lynette shouted.

"I don't have a girl. I have a wife, and she's right here," Craig said, as he grabbed me and pulled me into his apartment. "Miss, I don't know what you on, but you got two minutes to get from in front of my door. I should smack the hell out of you for disrespecting me and my wife. I don't know what you think this is, but I'ma show you." With that, Craig turned around to go grab his gun.

"Yo, y'all need to leave! Nakia, I'll call you later," I said as I closed the door and went to stop Craig.

"Yo, Craig, chill," I said as I grabbed his hand.

"No, this chick got you all bent out of shape, and now you think I'm cheating."

"Well, obviously y'all was doing something."

"Yo, I don't even know that girl like that. For real," Craig said in an angry voice. I knew he was lying, but something inside me wanted to believe him.

"And, Craig, you having sex with her with no protection? So you trying to bring something home to me?" I said.

"Yo, Jamila, the girl is lying," he repeated.

"Well, I hope so, but in the meantime, I just need some time to myself to chill," I said as I walked out the door.

Craig followed me and ended up taking me home. I was so hurt, the pain was almost unbearable. I couldn't believe Craig would cheat on me! The betrayal I felt cut deep down inside of me. I buried myself in my room for weeks, and I cried until I couldn't cry anymore. I wanted to just close my eyes and die.

Craig tried to meet me after school, but I changed my route home, and I refused all his calls. During that time I grew very depressed and sick. I was nonfunctional. My mother was concerned as I was no longer able to hold my food down. Everything I ate, I threw up.

"Baby, what's the matter with you?" Mama asked.

"Nothing, Mommy," I said.

"Baby, I know you. I can't stand to see you like this," she said as she sat on my bed and rubbed my forehead. Tears started streaming from my eyes.

"Mommy, he cheated on me!" I said as I bawled out, crying.

"Oh, baby," my mother said as she hugged me. "This is why I told you I didn't want you involved with no boys," she said as I broke down and told her the whole story.

My mother set up an appointment with her GYN to make sure I was okay after I admitted to her I was sexually active. Unexpectedly, at the doctor's visit, I discovered I was almost three months pregnant!

My mother and I cried the whole way home together. She felt she failed as a parent, and I felt I was just a screwup!

"How are we gonna break this news to your father?" my mother asked as I thought about it and cried again. This was all bad, and I couldn't imagine how it would end!

* * *

I ended up telling Craig I was pregnant, and surprisingly, he was happy! He would rub my stomach and tell me I was having his son and how laced his son would be. I always thought having a baby was cool, but now that I was fourteen years old and pregnant, I hated what I allowed myself to get into!

Craig showered me with gifts and often sang Jodeci's "Forever My Lady." *"So you're having my baby and it means so much to me. There's nothing more precious than to raise a family,"* Craig would sing to me as he rubbed my stomach. Time was quickly passing, and I was caught up between what I wanted to do. My mother wanted me to have an abortion, and Craig wanted me to keep our baby. My father was distraught! He couldn't even look at me. His baby girl had disappointed him. The look in his eyes killed me. I destroyed the innocent little girl perception my dad had in his head about me.

In the end, the final decision was up to me, and I chose to have an abortion. It was a two-day procedure and painful to endure as I had to be induced before I could have the procedure because I was so far along.

Craig begged me not to do it, but I didn't want to ruin my life by having a baby at fourteen years old. I cried for days after the abortion, looking at the pamphlets of the dead babies the protestors gave me outside of the abortion clinic. I went from making one mistake of getting pregnant to another, becoming a murderer! It took me months to heal from all that had happened in such a short period of time. My poor choices were finally catching up to me!

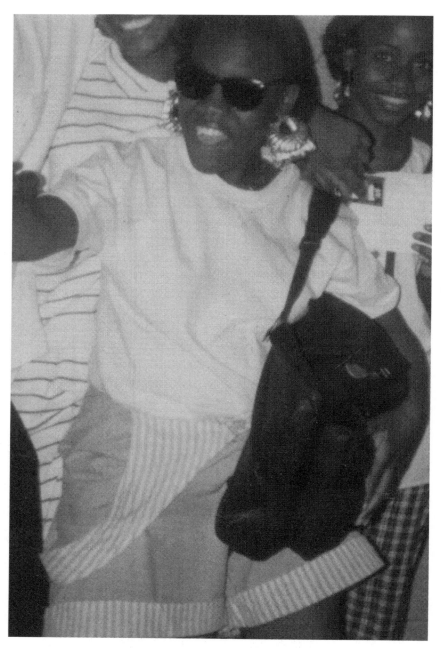

My friend Kim Walker at Martin Van Buren High School.

*S*ummertime approached, and I was happy to get a break from school. Getting up early and going back and forth from Queens to Manhattan had taken a toll on my body, so my first couple of weeks out of school I just rested.

After I had the abortion, my relationship with Craig became very shaky. We were still together, but in his eyes, I killed his baby, so he was still disappointed with me. We would see each other and spend time together, but nothing like we used to. We went from being inseparable to seldom seeing each other.

Most of my summer was spent with my three good friends, April, Qiana, and Talia. I grew to love them all dearly. They each had different characteristics and personalities, so I enjoyed spending time with them for different reasons, and I did different kinds of activities with each of them.

April was my best friend from junior high school. She was very loyal to me through thick and thin. She always had something positive to bring to the table. She got me involved in the Top Teens of America, and she even convinced me to pursue my talent and go to LaGuardia. Unlike the girls I had encountered in the past, April loved me just for me. She had her own things, and I had mine. She was content with who she was and never tried to compete with me or outshine me. April was always just April, which was her true self.

April was dark skinned, short, and heavyset. Her personality made her beautiful in my eyes, but her size made it difficult for her to get attention from boys. Instead of chasing boys, we just had solid fun doing girly things.

* * *

It was a hot summer day, and I got a call from April. She asked me to come with her to her choir rehearsal practice. A boy by the name of S.T. in our school formed a choir group which was composed of children who went to LaGuardia. They would travel all across the city performing at different churches and functions.

Since I started dating Craig, I totally backslid from the church. I knew fornication was against God's will so I felt like a hypocrite going to church. There-fore, I stopped going. I really wasn't sure about going to choir practice with April, but something inside of me convinced me to go.

April and I got on the train and went to Brooklyn to this church on Rogers Avenue where the choir practiced. We arrived at the practice late, so by the time we got there, the large choir was already singing. We could hear their powerful voices all the way down the street as we exited the train station. One thing about the children from LaGuardia, they were extremely talented. These kids had powerful voices and were professionally trained to sing every note on key.

"Oh, Lord, how excellent. How excellent. How excellent. Jesus is excellent. Excellent is thy name," the choir sang powerfully as we walked through the church doors.

April went up to the front and joined the choir, and I sat down in the back of the church. This choir wasn't just your typical choir. Our friend Jules, who was a music major, formed a band that was out of this world! They played all types of instruments behind the choir which made the performance even more extraordinary. The lead vocal-ist, Timiney, sang with such passion and anointing, that every word pierced through my soul. I thought I could sing, but my vocal skills were of no comparison to the LaGuardia vocal majors. They were trained to do such amazing things with their voices! Their soul-ful vocal riffs were new to me. I came from a traditional Baptist church where we sang traditional-style songs, nothing like how these kids sang. I became engrossed with the new Pentecostal traditions they taught and displayed in their performance.

As Timiney sang, tears streamed down my eyes. I felt totally convicted. I knew the new lifestyle I had been living was not pleasing to God. The choir practice wasn't just choir practice. The leader, S.T., was also a minister in training, so they had church in the middle of choir practice!

The children were dancing, singing, and shouting as they praised God. S.T. min-istered the Word of God while they practiced their songs. What I felt in the back of that church is unlike anything I had ever felt before. Suddenly, I began to shake, and my teeth started chattering. It's like I felt fire burning sharply inside of me!

The Spirit had hit, and children were speaking in tongues, prophesying, and falling out. This was customary in the Pentecostal church, which I had never seen before. Even though I had never experienced this type of demonstration of the Holy Spirit in the Baptist church, I couldn't deny the power of it—because I felt it! The Spirit of the Lord came upon me, and I could no longer contain myself!

"The Lord is speaking to me. He is saying there is someone in this building who has backslid. Someone whom He loves greatly. My daughter, you used to be faithful to me as a little girl. I enjoyed looking down from heaven watching you praise Me. You brought

Me such joy. Now, my daughter, you have turned your back on Me. You have a new god that you serve, and you show no attention to Me.

"I miss you, My daughter. I have great plans for you! Yes, you have made some mistakes, but I forgive you, and I will not hold that against you. All you have to do is repent and return home to your Father. I'm waiting for you, My daughter," S.T. prophesied over the church microphone, and I lost it!

I started screaming and crying loudly in the back of the church. I knew his message was for me. At that moment, I desperately wanted to repent and turn back to God. The choir members and S.T. came to where I was to console me.

"My sister, that word was for you. Now it's time to come back home to your first love, God. Repeat these words after me. Lord, I am accepting Your call. I repent of all my sins, seen and unseen. I realize without You, God, I am helpless. I need You, and I ask You to come into my life. Today, I accept Jesus Christ as my personal Savior. I believe He died on the cross for my sins and rose on the third day. Because Jesus lives, I am forgiven of all my iniquity. I am covered and washed in the precious blood of the Lamb. I will dwell in the house of the Lord forever. Amen," S.T. spoke as I repeated the powerful words after him.

"Congratulations, my sister, and welcome home!" S.T. said as everyone began to hug me. I was officially saved!

That day I decided to join S.T.'s choir with April, and we traveled all across New York City performing and praising God together. I felt so good deep down inside. I knew I was doing the right thing, and that made me proud!

* * *

Qiana had a very special place in my heart. She was in my drama class, so we often spent a lot of time together. Qiana lived in Grant Projects on 125th Street and Amsterdam Avenue in Harlem. She was raised by her older grandparents and had the freedom to do pretty much whatever she wanted.

Qiana was fashionable, pretty, and upbeat. She put me on to all the Harlem fashion trends and traditions. Across the street from her house was a Dominican beauty parlor. She introduced me in the early '90s to the Doobie wrap hairstyle. The Dominican women would set our hair on large plastic rollers, sit us under the dryer, take the rollers out, wrap our hair around our heads in a circle, and then place large bobby pins in it, designed in a crown to hold it down. Queens' girls weren't up on Doobies. At that time, we didn't have many Dominican salons in Queens. Qiana showed me how straight, silky, and healthy my hair would come out using the Dominicans' process, so I began going Uptown to get my hair done.

Qiana was very advanced and well experienced with boys. She knew all the get-money hustlers in Harlem and would introduce them to me. I loved going to 125th Street to see Qiana. There was always some kind of action happening in Harlem!

* * *

It was a nice summer day, and Qiana invited me to Harlem. I got dressed and took the train to 125th Street, where she met me.

I rushed up the train steps to the busy street setting. The blocks were flooded with street vendors.

"Come on, let's go to the Mart," Qiana said as we exited to go to the indoor flea market. The street was packed. I immediately noticed the flashy cars and cute boys that were on the street. As we walked up the busy street, we were constantly being solicited and approached by guys.

"Jamila, why aren't you taking any numbers?" Qiana asked.

"Qiana, you know I have a boyfriend!" I responded.

"And so do I. That doesn't stop nothing! You better get some numbers, girl," Qiana said as she twisted extra hard, showing off her cute miniskirt and her voluptuous shape.

"Qiana, I don't believe in cheating," I said.

"Girl, please. What he don't know can't hurt him! Besides, I know you don't think he ain't cheating on you," she responded in a strong sister-girl tone.

"No, I don't believe he is."

"Girl, don't be no fool. You already caught him cheating once, and that's what you know about. What about what you *don't* know about?"

"Well, um. I guess you have a point," I said as we entered the doors of the Mart on 125th Street.

"Yo, Shorty, come here a second," a cute brown-skinned boy called out to me.

"Girl, he is mad cute! You better get his number," Qiana whispered as she nudged me to go over to him.

"What's your name, sexy?" the boy asked me as we stopped.

"My name is Jamila."

"Hi, Jamila. My name is Gee," he said as he smiled.

"Where are y'all from?" he asked.

"Oh, I'm from Queens," I said.

"I'm from Harlem," Qiana interjected.

"Oh, okay. Well, me and my friend Tyquan, we are from Brooklyn. Can we hang out with y'all?" the boy asked as I looked at Qiana for direction.

"We sure can. What y'all want to get into?" Qiana asked.

"I'm saying we just come up here to go shopping. I don't really know Harlem well. How about you show us around?" the boy asked. I was reluctant, but Qiana was all for it!

"Y'all stay right here. Let me get my car and I'll pick y'all up out in front," the boy said as he walked away with his friend.

"Qiana, you tripping. We don't even know them," I said nervously.

"Girl, please! They ain't going to do nothing to us. Calm down. I got this. Besides, if there is any foul play, we'll just kick them in the balls," Qiana said as she laughed. "Yeah, they some cuties and they from Brooklyn! That gives us someplace to go and something to do!" she said as Gee pulled around the block in a brand-new Acura Legend.

"Oh my goodness, girl. Do you see his ride? Now you see I know what I'm talking about!" Qiana said as Gee pulled up, and his friend Tyquan opened the door for us to get in.

"So where y'all want to go?" Gee asked as we got in the car.

"Let's chill Uptown. Come on, let's go to Grant's Tomb," Qiana said as she instructed Gee how to get there. Gee's car was fresh! It had all types of buttons and compartments. It was no comparison to Craig's little Jetta. As we drove I took notice of all the functions the car had.

"So what you like to do in your spare time?" Tyquan asked Qiana.

"Nothing much. I like to chill and write, for the most part."

"Oh, you a writer?" Tyquan asked.

"Well, I ain't no real writer, but I do write rhymes," Qiana answered.

"Oh, word, Shorty? Are you nice?" Tyquan asked.

"Anything I do, I do it for real!" Qiana replied back in a feisty tone.

"Well, I rap too!" Tyquan interjected as we got out of the car and sat on the busy park bench.

"Okay, so what you saying? You want to battle or something?" Qiana said with confidence.

"Shorty, you don't want none of this!" Tyquan replied, and Qiana just started free styling. She rhymed with such poise and confidence. As she was rapping, crowds of people made a circle around her. Tyquan joined in, and they started battling. The crowd cheered and laughed as they joked on each other in their punch lines.

I had never seen a rap cipher up close and personal. I loved the energy the two of them had! Both of them could rap very well. The battle ended, and Qiana won! She killed Tyquan when she switched off into a Das Effects-style rhyme. The crowd roared as she continued to switch up her rhyming styles as she free styled. It was clear to me at that point that Qiana was a lyrical beast when it came to rapping! I always admired female rappers from Salt-N-Pepa days, but I had no clue how to write rhymes like Qiana did.

Qiana's personality won the boys over, and they constantly wanted to meet up with us after that day. I spoke to Gee on the phone a lot, but I didn't let it get serious. My loyalty was with Craig, and I didn't want to break my promise to be faithful to him. I did enjoy hanging out with Gee, and I loved riding in his car. As the days went by, the two of us became really good friends.

* * *

Talia became my partner in crime. She was a pretty, light-skinned girl with long hair who was very jazzy. I loved her Brooklyn swagger. Just like Tanya, Talia was very materialistic. She kept up with all the latest fashion trends. Talia lived with her grandparents who both owned several properties and had acquired a substantial amount of money in their many years in New York, migrating from Georgia. They spoiled Talia, and she got whatever she wanted. Talia was her grandfather's little princess. Disappointed by Talia's mother and his two sons who fell victim to drug abuse, Talia's grandfather wanted to see Talia become successful! All she had to do was pout, and she got whatever she wanted! Her grandfather would give her his credit card, and she would go shopping. Talia stayed in the mall!

Talia introduced me to Bed-Stuy, Brooklyn. I was fascinated with the brownstones and the fast-paced environment in Bed-Stuy. Talia's boyfriend, Rahmel, hustled drugs like Craig, so we often went to his block and hung out.

Brooklyn dudes were different than Queens boys. Like the girls, all the Brooklyn boys were into was labels. In that era, Polo was the #1 sought after name brand. Brooklyn boys draped themselves in Polo, from head-to-toe. You could tell by the way they dressed where they were from. Most Brooklyn boys hustled for a living, whether it was boosting or selling drugs. From a young age, most of them were getting bank! Unlike the silver spoon lifestyle in the suburbs where I lived, where the parents provided well for their children, most of these boys had to work for what they had. I was attracted to their drive and ambition.

* * *

It was a summer afternoon, and I convinced my mom to let me spend the night at Talia's house after she spoke to Talia's grandfather. My mother dropped me off, and I took my bags inside Talia's house.

Talia's grandmother and grandfather lived in separate brownstones, across the street from each other. They weren't together, but they were good friends and often spent time with each other.

Talia lived in her grandfather's brownstone on Macon Street. I liked spending the night with Talia because we could count on her grandfather, who she called Poppy, to be knocked out by 8 o'clock. When Poppy went to sleep, we snuck out of the house and enjoyed our nights on the streets in Brooklyn.

We had to carefully plan our escape. Talia's grandmother was nosey and often sat at the window. We had to make sure she was also asleep, then we would rush out of the house. Sometimes we would just chill on the stoops of the brownstones in Bed-Stuy, but this particular night, our plan was to go to the club.

Jamaican music was big at that time, and there was this club called the Golden Pavilion that all the older kids would brag about. Talia and I waited for Poppy to go to bed. Then, we got dressed to go to the legendary club we heard so much about!

We both were dressed to impress and fixed each other's hair in the mirror. "I look all right, girl?" I asked as I put on makeup to make myself appear to look older.

"Yeah, girl, you look good. What about me?" Talia asked.

"Girl, you know you fine," I said sarcastically as we both laughed.

"Here, this is Stephanie's ID. She's brown like you. Remember the date of birth just in case the bouncer asks you," Talia said as she handed me the ID, and I put it in my purse.

We studied Talia's grandmother's window to make sure she was asleep, then we tiptoed out of the house so we didn't wake up Poppy.

We both took a deep breath as we made it safely to the corner, where we flagged down a gypsy cab and headed to the club.

The parking lot was packed with all types of fly cars at the Golden Pavilion. We both got excited as we observed the atmosphere. This was my first club appearance in New York City!

The line wrapped around the block. "Man, Talia, look how long the line is," I said as we got out of the cab.

"Don't worry about that. All we have to do is find some guys at the front of the line," she said as she nudged me to follow her.

"Hey, sexy," Talia said as she flirted with some ugly dude in the front of the line. He was quickly mesmerized by her sweet talk and invited us in line with him. "I told you," Talia said as she whispered in my ear. Talia hugged on this boy and kept making him smile by her hand gestures. She even convinced him to pay for us to get into the club. After we got in the doors of the large club, she took off and ditched him!

The Golden Pavilion was large, and to me, it was spectacular! It was nothing like the little club I went to in Kinston. The music played loud, and you could feel the vibration from the speakers in your soul as the Reggae music played.

The Golden Pavilion was a Jamaican club, but there were some Americans there. The Jamaicans had on their linen suits with custom designs woven in them. The girls had big hard hairdos, and a lot of them wore short shorts. Each of their outfits looked like costumes. They took this party thing serious!

There was a large dance floor, where at first we just stood and watched the girls dance to the Reggae Dance Hall music. They were doing the Bogle dance and the Butterfly and all the other latest Jamaican dances. I enjoyed watching the girls and picking up new steps.

Talia convinced me to take a drink with her. She had the bartender fix me some special concoction of hers. I took two sips and got twisted! Then I really started getting into the music, and Talia and I took over the dance floor. She knew how to dance well. We danced together on the floor like it was our world! I zoned out, and so did she! She followed my lead in dances, then I followed hers.

We quickly got the attention of the entire club as the bystanders made circles around us. The regular dance-hall girls in the club got mad, and a crew of them surrounded us to battle.

"Oh, I know this cheap Flatbush Avenue-dressing girls don't want it with us!" Talia said as they heard her.

"Cha bumba clot?" the Jamaican girl cursed in her native language.

"The little Yankee chick want to romp with me," the girl shouted in her thick Jamaican accent as she assembled her crew. I quickly took notice of how numerous they were. They way outnumbered us! Talia didn't care; she was drunk and continued to pop trash.

"Yo, close your mouth. Your teeth are raggedy. Instead of buying that ugly outfit, you should have spent your money to get your teeth fixed," Talia shouted loudly as the girl lunged to grab her.

"Yo, chill, miss. We don't want no problems with you. My friend is drunk," I said as I jumped between Talia and the girl.

"She better watch what the ras clot she say," the woman boasted. I was able to diffuse the energy and calm the lady down. I was scared they would still try to jump us after the club, so I called Gee to come pick us up.

Gee dropped us off at Talia's, and we snuck back into the house. Poppy was still sound asleep. We quickly took off our clothes, put on our pajamas, and got in the bed like nothing ever happened. Poppy never had a clue we were ever missing, so we continued to sneak out of his house every chance we got!

* * *

School was back in session. I was officially a sophomore. I had learned all the ropes, so school became a breeze.

In school I was considered a "cool kid," so I enjoyed the privileges it carried. I got my props, or respect, at school, and I hung out with the other "cool kids" in our elite clique. I was never big on the boys that went to my school. Instead, I was attracted to the drug dealers and hustlers, from every borough. They were the ones with the money and the respect! In my heart, I desired to one day have what they had-power!

Me, at 15 years old, posing in my black Sherling at 60 Minute Photo, a
week before I got jumped and robbed for my earrings.

I just finished up my drama class. I got dressed in the locker room and went upstairs to the pay phone. Craig was heavily on my mind. I called his house, and a girl answered the phone.

"Hello. Can I speak to Craig?" I asked, trying to figure out the voice.

"He's not here. Who's this?" the girl said in a sassy tone.

"What! This is his wife. Who are you?" I snapped back.

"I'm Shaneeda, and I don't know who you are, but I'm Craig's girlfriend, and I'm having his baby, so I would appreciate if you don't call here anymore," she said and hung up on me.

I was furious! My emotions got so out of control I could hardly breathe.

I paged Craig with 911 behind the pay phone number, -back to back. I was determined to get to the bottom of this.

Craig called me back on the school pay phone with the girl in the background.

"Hello," I said as I heard the girl yelling at him.

"Tell her what it is, Craig," the girl shouted.

"Look, Jamila, you know it's been kind of rocky with us and, um . . . look, I ain't gonna beat around the bush. I'm with Shaneeda now, and she's pregnant!" Craig said, wasting no time.

"So all of this time and you gonna play me like that!" I said furiously, and I began to cry. "What does she have to offer you that I can't give?" I cried frantically.

"Look, Jamila, Shaneeda is seventeen, and she's got a job at the bakery. She makes good money, and she's an independent woman. I like her 'cause she's about something, unlike you. All you want is handouts. Shaneeda goes out and gets her own!" Craig said as he praised his new baby mother-to-be.

Craig's words cut, but it made me realize how pointless relying on a man was! All my dreams of spending the rest of my life with him shattered all at once. At first I was hurt, but my pain turned into determination. I was determined to do my thing and shine on Craig! If I didn't do anything else in life, I wanted to show him just who he

Chapter Forty-One

passed off on!

Nothing in this world can compare to the pain of heartbreak for the first time. Inside, I felt like I was lifeless. I couldn't believe the boy I believed was my true love would hurt me so bad. When I looked in the mirror, I no longer liked what I saw. I felt like I was missing something and I was less of a woman. *Maybe that's why Craig left me,* I thought to myself. I no longer felt confident about who I was. I desperately wanted to become more! I wanted to be noticed and appreciated. I wanted to make sure I never got dumped again for another female. I had to find a way to become great and gain my own power and recognition!

* * *

At school I became very close with one of the school aides, Mrs. Clark. I would sit with her in her office for hours laughing and talking. One day I convinced her to give me my working papers. I was only fifteen, and I needed to be sixteen to get my working papers. Ms. Clark altered my age on the papers, and I was able to work.

I went all around Manhattan putting in job applications, but after several weeks I still got no response. I refused to give up on my effort. I wanted to show Craig I could make my own money too.

One day I walked inside of the Häagen-Dazs ice-cream shop on Seventy-second Street and Amsterdam Avenue. It was a small store in the middle of a lot of action.

"Excuse me, sir, are you hiring?" I said as I walked in the store.

"Well, I'm really not hiring right now, young lady," the middle-aged white man with black hair said.

"My name is Jamila, and what's your name, sir?" I asked as I walked closer to him.

"My name is Howard. I'm the owner of the store," he responded.

"Hi, Howard. I'm a student at the High School of Performing Arts right up the street, and I really need a job, Howard. I'm a hard worker. I'm reliable, and I believe I could be an asset to your company," I said as I leaned over the counter to shake his hand.

"Oh, is that right?" he responded.

"Yes, sir, and I have charm and charisma, which could help increase your sales. And, Howard, I have a nice smile. See?" I said as I smiled for him, and he laughed. When Howard laughed, I knew I had him just where I wanted him.

"Well, we don't really need anyone now, but what time do you get out of school?" he asked.

"Three o'clock."

"Well, can you work the four to ten p.m. shift?"

"I certainly can," I said in an excited voice.

"Okay, come back and see me tomorrow, and I'll give you your hours. Congratulations, you talked yourself into a job!" Howard beamed.

"Thank you, sir. Thank you so much! I promise you, you won't regret your decision," I said as I shook his hand again and walked out the door.

I was so excited! I couldn't believe I finally landed a job! I had a tough time convincing my parents to let me work so late, but my father admired my desire to make my own money, so he convinced my mother it was okay. Look out, world, 'cause here I come. I'm Miss Independent!

* * *

Working at Häagen-Dazs gave me a new sense of self-worth. I took pride in making my own money, and my peers admired me. My friends would often come to the ice-cream shop, and I would hook them up with lots of ice cream.

My job was simple. I scooped ice cream and made shakes and sundaes. I worked directly across the street from the Beacon Theatre, so I would often serve famous actresses and actors. I liked to talk, so I made conversation with a lot of the customers, causing them to come to our store more frequently. Howard recognized my talent, and he loved having me aboard his work team.

Coming home late on the train at times was scary, but I learned to move with the crowd. Often at night, many of the cars in the train were empty, so I would keep walking down until I found a car with people in it.

I worked three nights during the week and one full day on the weekend. I pulled in quite a few hours, so I made good money. Every pay period I made three hundred to four hundred dollars, which was extremely good for a high school student, at that time. I took all my money and bought myself lavish gifts.

I became one of Benny the jeweler's best customers. I bought so much jewelry that it was insane. Every one of my fingers had rings on them. I bought several pairs of earrings, top and bottom gold teeth, a bunch of bracelets, and two large chains with medallions.

My jewelry made me feel good about myself. I loved the attention I would get from others when I wore it. People would stop to compliment me on my jewelry, and I loved it! I copied the trends of the rappers I saw on television. I had more jewelry than any other girl I knew!

Spending my time at Häagen-Dazs helped me to get over Craig. I was so busy with work and school that I had no time to think about him anymore. Whenever I felt lonely or depressed, I would go shopping. Shopping helped soothe my pain! I got a high going into the store, picking out designer clothes to wear. My jewelry and my clothes became the crutches I would use to cover my inner wounds. As long as I had on a fresh outfit and jewelry, I felt good about myself.

I quickly became the talk of my neighborhood. My style was different from the girls in my neighborhood. Going to school in Manhattan, I had access to all types of stores. I developed my own unique style and swagger. I no longer looked up to Kim and Nakia. Instead, they began to look up to me. I was doing way more than them because they were limited to Queens. We would see each other on the weekends, and they would admire my new stylish fashions. This made me feel good, yet I still felt incomplete. Something was still missing, but I couldn't quite put my finger on what it was!

One day while working at my job, I met this boy named William, who lived in Amsterdam Housing Projects, which were directly next to my school. I liked William's swagger, so we began to kick it. He would come pick me up every night from work and walk me to the train station.

William sold drugs in the projects, but he didn't make the type of money that Craig made. William was a worker. Craig was a boss! Even though William didn't make as much money as Craig made, I liked his personality. I would spend hours chilling at his apartment in the projects. He lived with his mother and his two sisters. His sisters were fly girls who were always into something, and William's mother was funny as hell. She would tell jokes and snap on people like she was a paid comedian on television. Their house became like my new home. I was always there.

The Amsterdam Housing Projects, on Sixty-sixth Street where William lived, was full of action and entertainment. You could count on someone acting up on the block. I loved to chill outside on the project benches with William and his sisters and enjoy the excitement of the hood. I was all into the action! For whatever reason, I was attracted to the different housing project of New York City, and they were also attracted to me!

* * *

As I spent time with Qiana, she taught me how to write rhymes. At first, it was difficult, but after a while, I caught on. We would spend hours together writing songs. She would start, and I would finish.

One day while I was sitting on my bed, this song called "Pocket Rockers" came into my head, and I began to write it. I couldn't wait to rap it for Qiana the next day at school.

"Yo, Qiana, listen to this," I said as I rapped the song "Pocket Rockers."

"Oh my goodness, Jamila, that's hard as hell. You wrote that?" she asked.

"Yeah, last night," I said with confidence.

Chapter Forty-Two

"Yo, they having a talent show next month. Let's sign up for it," Qiana suggested.

"So what we gonna perform?" I asked.

"Let's do the 'Pocket Rockers' song."

"Okay, cool," I agreed.

Qiana and I tried out for the talent show and we were selected. There were few rappers in our school, and almost none were girls. We couldn't wait to show off our talent!

*　*　*

Qiana and I were very close. She also had a friend named Dana from the Bronx. Dana was a short, fair-skinned girl. She was half Puerto Rican and half black. I was cordial to her because of Qiana, but I could tell Dana was envious of our relationship.

Right before the talent show, Dana busted in the drama dressing room and tried to call me out in front of everyone.

"Ah, yo, Jamila. Let me talk to you for a second," she said as she swung ferociously through the door. She caught me by surprise because we really didn't speak much.

"Yo, what's up?" I responded back.

"Yo, I heard you told somebody that I said I didn't like them and you told them you don't like me," she yelled loudly, gaining the attention of the entire locker room.

"What? I don't even know you, and for real, I don't care about you enough to talk about you," I said as I sized Dana up. I had on a red Guess T-shirt and my light denim Guess skirt to match. I really didn't want to fight, but I had learned from the fight I lost in junior high to Shavon that I couldn't let anyone punk me out. My reputation was on the line, and I couldn't risk losing my "cool kid" status.

"For real, Dana, I don't do all this 'he said-she said' stupid stuff. If somebody says I said something, bring them to me," I informed her as I stared her up and down.

"Okay, I will, and if I find out you said it, I'm gonna beat you up," Dana boasted as she pointed in my face.

"What, chick? Look, let me save you a trip," I said as I took my earrings off, gave them to Qiana, and swung on Dana.

I fought with everything within me, just like Kim showed me. Dana didn't even get a lick in. I wrapped my hands around her long hair, gripping by her scalp, and began hitting her head on the lockers. "Oh, so you want to pop crap to me. You better think about who you step to the next time," I said in syllables as I whopped on her. Qiana grabbed me.

"Yo, that's enough. Y'all gonna mess around and get suspended," Qiana said as she pulled me off of her. Dana tried to get slick and kick me as Qiana pulled me away. Then she had the nerve to start talking trash again!

"Yeah, you ain't did nothing to me. You can't handle me," Dana screamed to save her reputation.

"Oh, yeah?" I yelled as I broke loose from Qiana and rushed Dana again. I jumped on top of her, got her down on the floor, and started punching her repeatedly.

"Get her off of me! Get her off of me," Dana yelled as a crowd came to pull me off.

"Oh, this ain't the end. I ain't going out like that," Dana said as she got up looking like she was in a war at Vietnam. Her hair was all over the place, and her clothes were scuffed up.

"Oh, that's a threat?" I yelled as my friends held me back.

"Oh, no, baby, that's a promise!" Dana replied.

Dana left the locker room, and some of my friends said she had called her boyfriend who was supposed to be some ill dude from the Bronx, so I immediately left school and went across the street to William's house.

I cried to him, telling him how I beat Dana up and she was going to get her man. "Oh, word? Not in my hood it ain't going down!" William yelled, and it seemed as though he gathered the whole projects together.

When school let out, I stood out in front of LaGuardia with half of the Amsterdam housing projects. William's boys were ready to get it popping! Dana and her man never showed up, but the whole school talked about me for months!

"You don't mess with that girl Jamila! She ain't no joke. She can fight her butt off, and her boyfriend got the projects next door on lock," they would say.

That fight made my peers respect me! You couldn't tell me I wasn't about it!

* * *

It was the night of the talent show, and our large school auditorium was packed. Everybody invited their friends from different boroughs. William and all his friends from the projects came to cheer Qiana and me on.

The act before us was some dance majors who choreographed a hip-hop dance to a mix tape which kept switching songs. The crowd went wild as the girls shook their butts to the fast, up-tempo Luke music. *"I wanna rock, I wanna rock, I wanna rock right now,"* the Luke music blasted as the girls danced just like the girls in the video. They were on their backs and all over the floor. William and his friends were cheering furiously.

My heart pounded. This was my first performance at LaGuardia, and I was nervous. LaGuardia shows were serious, and the crowd was harsh. They even booed a couple of the acts.

It was our turn, and our music came on. Qiana immediately transformed, rousing up the crowd. *"Turn my mic up,"* she said as we bopped on the stage, and the crowd stared.

"Pocket rockers, the picketa pocket rockers, the picketa pocketa, picketa pocketa, picketa pocketa rockers. *What you call it? Pocket rockers, the picketa pocket rockers, the picketa pocketa, picketa pocketa, picketa pocketa rockers."* We rapped our hook passionately in the Das Effects rap style as the audience got in into it.

"Well, my name is Jamila, and I'm a picketa pocket rocker. When I go out with a guy you know I order the lobster. Dom Pérignon and don't forget the caviar. Scheming on the way to get the keys to his car.

"This reminds me of Tom, a cutie from around the way. He ask to take me out, and you know I said okay.

"I went out in the day he took me to the shopping mall. I put my scheming up in gear because there is no need to stall.

"Uh-oh, excuse me, I think I left my purse at home. Will you buy me that fat chain? I think I'd like to try it on.

"After I got the chain I knew I just couldn't stop. Had to finish up my mission and complete the pocket rock.

"Oh, those shoes are cute and that suit is type fly. Think I didn't get it when I did? You know my game is just too sly.

"As we walked through the mall I continued my approach. Def jewels and gear is for all I would search.

"After we left the mall we headed over to the restaurant. He handed me the menu, ordered all I could ever want.

"At the end of the night he asked me what he'd get for this. I thought to myself, and then I blew him back a kiss," I said my verse, and the whole crowd went crazy!

Qiana finished the song with her verse and not a single person in the audience was in their seats. William and the project boys were standing on top of their chairs dancing. We created a semifrenzy up in the building.

That day I tapped into a new passion. *Maybe I'll become a rapper,* I thought to myself as I enjoyed the energy my rapping created.

I became a minicelebrity at my school after the talent show. We didn't win, but we definitely represented. In my large school with so many talented kids from all over the city, we made a name for ourselves, and we were only sophomores. Everybody talked about us. The girls even sang the "Pocket Rockers" song in the hallway. The song was a big hit! My newfound fame felt good!

* * *

One late night coming from work, William dropped me at the subway. I stood on the platform with him, waiting for the train, when I noticed this really cute brown-skinned, tall guy who kept staring at me. I kissed William good-bye and got on the train and sat down. The boy walked over and sat across from me, and he just stared. I felt very awkward so I laughed.

"Yo, what you laughing at?" the boy asked.

"You!" I responded, and he began to try to rap to me.

I wasn't really interested, but he was so funny. He kept me laughing.

"Yo, that was your man?" the boy asked.

"Yeah, I got a man," I said in a feisty tone.

"I ain't trying to hear that, see. What yah man gotta do with me?" the boy rapped, imitating the popular song "I Got a Man," and we laughed together.

The boy introduced himself as Trini. He was born and raised as a little boy in Trinidad, but now he lived in Queens. He lived in the town right next to mine. His house was literally walking distance from my house. We rode all the way to Queens on the train together from Manhattan, laughing and talking the whole way. We finally arrived at our final destination, Parsons and Archer, and I hated to see him go.

"So you gonna give me your number?" Trini asked as we got off the train.

"Well, um, I told you I have a boyfriend," I replied.

"Listen, I'm not trying to get in the middle of all that. You are mad cool, and I want to be your friend. Can we be friends?" Trini asked as he charmed me with his beautiful complexion and wonderful smile.

"Oh, all right!" I said, giving in. I handed Trini a piece of paper with my number on it. At first I felt a little guilty, but Trini was only gonna be my friend, right?

* * *

Trini wasted no time. I got a phone call from him the very next day. He wanted to take me out to eat. I saw no harm in just hanging out, so we met in Queens, and I had a ton of fun.

I was fifteen years old, and Trini was twenty-two. His age allowed him the upper hand advantage of experience over me. Trini charmed me with his personality and his wit. He was also superfly! He moved to the United States with his mother from Trinidad when he was seven years old. They lived in the Bronx for many years. His mother got a good job, worked hard, and moved the family to Queens, looking for a better life.

Trini had an incredible swagger, and he dressed really nice. Not to mention Trini's olive complexion Indian skin tone, and his naturally curly hair. He dressed and looked like a model. At first I thought Trini was the nice, pretty boy-type, but boy, was I wrong!

Trini took me to hang out with him down on Second Street and St. Marks, in the Village area, downtown Manhattan. The area was composed of mostly white hippies, rockers, gay people, and drug fiends. The environment was different from anything I was accustomed to. At first, I didn't understand his ties to this area.

We sat on the stoop in front of one of the brownstone buildings and a bunch of black boys started coming up to Trini.

"Yo, what's it looking like out here?" Trini asked as he opened his jacket and leaned back on the stoop.

"Oh, it's money out here, boss," one of the boys said, as he handed Trini a knot of money.

"Yeah, I'm done already," another boy said as he passed Trini more money.

"Oh, all right, let me see what I got left out here," Trini said as he took me into a house where he stashed his drugs.

Trini turned out to be a minidrug kingpin! He and his brother Lenroy ran the drug trade in a whole section downtown Manhattan. I thought the projects in Queens were making serious drug money, but it was nothing compared to the busy blocks of downtown Manhattan. *I landed me a good one!* I thought to myself.

I was intrigued by Trini. He introduced me to a new lifestyle. I began to hang out on the streets of Lower Manhattan, picking up money and dropping off packages for him. Trini also hung out a lot in the Bronx. His brother Lenroy still lived right off E. Tremont Avenue and 177th Street. Trini and I spent a lot of time in the Bronx with Lenroy. I even ended up hooking Lenroy up with my friend, the twin, Michelle.

Trini and Lenroy competed with each other, showering Michelle and me with gifts. Although Michelle was a light-skinned, pretty girl, she wasn't accustomed to getting money from dudes. Lenroy was open, off of Michelle and her beauty, so she became his trophy, and Michelle got whatever she wanted! Her new sudden wealth got to her head, and I had to check her a few times, reminding her who put her on!

I broke up with William with no explanation. I became heartless. I did to him exactly what Craig did to me. At the time I didn't even care. I was into Trini, and nothing else mattered! Living the lavish life with Trini helped me to quickly get over Craig. To me, Craig was no comparison to Trini, and I loved the fact that I had stepped up my choice in men.

Time went by, and Trini helped turn me into a new monster! He taught me all about the drug business from inside out. I would even go with him to 145th Street and Broadway as he copped kilos of cocaine from the Dominicans. He thought it was important that I learn the business. I guess you can say, I became a silent partner.

I hardly ever went to school. I was too busy chasing behind Trini. I was his Bonnie, and he was my Clyde. After I got off from work, I had to stop at the block, pick up the money that was made that day and bring it back to Queens.

I was fifteen years old, collecting anywhere between three thousand to ten thousand dollars a night off the block. Trini knew he could trust that I would do the right thing with his money. No matter how much money Trini gave me, I refused to quit my job. I had learned my lesson from Craig, that I had to still get my own money. Trini liked that about me.

"Yo, my girl is about it. She gets her own money too. She's my little independent woman," he would brag to his friends. I quickly learned if I didn't keep my own source of money, I could be dispensed and fall off at any time!

My exposure to so much money increased my passion and love for it. I loved to just look at the money and count it. Trini had a money machine that I would use to help him count it and stack it up. Oftentimes, the drug fiends would use singles and fives, so we had stacks and stacks of singles and fives that we would trade in to the store owners for large bills.

I wasn't familiar with the drug trade, but I had a natural sense for business, so I helped Trini establish a system to keep a track of his money. It made the business run more smoothly. He began to listen to my suggestions, which just put me in greater esteem with him. Trini fell in love with me, and I fell in love once again, with him.

The money I got from Trini took me to a whole 'nother level! I was literally shopping every single day. I seldom ever repeated an outfit. Trini was very flamboyant and liked to show off his money. He would come to my school and pick me and all my friends up, and take us on shopping sprees and treat us all to dinner and the movies. My friends envied me, and they loved Trini. When they saw Trini, my friends knew they were going to have a good time!

The more money I had, the more clothes and jewelry I bought. I came to school looking like movie star. The world became my stage! Motorola had just come out with the first version of the flip cell phone. It resembled a small, plastic, gray container, and it had a large black antenna. Trini bought himself and me matching cell phones, and everybody at school talked about me chilling on my phone going up the escalators.

I was officially that notorious "fly chick." I became everything I desired. I came to school every day dressed fresh to death, and I always had knots and knots of money in my pocket. I was no longer naïve and innocent. Overnight, I turned into a little "queen pin."

I became very close to my friend Shalon, who I knew from Bernice Johnson's Dance School. She was a pretty, creamy-white-skinned, slim girl, who I began to take with me around Trini and all his friends. Shalon didn't have many clothes, so I made it my business to buy her all the same type of clothes I wore. She lived in Queens, so we began to do everything together, including picking up money on Trini's block.

Life for me was all about fashion and fun. I lost my interest in anything else, even school. I mastered bobbing and weaving through the academic school system. I would only go to school when it was test time. I'd study the textbooks at home and aced my tests, effortlessly. My grades remained good, so my parents really didn't have a reason to complain.

Passing academic classes was easy, but it wasn't the same for drama. My sophomore drama teacher couldn't stand me. She hated my arrogance. She told me I felt the world revolved around me; and guess what? I probably did. I didn't care about drama or even school, for that matter. I got turned out by Trini and fast money. I would stay in school until Trini said he was up, then I would leave and make my way to him.

Qiana and I were drama partners, and we had to do a skit together from *A Raisin in the Sun.* All the classes came to watch us perform, and our performance determined our grade. Qiana got on the stage and forgot her lines, so she started acting stupid, making jokes to cover up her mistake. The audience started laughing, and I did too! I thought it was funny, but my drama teacher sure didn't think so! She failed Qiana and me, meaning, we would both have to repeat sophomore drama. I was so humiliated!

I went home and cried to my mother. My mother knew I never failed a class in my life, so she took my side and came up to the school to go to bat for me. My mother even threatened to sue for discrimination and every other thing under the sun, but my drama teacher wouldn't budge! I was going to have to repeat sophomore drama.

Upset by the final decision, I decided to go to night school and summer school to get my academic credits, so I could graduate early from high school. I no longer cared about obtaining a Certificate of Completion in Drama. I just wanted my high school diploma. I barely ever even attended drama classes anymore; instead, I left the house each morning and went to Trini's house and got in the bed with him until he woke up. Then, we would hit the block.

* * *

One day I was shopping in Green Acres Mall in Queens with Trini. He went into the dressing room to try on an outfit he was gonna wear to a party. Trini and his brother Lenroy were West Indians that loved to party. They took parties very seriously and bought elaborate designer outfits to wear to them. The two brothers were always competing with each other. This particular day, Trini was trying to buy a better outfit than Lenroy.

"Jamila, what do you think about this one?" Trini said as he came out of the dressing room, posing in his designer men's suit.

"I guess it's all right," I said checking him out.

"Oh, I forgot, you're a Yankee. All you know about is sneakers and jeans," Trini said with an attitude because I wasn't into his suit.

"Yeah, I guess that's why you so into me, right?" I said snapping back. Just as we were talking, I noticed Craig walking with a girl who was pushing a stroller. My heart dropped. I hadn't seen Craig in such a long time. I wondered if that was the girl who I spoke to over the phone and if that was his baby.

"Yo, what you looking at?" Trini said as he saw me take notice of Craig.

"Yo, Trini, that's my ex-boyfriend, Craig, that I told you about," I said.

"Oh, him," Trini said as he checked him out.

Trini went back in the dressing room to change, and my eyes were glued on Craig. He didn't see me, but I saw him. He and the girl were in the junior's section, and she was picking out an outfit.

Trini came out of the dressing room and noticed me still staring at Craig.

"So you still don't have any closure. You want to get him back for what he did?" Trini asked.

"Hell, yeah," I said.

"Okay, follow my lead," Trini instructed as we walked over to the junior's section. "Jamila, pick out whatever you want. You know Daddy's got it!" Trini said as we walked over, and Craig took notice.

"Oh, that's why I love my daddy," I said as I stopped and gave Trini a kiss on his lips. I could tell by the look on Craig's face he was sick to his stomach. Trini pulled out his cell phone and began to talk big money talk to his brother Lenroy while I picked out every outfit I thought was halfway decent. As I filled up my hands, I passed the items to Trini.

"Baby, that's all you want?" Trini said as he told Lenroy to hold on.

"Oh, maybe I'll get a few more items," I said as I stared at Craig and showed off. I tried my best to get a glance into the baby carriage, but I couldn't see the baby.

Trini purposely went to the counter directly in front of Craig and the girl to ring up all our items. He pulled out like four knots of money.

"Damn, baby, we got to go home and put some of this money up," Trini bragged as he counted out his money and even tipped the cashier.

Craig's face said it all! I couldn't have paid for a better revenge! I felt so good as Trini and I left the store. We laughed about Craig's facial expressions all the way home!

Shortly after I got back home, my phone rang. It was Craig.

"Oh, so you stuntin' with your new little dude. Y'all lucky I didn't have my gun on me.

I would have robbed you and him!" Craig said as I laughed.

"Why are you calling me? Ain't you happy with you and your little family?" I rubbed it in. "You're happy, and you know I'm extremely happy," I said as I gloated on the phone.

Trini's plan worked! All of a sudden, Craig wanted me back, but strange to say, I wasn't interested. I liked the attention and the fact that he wanted me back, but I couldn't forget what he had done. For goodness' sake, Craig was now a father!

L ife was grand! I lived a care-free life. I sported my fly clothes and my jewelry, and I rarely took precautions. I felt like everyone knew who I was, so I would never be tried or have problems. Boy I was wrong!

One day I was on my way home from school, and I stopped off to go to Trini's house in Queens. I had on my black Sherline coat, my large twisted hoop earrings that just came out, my mother's black Gucci bag with the small *G*s, and some black high-top Reeboks. I looked cute, and I knew it, so I walked with confidence. I had just gotten off the bus and had two blocks to walk to get to Trini's house when I saw this group of girls headed in my direction.

"Excuse me," I said as I tried to get by them, but they wouldn't move. They just stared me up and down. After waiting a couple of seconds for them to respond, I pushed my way through them and kept walking. I didn't think anything of it, especially since I had successfully walked a whole block past them.

All of a sudden, I saw three girls running toward me. Two of them were thick, and one of them was skinny like me. "Ah, yo, give me them earrings," one of the thick girls said as I dropped my bag.

"What?" I screamed, and the three girls began to jump me. One of the thick girls took my earrings and ran. I quickly grabbed the skinny girl, and we got it in! I held on to her with all my might, and I wouldn't let her go! I gripped her hair and wrapped it around my fist and took her with me as a bigger girl pounced on me.

"Get her off of me!" the skinny girl yelled, but I refused to let her go! The thick girl tried, but she couldn't get me off of the skinny girl.

"Oh, so y'all want to rob me? So what you thought, it was gonna be easy?" I said as I continued to fight with all my might. I prayed Trini would hear the chaos and come outside. We were only a few doors down from his house!

The girls and I fought for about ten minutes, and finally, we grew tired. I still refused to let the small girl go. We would have continued to fight, but a man came outside and unhooked me from the girl.

"Yo, mister, they just robbed me!" I said as I let go, and the girls took off running to the bus stop. I was furious!

I ran to Trini's house and rang the bell. My hair was all over my head. "What happened?" Trini said as he opened the door.

"These girls just robbed me!" I screamed.

Trini got his brother Lenroy, and we ran out of the house and got into the car to find the girls.

They were no longer standing at the bus stop, so Trini rode through the back streets to catch up with the bus.

We spotted the bus about fifteen blocks up the street. Trini blocked the bus off with his car, and he and Lenroy ran up on the bus with me.

"Nobody move," Trini said as he pulled out his gun. The older people on the bus started screaming.

"Yo, where the girls at?" Lenroy said as I looked all the girls on the bus up and down, but I couldn't find them.

"Yo, them girls that robbed your girl just go off the bus at the last stop. They go to Andrew Jackson High School," one of the boys spoke up and said.

We exited the bus with disappointment. For about an hour, we rode around looking for the girls, but we never found them. I felt violated. I couldn't believe I got robbed, and by girls at that!

Trini saw the pain in my eyes and immediately took me back to Benny the jeweler to buy me another pair of earrings. The earrings had just come out, so he had to order them. It took me like two weeks before they arrived. Before those two weeks were up, Trini and Lenroy did their own private investigation and found the girls that robbed me. They had bragged to some of their friends, telling the story about how they robbed me, and it got back to Trini. Trini slapped the girls and paid some other girls to beat them up.

I didn't get my earrings back from them, but I did get the same exact pair when my order came in. It taught me one valuable lesson. I had to be on alert for robbers. The city of New York was rampant with thirsty people waiting to take what they wanted.

I started taking off my jewelry when I went into certain neighborhoods, and I tucked my chains in when I went to other areas. I was determined to never be robbed again! It wasn't a good feeling.

* * *

Qiana cried in my arms after getting the news. She had been sick for weeks, but mistook it as some sort of cold. By accident, she found out she was pregnant, but she was too far along for a regular abortion. She would have to get a two-day procedure, which only a few abortion clinics administered.

Qiana found an abortion clinic in Queens called Choices. We met each other early one morning and headed for Choices.

We arrived at the building on Queens Boulevard, greeted by angry protesters who marched with their signs.

"Baby killers!" a woman yelled as we went into the door of the clinic.

"You don't have to kill your baby. There are options," another lady shouted as she attempted to hand us a pamphlet.

"Get out of our way," I demanded and I escorted Qiana through the doors.

Qiana was clearly nervous. She didn't want to be a baby killer, but she also didn't know how to tell her grandparents that she was pregnant.

We sat in the crowded waiting area for hours before they called Qiana's name. "It's going to be all right," I assured her as I squeezed her hand tightly before she went into the office.

Qiana came out about a half hour later. "Let's go," she said as she grabbed her belongings.

"What happened?" I asked as she stormed out of the busy clinic.

I followed Qiana out into the hallway of the building, where she collapsed in my arms. "Jamila, I'm over five months pregnant. I'm twenty-six weeks, and the lady said it's too late to have an abortion. There's nothing I can do." Qiana cried profusely in my arms. I began to cry with her. This was so real! We were both fifteen years old, and Qiana was about to have a baby.

"Qiana, you're not alone, I promise, I'll be there for you every step of the way," I said as I cried with her.

We sat in the lobby of the clinic for about half an hour until we got ourselves together. I rode with Qiana back to her apartment building in Harlem, where she broke the news to her grandparents, who, of course, were very angry.

It was official. Qiana was having a baby! The news spread rapidly throughout our school, and Qiana became the talk of all the students.

"Girl, she's pregnant. What a shame," some of the students said.

"If it was me, my mother would kill me," some of the girls would comment as Qiana walked by.

I didn't care what anybody said. I could have easily been Qiana last year. I loved my friend unconditionally and started spending my money on my new godchild-to-be.

As her due date approached, I grew anxious for her baby to arrive. My godchild was going to be fresh to death. I would make certain of it!

Me, at age 16, attempting to kiss my dad in front of
my grandmother's house.

*I*t was my birthday, July 11, 1993, and I was sixteen years old. My mother wanted me to have a big Sweet Sixteen party, but I opted to spend my day with Trini on his block, St. Mark's, in Lower Manhattan.

I sat between Trini's legs on the stoops of the building he hung out at. As he wrapped his arms around my shoulders, I felt special. Trini made me feel loved and protected. He gave me the lifestyle I secretly aspired for all my life. I was finally the drug dealer's wife! It felt good to accomplish my mission, and I did it with excellence! Trini made more money than C.B. and Donnell combined, and he loved me. What more could I ask for?

I was sixteen years old, and I had everything a girl could want. I switched from working at Häagen-Dazs to the Love Store, which was a chain of drugstores in Manhattan. I made my own money, and I still got whatever I wanted from Trini. I should have felt complete, but deep down inside, I was still missing something.

I was well-known in many boroughs of the city, in many projects, and on many blocks. I was well respected and liked, but I wasn't known as the pretty girl, like Renée, Michelle, Talia, and Qiana. I was known as Jamila, the "fly girl!" When I looked at myself in the mirror, I didn't feel pretty. So I used designer clothes, jewelry, and money to make up for what I felt I lacked in looks. I went extra hard to contend with my competition, which, for the most part, was the light-skinned girls. In my era, light-skinned girls were in. Traditionally, you had to be light skinned with long hair to catch the attention of the premier hustlers. I was a brown-skinned girl who defied the odds! I was determined to get my respect and have all the grand hustlers drooling after me. That was my goal, and I was sticking to the plan!

* * *

As time went by, my relationship with April dwindled away. We no longer had much in common. She was living the life of a good high school girl, and all I was interested in doing was picking money

Chapter Forty-Four

up from the block. Life for me became all about money and how I could get some more. No matter what I had, it was never enough. I had to always be grand and over the top. I became a certified label queen and a jewelry fiend. Whatever was new out, I had to have it first, even if I didn't really like it. It gave me a rush when people would say, "Oh my goodness, she got the new such-and-such on. I haven't even seen it in stores yet." I loved the attention that I got as a "fly girl," and I was determined to keep my status!

* * *

Qiana was big and pregnant. Her baby's father, Jason, a dude from Brooklyn, kept her locked up in the house for the most part, so she couldn't do much. I would visit her at her grandparents' house in Grant Projects and bring her all types of food that she craved. My loyalty to Qiana was very strong. I promised I was going to ride out her pregnancy with her, and I meant it!

* * *

After I hooked Michelle up with Lenroy, I became close again to the twins, Renée and Michelle. I was cooler with Renée than I was with Michelle. Michelle switched up after getting with Lenroy. The money went straight to her head! I would see Michelle a lot because she was always with Lenroy, and Lenroy hung out frequently with Trini. Michelle always seemed to be in competition with me. Everything she saw me with she tried to get Lenroy to buy her. After a while, that got played out to Lenroy. I also worked, so I had my own money. If I asked Trini for something and he said no, I would simply buy it for myself. Michelle didn't have that option, so she couldn't keep up with me. Deep down inside, I believe she resented me for that.

The twins went to Springfield High School in Queens, and they stayed beefing with some girls over their boyfriends. Qiana and I even went up to their school on several occasions to help them fight. The twins definitely weren't any punks; they both would fight, but they got tired of all the drama which caused them to eventually drop out of high school.

Lenroy would get on Michelle about not going to school. Then Trini would brag to Lenroy about how smart I was an he'd talk about my grades. In turn, Michelle would be put down by Lenroy, causing her to resent me even more. I stopped caring about how girls viewed me. I quickly learned shining on them was my best revenge! Every day I walked out of my house I stayed fresh! When others were at their worst, I managed to stay at my best. When they saw the sparkle in my eyes, my independence, my intellect, and my man, there was no denying that Jamila had the complete package! I worked hard to gain my reputation and maintain my sought after image!

Renée and I remained cool. She ended up hooking back up with T'chaka from Bernice Johnson's dance school. T'chaka made it big and became a part of a rap group called "Mobb Deep." He no longer went by the name of T'chaka; he was now Prodigy.

Prodigy and his rap partner Havoc would come by the twins' house, and we would all go out to chill and have fun. Prodigy was the first person I saw with a Lexus. He sported his car around town, and everybody loved it. He got the attention of the whole neighborhood when he came around. Renée would say, "I want to drive his car." I would say, "Girl, I want to drive my own Lexus," and I was serious! I was determined to find a way I could make my own ends and buy me a fly car too. I had everything else, but I didn't have a car. I had to find a way to step my game up!

* * *

School came back in session, and for me, it was business as usual. I was left behind to remain in the sophomore drama class, and Qiana no longer went to my school. She transferred to an alternative school for teen mothers so she could catch up with all her credits and graduate on time. Staying behind in the sophomore drama class brought me great humiliation, so I hardly ever went. Instead, so I could graduate early, I took as many classes as I could at Jamaica High School's night school program in Queens. I was anxious to finish school so I could move on with my life. I had dreams and aspirations of going away to college and making something of my life.

I stopped taking the regular subway to school and began to take the Long Island Railroad. Although it cost more money, the railroad had less stops and was faster than the subway train ride. Each morning I would bump into Jules, who was one of my talented guy friends that played almost every instrument you could think of. Jules was the leader of the Gospel choir at school and had just written the hit gospel song, "I Still Hear You Calling My Name," for Hezekiah Walker and the Love Fellowship Crusade Choir. Jules was a church boy, but had a little swagger with him, and he always had money. Jules played for his church choir and got paid in cash every week from his church, plus, he got residuals from his songs that topped the Gospel chart. Jules was a gentleman and always paid for my train ticket when he saw me at the railroad.

"What up, Milla?" Jules said as I waited at the ticket counter at the Long Island Railroad Station on Suptin Boulevard in Queens.

"Hey, Jules," I said as I sipped on my hot chocolate.

"Smile for me," he said.

"Why?" I asked.

"Just smile," Jules said as I gave him a stupid grin.

"Oh, I wanted to see if you had them stupid gold teeth in your mouth while you are drinking," Jules commented as we approached the ticket line and he paid for our tickets.

"Jamila, you are a nice-looking girl. Why do you wear all that stupid gaudy jewelry and them gold teeth? Yo, you killing me!" he said as we walked up the platform to catch the train.

"Everybody likes my jewelry except for you," I said back in a feisty tone.

"I'm saying, can you cut down? Just a little?" he asked.

"For what purpose?"

"So your true beauty can shine," Jules said in a charming voice, causing me to smile.

"So what, you been listening to that Apache song, 'Gangsta Chick,' and took it seriously?" he asked.

"Listen, Jules, I am what I am. You don't see me getting on you about your church boy pants and all that," I said as we both laughed and got on the train.

"Now, Jamila, there is something special about you, and I just feel like you going in the wrong direction. You don't even sing with the choir no more," he commented.

"Look, Jules, I ain't no hypocrite. I love God. I really do, but I know what I'm doing isn't right, so I am not about to be all phony, falling out in church when I know I'm going home to be with my boyfriend."

"Listen, it's not all about that. God knows your heart, and He sees everything you do. God is forgiving and merciful. I'm not saying you got to go to church every Sunday, but come once in a while. If not for anybody else, just come for me," Jules said as we rode on the train.

"We'll see," I said faking a deep breath as my heart felt convicted by his words.

Every time I saw Jules, I was reminded of all my sins. I was enjoying my new life-style, and I really didn't want to change. But, at the same time, I knew what I was doing was wrong. Jules became my voice of reason. He was that friend who was determined to keep tugging on me until I finally turned back.

"Milla, you know I got a big Gospel concert coming up at LaGuardia. If I'm your friend, just do me one favor. Please come," Jules said as he grabbed my hand. I took a deep breath and responded.

"Well, okay, if you insist."

"Milla, it's gonna be crazy! I got a lot of people coming out. I'm sure you're going to enjoy it," he said as he pulled two tickets out of his book bag and handed them to me.

"I'm sure it's gonna be good. So I'll come and support you. Boy, you have a way of always trying to bust up my little fun," I said to him as we both smiled and laughed.

Jules knew how much I really loved God. He also knew if he could get me back near the church and the choir, I would be convicted in my spirit to change my bad ways. Jules's voice had a grand effect on my life. He was indeed God's little messenger.

* * *

One day I was sitting in my math class and my cell phone rang. I quickly grabbed my bag and headed out of the class. Everyone knew not to call me while I was in school. I answered the phone with an attitude.

"Hello," I said.

"Yo, Jamila, I had the baby. It's a little boy. His name is Cory," Qiana zealously shouted.

"Oh my goodness. We have a little boy!" I ran through the hallway screaming with excitement.

I couldn't wait to see my new little godson Cory. I had to work that evening so I couldn't go to the hospital that day. The following day they let Qiana go home from the hospital, and I was one of her first visitors at home.

As I held little Cory in my arms, I began to cry. I couldn't believe Qiana had a son. Time seemed to shoot by so quickly. I also couldn't help but think about the baby I aborted. All types of mixed feelings came over me as I held little Cory in my arms. He was so cute and so precious. I bought everything I could find that was for babies. Qiana and Cory lacked nothing! Cory was draped in the cute Baby Gap outfit I bought him with the matching little booties. He was a couple days old, and he was styling.

I stayed at Qiana's house for hours just staring and looking at my new little guy!

* * *

It was a Saturday night, and the night of Jules's grand Gospel Choir concert. LaGuardia's gospel choir was well-known for their voices and extraordinary performances. When I arrived at the doors of our school, there was a line wrapped around the entire block! Everybody was trying to get through the doors to see this show.

I finally made it in and took my seat toward the front, using the tickets that Jules gave me. The curtain rose, and the show began. Jules was a master songwriter. He wrote and arranged all the songs in the performance, and they were spectacular! The vocal arrangements of the choir were absolutely incredible. They hit every note on key. The entire audience was up out of their seats clapping and acting as if it was a Sunday morning church service, including me. I was all good till the music slowed down and Timiney took the mic.

This girl's voice was so anointed! As she sang, chills went up my spine. I tried to shake it off, but her spirit, through her vocals, invoked the Holy Spirit to come into the room. When the Spirit hit, there was no place I could run. I had to throw my hands in the air and just begin to surrender. Jules smiled at me as he watched the tears flow down my eyes with my hands in the air. I guess at that moment he knew his plan worked!

Immediately after Timiney sang, Jules went into his shout music. The whole audience stood up in a frenzy! Both young and old were shouting all over the school auditorium, a sight that especially the white people had never before seen. You could tell by my white principal's face he wasn't sure how to act. He also stood to his feet and began to clap and follow the vibe of the audience.

Once again, I was convicted! I was caught up between the streets and the church. I loved both of them, but, sad to say, I didn't know which one I loved more. I was split between two worlds!

After the gospel concert, I started hanging out more with Jules, who refused to give up on me. He finally convinced me to start going to church again with him on Sundays, and I couldn't help but to, once again, recommit my life to the Lord!

* * *

I got back into the church, and life for Trini and me changed. I no longer felt comfortable having sex with him, so I avoided it. I was always too tired, on my period, or had something to do. Trini quickly noticed the difference and began to fight with me.

"So you messing with the church boy, and now I can't get none," Trini would say as he argued with me. The more I stayed in the church, the worse our relationship got. We almost never saw each other anymore. I was really trying my best to get right with God.

I began traveling the city watching Jules play at all types of Gospel events and concerts. I loved church, and Jules just seemed to always be affiliated with the best of them. When we were together we had good clean fun. It was an environment where I was comfortable and able to be myself. Jules always knew just how to bring the best out of me!

* * *

With the extra credits I gained at night school, I was a couple credits short of being able to get my high school diploma. Jules put me on to this private school in Queens named Christopher Robbins Academy, which had Saturday classes. I went to Saturday classes with him for twelve weeks and completed all the credits I needed to graduate, so I ended up graduating early, completing high school in two-and-a-half years instead of four. I felt proud of my accomplishment and couldn't wait to take over in the real world!

I combed the local newspaper looking for a better job now that I officially was done with school. After several interviews, I landed a job as a vault representative at EAB Bank in Rockefeller Center Plaza in Manhattan.

I worked part-time, letting wealthy Jewish jewelry storeowners in and out of their vaults, where they stored their valuables. I liked watching the behavioral patterns of my rich customers. I wanted to see how they functioned and how they were able to obtain all they had. We both had something in common, a well appreciated friend—money!

Working inside the bank around money all day helped increase my passion for it. The money I was accustomed to was kibbles and bits compared to the money that my wealthy customers had. I was determined to discover their secrets and obtain the same things they had!

* * *

After I graduated school, Talia found out she was pregnant. Like myself, she had an abortion, but she stayed with her boyfriend Rahmel. She got pregnant again, and this time, she decided to keep it. Her grandparents were devastated, but Talia clearly ran the show when it came to them.

Talia left LaGuardia and went to Ida B. Wells High School in Queens, which had an alternative program for teenage mothers.

Around that same time, the twin Renée got pregnant too! It seemed like all my friends either had children already or were pregnant! Trini wanted me to have a baby too, especially after he saw me with Cory so much. I liked the idea, but my aspirations for college and a good life were far greater. I had also seen how bad Qiana had it after Cory was born. She couldn't do the things she used to do. Instead, she was stuck in the house babysitting. I had too much to do to be stuck in the house with some baby. Instead, I would just pick up the babies when I wanted to have a good time with them, spend money on them, spoil them, and then drop them off! That became a normal routine for me!

* * *

Trini's and my relationship became distant, but we were still together, refusing to let each other go. One day after work I went to his house and discovered a girl's telephone number in his coat pocket when I reached in to get some money. I grabbed the number, folded it up, and put it in the back pocket of my pants.

I couldn't wait till I got home so I could call it. I shook frantically back and forth on the ride home in the cab. I didn't want to believe Trini was cheating on me, but deep down inside, I knew it was the truth. I went home and got up enough nerve to call the number.

"Hello, may I speak to Jennifer," I said as a girl's voice answered.

"Yes, this is Jennifer. Who is this?" the girl asked.

"My name is Jamila. Do you know a boy name Trini?"

"Yeah, I do. How did you get my number and why are you calling me?" the girl asked with an attitude.

"Listen, I don't mean to disturb you, and normally, I would never call you, but I'm Trini's girlfriend and—" I said as the girl interrupted me.

"His girl! He said he doesn't have a girlfriend," she shouted.

"Well, me and Trini have been together for a little over a year," I said.

"A year? Oh my God. I met Trini in the Village, and we've been going out for a little over three months, and Trini asked me to be his girl!" Jennifer yelled.

"Whoa," I said as I just shook my head in disbelief and disappointment.

It was the Lynette thing all over again! Instead of Craig, this time it was Trini. I was hurt, but I had promised myself I would never let another boy hurt me like Craig did.

The negative energy I internalized from Trini cheating on me just turned into an inner passion to excel. It made me coldhearted when it came to men. I made up in my mind I would use them for my purpose, and then drop them like hot cakes. In my eyes, it didn't pay to be loyal to men because they weren't going to be loyal at all. Cheating seemed to be in their nature. No matter how much they said they loved you, they always needed someone else to satisfy them.

I spoke to Trini, and he admitted to his relationship with Jennifer. First, he tried to flip on me for going in his pocket, but I quickly flipped back on him. Instead of being angry, I was smooth, calm, and collected.

The calmer I was, the angrier Trini seemed to get. I didn't care. I already had it made up in my mind that revenge was my only option. I had to do to Trini what I learned to do to everyone else who ever hurt me—shine on them! Me doing my thing would become my greatest weapon of revenge!

*G*oing to work one morning, I bumped into a cute boy standing at the bus stop. He began to flirt with me, and we started to talk. His name was Gary. He lived three streets down from me, and he was a freshman at the Borough of Manhattan Community College. Gary and I exchanged numbers, and we began to talk frequently.

Like all the other dudes I was accustomed to, Gary hustled. He didn't sell crack, but instead, Gary sold weed. I already knew the crack business inside and out. Gary came along and introduced me to the marijuana trade.

"Jamila, coke money is good money, but it comes with too much risk. If you get caught with a bunch of coke, you might go to jail for life, but if you get caught with weed, you'll get a slap on the wrist. Weed money is safe money," he would say as he schooled me.

Gary's parents were from Haiti. Although he was born in the U.S., he spoke Creole perfectly. Gary lived with his parents, and I would go to their house to visit him. Every time I came over, it seemed like his mother was beefing, but I didn't understand what she was saying because she spoke in Creole. After a few times of experiencing her vibe, I broke down and asked Gary what she was saying. He kept it real and told me his mother didn't want him dating an American girl. She felt like African American women were lazy and no good. After I found out the facts, I simply ignored his mother's ignorance. I was determined to show her he would be with me, whether she liked it or not! It was clear she didn't like it!

I began to spend a lot of time with Gary. That was my way of getting Trini out of my system. I was a sucker for knowledge, so I loved learning more about another way to make money. Gary showed me how to cop, break down, stretch, and bag up weed. I quickly caught on and began helping him with his work. My eagerness impressed Gary. He wasn't used to girls who wanted to be involved in his business. Not only did I want to be involved, I actually wanted to take over. I was sure I could school Gary on more ways he could make more money, just like I did for Trini. Over time, I did!

Chapter Forty-Five

Trini had taught me all the spots to cop coke from, and I had a lot of contacts and connections from Trini. I gave Gary some of Trini's connects, and Gary took them to the top!

Just like me, Gary liked to shop too. One day we went to Manhattan on the train to go shopping. We bought a bunch of clothes, and I had several shopping bags on me. On the way back home, we bumped into Trini on the train. It was like déjà vu all over! Trini was sick to his stomach. He couldn't believe I decided to move on so quickly. It had only been a couple of months since we had broken up. When Trini saw me, I was happy with Gary, as if Trini and I never existed.

Just like Craig did, Trini began to call me uncontrollably after he spotted me with Gary.

"Jamila, I love you. I miss you, baby!" Trini would plead on the phone. I quickly recognized the pattern.

Men didn't really take women seriously until they saw someone else wanted them! *Okay, so I guess to win this game I'm always gonna have to keep different men wanting me*, I thought to myself. To me, it became all a big game called the chase. If I could keep them chasing, then I would always end up on top! I refused to let my feelings or emotions get me caught up into anyone. Love wasn't real. It was only an illusion! I had to learn to win the chase. Always cut them off before they cut you off. When you see the signs coming, break out! Leave him before he leaves you! Say good-bye and never give an explanation why. When you do that, they will continue to chase you! If I could keep them chasing, then I would always win! I wasn't playing to lose anymore. This go-around, I was playing to win!

* * *

Overnight I became a female mack. I accepted calls from everyone, including Trini and Craig. I saw them when I wanted and controlled the relationship by keeping it on my terms only. When I felt like Trini, it was Trini! When I felt like Craig, it was Craig! When I didn't want to be bothered, it was no one!

As I began to play the game my way, everyone seemed to be in love with me. I entertained them all and committed to no one, making me a hot commodity!

Playing the game was easy with Gary because he refused to make a commitment. He said I was his "special friend," and he refused to make me his girl. Not having Gary on my terms intrigued me more. I was determined to break him down and get him the way I wanted him. Gary became a challenge, so he was able to stick around for a while. Craig and Trini became a part of my rotation. I played them both just like a violin. I kept both of them spending their money on me and chasing behind me. They both were clearly dealing with other females, but I made sure Jamila always stayed on their minds!

* * *

Growing up, I could pretty much convince my dad to do anything for me that he believed would help me. I left my job in Manhattan as a vault representative for a job closer to my home in Queens. When I got the job as a bank teller at Ridgewood Savings Bank, I decided I needed a car. I was tired of the bus, the train, and cabs. I wanted my own whip, and the only way I knew how to get it was to convince my dad to buy me one.

I didn't even have my permit. First, I had to convince my dad to teach me how to drive. That part was easy, but his driving instructions were not!

I studied the New York driving instruction manual for a whole week. Then I went to Motor Vehicles, and I aced the test! I finally had my driver's permit, and now I was ready for my dad to teach me how to drive!

It was my first day behind the wheel. I was nervous but excited. I got behind the wheel of my father's Ford Taurus, and he got in the passenger seat.

"Okay, Jamie, the first thing you do when you get in the car is put your seat belt on, check your mirrors, turn on the ignition, and then you can put the car into drive," he instructed.

"Okay, Dad. My seat belt is on. I've checked my mirrors. Let me turn on the ignition and we're ready to go," I said in an excited tone repeating his directions. I started to drive, but I got scared so I pressed the brakes hard, and we stopped short.

"Jamie! Don't press the brakes hard like that!" Dad scolded.

"Oh, I'm sorry," I said as I continued to follow his directions as best as I could.

"No, no, Jamie! I said turn the wheel like this," he shouted again. He got me so nervous I could hardly function.

"What are you, an idiot? You can't follow simple instructions?" he yelled as I almost backed into the neighbor's car.

"Okay, Dad. I'm not ready for this. We'll do it again another time," I said as I hopped out of the driver's seat so he could drive us back home. I didn't want to take any more lessons from him.

I was so discouraged! I didn't think I would ever learn how to drive. I made so many mistakes. For goodness' sake, I almost crashed! I lay down on my bed depressed, thinking my hopes of getting a car were over. As I moped, my mother came into my bedroom.

"Jamie, how was your lesson?" she asked.

"It was terrible! Dad made me so nervous. He kept yelling at every little thing I did," I said angrily, and my mother laughed.

"Why are you laughing? This is far from funny," I said.

"No, I'm not laughing at you, Jamie. I'm laughing at your father. He did the same exact thing to me when he tried to teach me how to drive. I had to go to driver's school so I could learn, and guess what?"

"What?" I replied.

"If you want your driver's license, you'll have to go to driver's school too. Let me get the phone book and find a good school in our neighborhood," Mama said as she hugged me, and I quickly perked up.

The driving school turned out to be a great suggestion. I was ready for my road test after just five lessons with the driving instructor. I couldn't believe I finally knew how to drive!

I took the road test and passed it on my first try. I was sixteen years old, and I had my driver's license! The only thing I was missing was my car. Buying a hot car became my obsession. I couldn't sleep until I had accomplished my mission!

* * *

My goal in life was always to become an adult so that I could be independent and on my own! I raced through life doing everything at an early age to achieve this goal.

Obsessed with shopping, I was intrigued with the plastic credit cards people used to purchase their items. I wanted in on their purchasing power, so I figured out a way to get a credit card. I lied on my credit card application about my age so I started developing credit at fifteen years old. I spent so much money shopping and I kept using the cards and paying them off, that by the time I was sixteen-and-a-half, I had A-1 credit, and over ten established credit accounts.

When it was time for me to get my car, I knew my good credit would help me with my purchase. I visited every new car dealership I could find, browsing the showroom floors looking for a brand-new car. My dad said I was a new driver who was bound to have a couple of accidents and that a new car would be a waste of money. I was totally upset with his assumptions, but I knew if I wanted a car I would have to follow his lead.

I went to the used car lots on Hillside Avenue in Queens and found a beautiful burgundy red Audi 80. The car was only a couple of years old, and it looked better than most of the brand-new cars I saw at the dealership. I put a deposit on the car and ran home to get my dad.

"Daddy, Daddy, I found my car," I said zealously.

"I told you I'm not helping you get no brand-new car, Jamie," he replied.

"No, Daddy, it's used, but it's beautiful. Please come with me to see it," I begged.

My dad got dressed and took me to the used car lot, and surprisingly, he liked the Audi too! It took about a week to get the financing, which we obtained through the bank I worked at, and I got my employee financing discount rate. My dad and I got the check, and we went together to pick up my new car!

I was so excited that my palms were sweaty. I got behind the wheel and drove off. Before I could hit the light, I had a carload of boys honking their horn at me. "Nice ride!" they yelled as I rode past them.

I knew at that moment I had made the right decision. My car was hot, and I knew it! It brought me so much attention and recognition that it was incredible!

My girlfriends and I hit up every hood we could think of and drive to. I met so many new people who were fond of me and my ride! Then I became Jamila, the fly chick with the red Audi!

On any given day I would be driving through Jamaica Avenue in Queens, Flatbush Avenue in Brooklyn, 125th Street in Harlem, or Fordham Road in the Bronx, with my sunglasses on and my car seat leaning to the back. My stereo would be booming Mary J. Blige's "Real Love" cassette or SWV's "Right Here" tape on repeat. I was sixteen years old, doing my thing, and I wanted everybody to know it!

I began to collect telephone numbers for fun! I would compete with myself on how many guys' numbers I would get in a day with no effort. Driving actually stepped up my access to the premier hustlers. I would drive down the street and Lexuses, BMWs, and Benzes would pull up next to me.

"Yo, Shorty Audi, what's good. Can I get your number?" was a common phrase I heard. I loved every bit of my newfound attention.

School was still in session for my peers, so I would often go up to LaGuardia and pick up Shalon from school. Heads would turn as I bumped my car system as loud as I could. "Is that Jamila? Dag, she got an Audi now?" LaGuardia students would say.

"No, that's got to be her man's car," others would comment.

I didn't care what they said as long as all eyes were on me, and they definitely were!

I loved cruising through 40 Projects in South Jamaica Queens. All of Craig's boys would be on the block and watch me intensely as I pulled up.

"Damn, your old shorty is fly as hell. Now she got an Audi. Oh, you messed up, Cee," Craig's friends would say.

I finally felt vindicated. Eat your heart out, baby! Jamila is on the scene, and this young chick is ready to take over!

* * *

June came around, and it was time for graduation. I already had my diploma, but my mother insisted that I participate in the ceremony.

Talia had a baby boy named Nyquan, a few months premature. She completed her classes at Ida B. Wells and also was allowed to graduate with our graduating class.

I could care less about the ceremony, but I participated for my mother. I stood side by side next to Talia in our white gowns at Lincoln Center's Avery Fisher Hall, which brought back memories of my Bernice Johnson Dance recital days. Talia went onstage right behind me, and we got our diplomas. It was official. We finally made it! We played hard, but it was clear we worked hard too!

Chapter Forty-Six

I t was the summer of '94, and my parents decided to go on vacation to Kinston, North Carolina. I hadn't been to Kinston in years, so I decided I would drive down behind them. I had never driven out of state, so I wanted to gain the experience.

I followed behind my parents the whole way, and my brother drove in the car with me. We took turns driving until we reached our destination: Kinston, North Carolina.

It was early evening when we arrived in town. I couldn't wait to see my grandmother who I hadn't seen since Aunt Carolyn's funeral. I ran to the door just like I did when I was a little girl, and my grandmother opened the door with her same excited expression. "Hey, baby!" my grandmother said as she hugged me tightly.

"Hi, Grandma. Come see my new car," I said as I escorted her out of the house.

"Oh, baby, this is nice," my grandmother said, climbing behind the wheel and checking out my vehicle. "Grandma might have to borrow this nice thing here," she said as she checked out all the gadgets on the car.

As my grandmother was checking out my car, Donnell pulled up with Billy, Dino's brother.

"Oh my goodness. My favorite boy cousin," I shouted as I ran up to Donnell and hugged him. I was so happy to see him!

"Hey, little cuz," Donnell greeted me as he hugged me back.

"Donnell, come see Jamie's new car," my grandmother shouted.

"Oh, shoute. Billy, look! Jamie's got a brand-new Audi," Donnell said to Billy who got out of the driver's seat of the car. They all swarmed my vehicle, pushing the buttons and checking out my hi-tech car.

"Yo, you know my brother Dino is home," Billy said to me.

"Oh, for real?" I replied.

"Yeah, he just came home from prison a couple of months ago. You know he always asks about you," Billy said.

"Oh, man, I got to check him out," I replied.

"Yeah, he is going to love to see you," Billy said.

The boys helped me get my luggage out of the trunk and brought my bags into the house.

I chilled with my grandmother for a little while, catching up on things and reminiscing about old times.

"Jamie, take me to the store real quick," my cousin Donnell asked, and we left the house and rolled to the other side of town.

We approached the Front, which was the spot Donnell hustled at. Nothing had changed. It looked exactly the same as it did when I was a little girl. Before we arrived, word had already spread that I was in town. Dino came out of nowhere, rolling up on a dirt bike to the driver's window of my car.

"Ah, yo, what's up?" Dino said.

"Hey, Dino, I haven't seen you in so long!" I said joyfully. Dino was nice and buffed. His smooth chocolate skin glowed, and the waves on his Caesar-cut spinned. Dino still looked good!

"Get out of the car," Dino said as he opened my door and grabbed me, pulling me into his arms as he hugged me.

"Girl, where you been? I always ask Fishkell and Solo about you."

"Well, I ask about you too. I didn't find out until way later that you were locked up."

"Yeah, I was down for like four years," Dino said.

"I know. Are you okay?" I asked.

"Yeah, I'm fine now that I have my wife here," he said as I smiled from ear-to-ear. It was clear he hadn't changed.

"So what's going on with you?" I said as I checked out Dino's dingy outfit.

"Nothing much. I'm just hustling hard trying to make some money. There's a bunch of young kids out here, so money ain't like it used to be."

I ended up spending most of my vacation chilling with Dino. In a week's time we became the talk of the small town. I went out to the club with him, and the whole little town began to gossip. The attention I received in New York was nothing compared to the attention I got in Kinston. It was like I was a celebrity or a princess, and Dino, freshly home from jail, was the prince. The people seemed thirsty to watch us perform, so I decided to give them what they wanted: a show!

Dino knew how to hustle, but he didn't have anybody to put him on. I had access to drugs, but I didn't know how to hustle, so together, we made a perfect match. I convinced him to get out of the coke business and go into the marijuana business instead. I promised to supply the weed if he would help to distribute it. We would become 50/50 partners, and he and I both would get on our feet. Dino agreed, and I went back to New York to set my plan in action.

When I came back to New York I gave my job at the bank a two-week notice, and I used my last two paychecks to cop a pound of weed from Gary. Gary got me the weed, and I convinced Shalon to ride with me back down to Kinston.

I was nervous, transporting the strong-smelling marijuana to Kinston, but the thought of the big money I would make kept me driving. Shalon didn't know how to drive, so I had to make the eight-hour drive on my own. It was difficult at first, but I made it!

I arrived in Kinston and went straight to Dino's mother's trailer home, where I stayed until the pound of marijuana was done. I tried to be discreet because I didn't want my family to know I was in town. My mother and father would go crazy!

Dino and I broke down the good weed which literally was gone in a couple of days! We were on to something. Everybody in Kinston had access to coke, but very few people had weed, and the ones who did have it, had poor quality weed. Everybody smoked weed, so it was in popular demand. We quickly flipped the weed which I transported into the small Southern town. And, in no time, I went from copping one pound of weed to copping five pounds at a time.

Dino's wish of coming to New York finally came true. He began to ride up with me to cop. I took him to 125th Street in Harlem, and we went on a shopping spree. I helped him pick out his clothes, and he got fresh to death! I had Dino looking like a New York boy. He would have fooled you . . . until he opened his mouth and spoke in his thick country accent. I met my match. I finally had a real partner in the game. I was officially a drug dealer!

My mom, my dad, my brother Kee and me (at 16
years old) at my grandmother's house.

*D*ino and I quickly became envied by many in the small town of Kinston. We were making thousands of dollars every couple of days, and word quickly spread about what we were doing. I could no longer hide the fact that I was in town. My whole family started to talk about me and Dino being together, and me selling drugs. We began to make so much money that my brother Kee and my cousin Donnell wanted in on the action. I started copping more weight and hitting them off with packages on consignment.

After a few months, I had several people working for me. I found it faster to flip my money with more people moving my product. I created incentives for my workers. I made them feel appreciated and loved as they worked for me. I gave each of them quotas, and as we hit our quotas, I took all my workers on shopping sprees at the mall.

I quickly had more money than I knew what to do with. I began to help all my poor family members. I bought televisions, furniture, paid rents, and bought food for all my aunts, cousins, and even my grandmother.

My grandmother didn't like what I was doing, but as I kept giving her money, her eyes turned away from my actions.

Dino's entire family loved me. I began to take good care of his mother and his grandmother, who were struggling and very poor. I practically moved in with them so I had to make sure they were okay. Nobody around me did without. As I got on, I made sure everybody was on around me. It felt good to finally have my own money!

Life with Dino was cool, but we often fought. Dino felt like I was bougie, and he accused me of looking down on him. The truth is, I wanted Dino to step his game up and be a boss. With my access to the product, we had the potential to shut the whole town down.

I was thirsty and hungry to get money. Dino was laid-back and reserved. After we made a certain amount of money, he would slack off and want to rest. For me, there was no time to rest. We had to get this money while it lasted. I showed Dino all the ropes Trini and Gary showed me, and I expected him to implement them! Things didn't work out quite the way I expected. Dino would smoke up the weed and mess up our money, which greatly disappointed me. I refused to smoke weed, because I knew if I got hooked on it, it would cut into my profits. Money meant more to me than getting high, but that wasn't the case with Dino. Dino was constantly going in our stash, taking out ounces of weed to smoke with his friends. It got so bad that I had to move the stash!

Dino didn't like my control. He knew if I left, the product left too. He couldn't control me like he wanted to, so he began to try to verbally abuse me to break me down! I wasn't no weak chick, so we would argue, and sometimes it even got physical.

Word got back to my grandmother about Dino's disrespect toward me, and she had a fit. One day I went to her house to drop her some money, and she had a long conversation with me.

My grandmother stood over the stove, cooking my favorite dish, fried chicken. Before she spoke, she cleared her throat. "Baby, I don't know what you're doing, but Grandma don't like it. Jamie, you always been such a good child. Now it's like you done gone crazy. That Jones boy, baby, he ain't no good. He ain't smack. His Pappy won't smack, and his Pappy's Pappy won't smack neither. I know them boys, their daddy, and their whole family. They are cut from a different cloth than us Davises. I don't want you ruining your life with that ugly black boy. Jamie, you are so pretty and so intelligent. You deserve so much better for yourself."

I listened to my grandmother's words, and I knew what she said was true, but I had fallen in love with Dino, and it was too hard to let him go. My grandmother saw that her talk didn't help, so she had no choice but to call my parents, and they paid me a surprise visit in Kinston.

Early one morning, I heard a knock on Dino's trailer home door. It was Donnell.

"Yo, your parents are in town, and they want me to bring you to the house now," Donnell said.

"Oh, man. Okay. I'll be over there later," I said in my morning voice.

"No, get dressed. You're coming now!" Donnell demanded as he barged his way into the house and waited for me to comply.

I jumped in the shower, put on my clothes, and reluctantly followed Donnell to the house in my car. I was nervous, but I was grown now, or so I thought. *What can they possibly do to me?* I thought to myself.

My mother stood with her arms crossed and her face screwed up as I walked through my grandmother's door.

"Jamie, what the hell is wrong with you? Have you lost your rabbit-behind mind? You down here selling drugs with that black, crusty, ugly boy!" my mother scolded in a high voice.

"Jamila, I'm very disappointed in you. You were doing so good . . . and now this," my father interjected. I knew when my father called me Jamila instead of Jamie, I was in deep trouble!

My parents lectured me for over an hour! I denied most of their allegations, and they saw they weren't really getting anywhere.

"Okay, listen, we see you like North Carolina. Do me a favor. Please go to college! There is a good college called Saint Augustine's in Raleigh. It's a really prominent black historical school. Baby, will you please check it out for me, please," my mother begged, and I agreed.

Since it was clear that I wasn't going to leave North Carolina, the compromise was that I would go to college. My mother hated Dino. She felt as if he was the one causing me to act out as I did. Every chance she got, she called him every name she could think of, even to his face. All this did was make Dino criticize me even more.

"You and your uppity mother, y'all think y'all all that. Y'all ain't better than nobody else," Dino would say when he was mad at me.

The more Dino and I fought, the more I fell in love with him. In my strange mind, I felt as though him fighting me was an expression of his love. We would fight hard, and then make up like nothing ever happened. It was an ongoing routine that seemed like it would never stop. No matter what anyone said about Dino, it didn't faze me. To me, Dino was my lover, my friend, and my partner! Nothing and no one could separate us, but they surely tried!

*　*　*

I went to New York to cop, and I got a call on my cell phone that Dino got locked up. He was in a house, with some boys, that got raided raided, and there was a bunch of drugs in the house.

I had just used all of our money to re-up on product. I raced back down to Kinston to try to get my boyfriend out of jail. I had very little money and a bunch of product, so I quickly broke down the packages of weed to raise enough money to bail Dino out. My workers weren't moving fast enough, so I decided to hit the blocks myself. I stayed up all night on the street, raising the money for Dino's bail.

Dino was only locked up a couple of days, but I felt like it was a lifetime. I was so used to him lying next to me in the bed, and I wanted him home desperately. My desperation kept me driven.

I did what I had to do to raise the money for Dino's high bail. The magistrate set his bail so high, because Dino had just come home from prison. I went to the bail bonds, with all the money I raised, along with Dino's mother who had to sign the bond.

I stood and waited patiently all evening for Dino to come out of the jail doors. He finally walked out of the jail and hugged me tightly. He told me how much he loved and appreciated me. His words meant everything to me! I felt so good about what I had done.

Dino didn't waste any time hitting the streets. I was tired from staying up hustling with no sleep, so I wanted to go to the house and rest. Dino wanted to go to the club. I agreed because I was so exhausted anyway. I went back to the house, and Dino celebrated his coming home from jail.

All the girls in Kinston were on Dino, especially after I spruced up his appearance. I was never worried or intimidated 'cause I knew he wasn't leaving his prize princess, especially for no local girls, so I never tracked Dino's whereabouts or cared about him spending time in the club.

It was about 3 o'clock in the morning, and I jumped out of my sleep. I rolled over and notice Dino wasn't there! The clubs in Kinston closed at 2 o'clock, and he promised he was coming straight home. I waited up about thirty minutes and he still didn't show. I began to worry. *What if he got locked up again?* I thought to myself as I began to put on my clothes.

I got dressed, left the house, and searched for Dino. The club parking lot had cleared out, and no one was outside. I rode past the Front and bumped into Dino's friend Mike.

"Yo, Mike, have you seen Dino?" I asked as he approached the car.

"Yo, got some weed on you?" Mike asked.

"Boy, you talking about weed and I'm worried about Dino," I shouted.

"Look, if you give me a bag of weed, I'll take you to where he is," Mike said as we made a deal, and I reached in my bag and gave Mike a dime bag of weed.

"Look, Jamie, you a good girl. Dino ain't good for you. You better never tell him it was me that took you here," Mike said as my heart pounded. I had no idea where I was getting ready to go.

Mike directed me to drive to a small project building in the back of the town. We pulled up, and Mike got out and knocked on the door. I pulled the car up so Dino couldn't see me and hid on the side of the building.

To my surprise, Dino came to the door in his boxer shorts. He was spending the night with some ugly, nasty-looking, fat girl he had been messing with for years!

As I saw Dino come to the door, I jumped out from behind the building. "Oh, *this* is how you repay me! I hustle all day and night to get you out of jail, and you at some chick's house," I hollered as Dino's jet-black face seemed to turn red.

"Oh, yo, Jamie. It's not what you think. I, um, I . . ." Dino shouted.

"There's nothing you can say to me. You're caught red-handed. I'm out. It's over!" I yelled, and I broke down and cried. I was so hurt. I couldn't believe my eyes!

Dino ran back in the house, put his pants on, and started running after me. "Jamie, Jamie," he shouted.

"Yo, it's over! Kick rocks," I rebutted.

"Oh, so you think it's gonna end like that? I'll kill you first," Dino said as he pulled out his gun. I thought he was playing, but I quickly found out just how serious he was. As I turned my back on him, I heard shots fire behind me, and I began to run.

I was taken away because I never expected for Dino to try to kill me. What the hell had I gotten myself into? I left my car and ran on foot back to Dino's mother's house. By the time I got to the house, I was out of breath. I quickly closed the door behind me and sighed in relief. I thought it was over.

Wrong!

Moments later, Dino came in the house behind me and began to beat me like never before. He beat me so bad that I saw stars flying around my head.

"You ain't going nowhere. You are staying right here with me!" Dino said as he stripped me of my car keys and all my money.

Dino tortured me and fought me for hours until Billy, his brother, showed up.

"Billy, Billy," I screamed as Billy came in the room.

"Yo, what are you doing to her?" Billy shouted as he grabbed Dino off of me. I told Billy the story and broke loose from Dino and ran around the corner to where my brother Kee hustled at.

Fortunately, Kee was on the porch, and I ran up to him and threw myself in his arms.

"Dino beat me, Kee. He cheated on me. I caught him, and he beat me!" I cried in Kee's arms. As we were talking Dino came around the corner looking for me.

"Oh, so you want to hit my sister?" Kee yelled as he jumped off the porch and charged at Dino.

"Hit *me*, you punk!" Kee shouted as he and Dino began to fistfight in the street.

They fought like professional fighters. Both of them could box real good, but Dino had more skills than Kee. The fight got so intense that I had to jump in the middle of it.

Dino grabbed me, and Billy came from around the corner.

"Ah, yo, Kee, I know that's your sister, but that's my brother's wife. He shouldn't hit on her, but let them work that out," Billy suggested.

"Yo, Kee, I love your sister. I didn't mean to hit her. It's just so much going on," Dino said as he broke down and cried, sitting on the curb. Dino's tears to me meant he really loved me. *Maybe he is sorry for real,* I thought.

"Dino, don't cry," I said as I sat next to him.

"I love you, Jamie. I didn't mean to hurt you. I love you so much. I just never want to lose you. You mean everything to me," Dino said, and I hugged him, and we went back to his mother's house.

Dino and I made up, and Kee didn't speak to me for like two weeks. It was clear my life had gotten out of control!

As I stared at my black eyes and my bruises in the mirror I knew I had to find a way to escape. Saint Augustine's University seemed like my only way out!

I called my mother, and she sent me the application and brochure. I wanted something better for myself, so I decided to attend college and try to get my life back on track.

*I*t was a hot summer day in August of 1994. My mother flew into Kinston to take me down to Saint Augustine's University to complete my enrollment in school. She was more excited than I was.

"Oh, this is the day I waited my whole life to see! My baby is going to college," my mother said proudly as we traveled on Highway 70, headed to Raleigh, North Carolina.

After several attempts, I finally got the nerve up to break off my relationship with Dino. Rumor had it, the girl that Dino was cheating on me with was pregnant with his baby. He said it wasn't his, but I knew better! That was the final nail in the coffin. I finally came to the realization that I didn't want to spend my entire life broke, busted, and disgusted, playing games with Dino, who constantly messed up our money. Therefore, I decided to pack all my things into my Audi, and one night I just left.

Dino's brother, Billy, lived in Raleigh with his girlfriend Wanda, who was also from Kinston and did hair. I told Billy I was going to go to Saint Augustine's, and he introduced me to his girl Wanda. I drove down to Raleigh a few times to check it out before I signed up for school, and Raleigh was all right. It was only an hour and twenty minutes from Kinston, but it was like night and day compared to Kinston.

Raleigh was a big city and had a lot of action going on. Billy's girlfriend, Wanda, was one of the top hairstylists in Raleigh. Her shop stayed packed with the town's "who's who." I enjoyed hanging out with her and her friends, so I looked forward to my experience away at school.

My mother and I arrived in Raleigh early in the morning. We stood together in the long line wrapped around the registrar's office to pay my tuition and get my program schedule. My mother was proud to cut the check to pay my tuition. She took my achievement of going to college seriously, just as if it was her very own.

"Jamie, you gonna love this school. I went to North Carolina Central in Durham. We always competed with Saint Augustine's. They have tons of activities here, Jamie, and maybe you'll become a Delta Sigma Theta, just like I did!" my mother said in an excited voice as I checked out the environment.

"Mom, I don't want to stay on campus. I want my own apartment," I said as we stood in the crowded line in the Student Union building.

"Now, look, Jamie, we already went through this. You just turned seventeen years old. I'm not comfortable getting you no apartment yet. Let's get through this semester, and if you do good, we'll see about an apartment," she replied.

"Well, okay, but I ain't really feeling these girls. I don't want no corny roommate," I pouted.

"Let me handle this, Jamie," my mother said as she took charge in the enrollment office.

"Ma'am, is there any way I can pay extra so my daughter has a room by herself, please?" she addressed the clerk.

"Well, a . . . um, let me see. I'll be right back," the lady said as she went to check with her supervisor.

My mother was determined to keep me happy away at school and out of the streets. She was willing to go to any level to ensure my success.

I was able to get my own room in Baker Hall, which was an all-female high-rise dormitory on campus. Most of the girls who went to my school were from the South. Everybody seemed so country. I wasn't sure what my experience would turn out to be, but I knew I had to make the best of it.

My mother helped me unload all my things into my dorm room. We rode together to the local Walmart, and my mother bought me everything she possibly thought I might need. I got a brand-new twenty-inch television, a radio, a microwave, a small refrigerator, and all types of utensils and trinkets. My mother stayed and helped me decorate my room.

"See, Jamie, it's not that bad," Mama said as she set everything up.

"Yeah, Mom, I guess you're right," I said as I felt more at home in my newly decorated room.

I dropped my mother at the airport and went back to my dorm room to experience my new life at Saint Augustine's. I really wasn't a social butterfly, but I didn't have to be. The Southerners were all naturally friendly. They had great Southern hospitality. The girls would speak every time they saw me. They weren't like New Yorkers who would pretend they didn't see you. If I saw those girls five times a day, they would speak five times a day. Sometimes it was cool, but sometimes I didn't feel like speaking. In that case, I would have to try to tip by so that they wouldn't notice me.

My Audi quickly gained me attention on campus. I had one of the flyest cars out of all the students in the school. I would bump my music and ride by slow, gaining the stares and admiration of my peers.

"Oh, look at her tags. She's from New York," they would say. Being from New York came with a great advantage in the South. Everyone seemed to be fascinated with New Yorkers.

"Can you talk for me?" "Say 'New York.'" "I love to hear New Yorkers talk," were some the comments I would get. Everyone wanted to hang out with the New Yorkers.

All the college kids from New York stuck together. They immediately introduced themselves, and we began to chill together. Shalon's long-term boyfriend Gordy went to Saint Augustine's too. He introduced me to all the people from our area, and all his friends. Gordy was a star basketball player, who was well-known at Saint Augustine's. I constantly had to chase girls away from him, looking out for my friend, Shalon.

After about my first week or so, I started to enjoy myself. I would spend hours in the Student Union building, hanging out, playing games, and watching television with my friends from New York. When we got tired of just hanging around, we would get in the car and cruise through Raleigh to pass time.

The first place in the town I had to learn how to get to was the mall. I knew once I found out how to get to the mall, I could escape whenever I wanted and have a good time. Raleigh had two big malls. They weren't like the malls in New York, but they were okay. My favorite one was the Crab Tree Mall.

Mostly all the "cool kids" at Saint Augustine's belonged to a sorority. They had step shows all the time right on the school grounds. I watched the girls step, and I wanted in! I wanted to become a Delta Sigma Theta, just like my mother. I loved their red and white colors. I watched the girls for a while, waiting for my opportunity to try to get in their exclusive clique, but I couldn't get over the disrespectful way they treated the girls on the line who joined. My ego wouldn't allow me to be dogged out by a chick, so I refrained from joining them.

I purposely scheduled all my classes in the evening. I wanted to chill and enjoy myself, so I didn't want to be a part of the morning college rush. I enjoyed going to school at night. It was laid-back and reserved.

My classes were cool. I loved my Humanities professor the most. History was my thing. It was so intriguing for me to study all that happened in the past. Just like high school, I excelled in all my classes, effortlessly. For the most part, they were enjoyable, so I listened to what the professors said, took notes, studied, and aced the tests.

Like any other school dorm, there was always drama in our dorm. From the door, I had to set the record straight and let them know just who they were dealing with!

* * *

I learned quickly if a girl thinks she can try you, she will! I rocked my baggy designer clothes and all my jewelry. I walked with a New York swagger and stayed with an ice grill on my face. I never played chicks too close. I didn't trust them!

My next-door neighbor in my dorm was a girl named Monique. She was a pretty, short, brown-skinned girl with long hair from Philly. We got cool with each other and hung out a lot. We also had another really good friend who used to chill with us. Her name was Enith. She was a light-skinned girl with hazel eyes from Charlotte, North Carolina. Enith had a brand-new Acura Integra. Her parents were successful executives in Charlotte, and the girls in my dorm were extremely jealous of her.

One day when I was on my way out of the building I saw Enith in the hallway slumped down, crying. "Enith, what's the matter?" I questioned.

"Nothing, Jamila. I'm just tired. I want to quit school," she said in a tearful voice.

"Quit school? Yo, you bugging. What happened?"

Enith continued crying. "These girls, Jamila. Sheila said she's gonna beat me up! They just keep on messing with me for no reason. The girl asked me to take her to Bojangles, and I said no. I take her all the time, and I just didn't feel like it that day. Now they all saying nasty things to me when I pass them in the hall. I tried to ignore them. Then, Sheila jumped all in my face in front of everyone."

"When did this happen?" I asked.

"Just a few minutes ago."

"Oh, okay. I got this. Come with me." I curled my finger, beckoning Enith to follow me onto the elevator, and we went up to the sixth floor, where Enith and the girls lived.

When we arrived on the sixth floor, the hallway was packed with girls. They looked surprised to see that Enith wasn't by herself.

"Ah, yo, what's good? I don't know what y'all think this is, but it ain't going down like this! Whoever got a problem with Enith got a problem with me, and we can certainly do this whichever way y'all want," I said at the top of my voice in the hallway as the frightened girls began to scatter.

Enith, who was standing nervously behind me, then got the courage to step beside me. She placed her hand on her hip with confidence as the girl, Sheila, dropped her head and went into her dorm room. The hallway was totally clear!

"Come on, Enith, let's finish this up," I said as we went down the elevator to the first floor, and I grabbed the dorm microphone and pressed the button to reach all the floors.

"Listen up, this is a public announcement. Any of y'all chicks who have a problem with Enith come to the lobby now. I want to see who's really gangsta around here. For the record, it's Jamila aka Shorty Rock New York. Whoever—and I repeat *whoever*—wants it can get it! Meet me in the lobby now!" My message blasted loudly over the PA system and was heard throughout the entire dorm.

Nobody came out, and after that day, Enith never had a problem again! The girls became very friendly with Enith, and when I came around, everybody dropped their heads. I became to them that crazy chick from New York. I didn't care what they thought. Enith was my friend, and I took all my friendships seriously. Nothing was popping off on my shift!

* * *

The basketball season was approaching, and they announced tryouts for the cheerleading squad. My friend Monique convinced me to try out with her.

All the cheerleaders were considered the popular "fly chicks" in the school. I felt like cheerleading was a good way to get recognized, and I could have fun at the same time.

Tryouts were scheduled for 3 o'clock in the dance center. I couldn't wait to show off my dance skills to the squad. These country girls had no idea what they were in for. I intended to show them what this New York chick was all about!

I got to the tryout practice early to warm up and prepare for the action! I had my leotard outfit and tights on. It felt good to be back on the dance scene.

All kinds of different classes of girls came into the room. The room quickly got crowded with freshmen to seniors, who wanted to be cheerleaders. The cheerleading squad had three empty spots from three seniors who graduated the year before.

I sat back and observed all the ambitious girls doing their dance and cheer moves in front of the mirror in the practice studio. I was warmed up and ready to go! *This should be easy,* I said to myself as the cheerleading captain came into the room. Her name was Trina. She was a short, slim, brown-skinned girl from South Carolina. She had a strong country accent and a sassy swagger.

"All right, girls," Trina said, "let's begin. We have three spots on the cheerleading squad to fill. My name is Trina, and I'm the team captain. Before we get started, I want to make this clear. I only want serious, reliable girls on my team. Cheerleading is not just about looking cute and being cool. We take our job serious, and we practice hard. If you are not a hard worker, you might as well leave now," Trina said in her deep country voice as she took her towel from around her neck and dropped her bag.

"Okay, I'm gonna teach you all a routine, and I need to see how fast you catch on," she said. She popped in a cassette and started to dance.

Trina wasn't doing any easy steps like I expected. They were sort of hard and intricate, even for me. I intensely studied her feet, trying to get the moves down packed. It startled me how awkward I felt dancing. I guess I hadn't danced professionally in years, and I was lacking in my skill set.

"Oh, no, Miss Honey. You look stiff as a board," Trina said as she called me out.

I was so embarrassed! I took a deep breath and regrouped, determined to catch on to the steps.

Trina walked around the room insulting all the girls. She was worse than Bernice Johnson at the dance studio back home! She had all of us under pressure, and many girls began to fold. I managed to hang on, but it was only by the hair of my chin.

"Look, y'all all look hideous! I'm gonna give you all a week to learn this routine. We'll meet back here same time, same place, next week," Trina said as she grabbed her stuff and left.

I felt so stupid! It was like I dropped the ball. I couldn't believe I let this Southern belle outshine me!

* * *

In my spare time I often went to Wanda's hair salon, called Crown of Glory. Wanda had recently gotten saved, and she was heavily into the church.

Her shop stayed packed! She did hair better than any New York stylist I had ever seen. All her cuts were funky! She did all types of styles and curls. Southern girls were serious about their hair! Even if they had on a cheap outfit, they kept their hair right! Wanda's clientele was so extensive, they had to make their appointments almost a month in advance.

Wanda kept my hair laced! I was drawn to her spirit. She became the older sister I never had. Wanda got me going back to church every Sunday. She would pick me up from school and keep me focused on the right track.

One day while I was sitting on Wanda's couch in her house, she was playing Gospel music on the radio. As the music played I thought about the good ole days when I used to sing in the Sunbeam Choir at Maranatha Baptist Church. I thought about how far I had strayed away from God, then I heard a familiar voice sing! It was Timiney Figeroua singing "Calling My Name," with Hezekiah Walker and the Love Fellowship Crusade choir, the song my friend Jules had written. It was announced as the number-one Gospel song in the country.

Tears rolled down my eyes as I heard Timiney's familiar, anointed voice, and I thought about Jules's major accomplishment. Once again I felt convicted about my lifestyle. I knew I should be doing more for God, but I was all caught up!

It seemed like every time I tried to do the right thing, I got sidetracked somewhere and went wrong! I wanted to live for Christ, but at the same time, I had a deep passion for men and money. I felt so confused, struggling with which side I wanted to be on.

As the song played I thought about all the conversations I had with Jules. I wanted to be able to see him again and make him proud of me. I knew I had to make a decision and be strong about it! I decided I would do my best and follow the way of the Lord!

The more I was around Wanda, the more rooted I stayed. I started to take church seriously and got actively involved in it.

I was an extremist. Either I was all the way in, or I was all the way out! When I was serving God, I was serious about it. I attended all the meetings and would even participate and testify about God's goodness and mercy. I got such an inner fulfillment in church that I was unable to get anywhere else.

I made a promise to God that I would give up fornication and that I would live right, and I meant just what I said. I gave up all of my wild ways, once again, and I tried my best to be a good schoolgirl.

Wanda was proud of me. She saw the drastic changes I made, and she encouraged me to stick with my new regime. We both had the same major struggle, fornication. Wanda fought her urge to be with Billy, and I fought mine. Together, we would laugh about how difficult it was to refrain from having sex.

"Once you start, it becomes like an addiction! It's so hard to let it go. Girl, Billy be so mad at me. He's constantly trying to get in the bed with me. Deep down inside, I want to let him in, but I don't! He can't stand this church thing, girl! He said church caused him to lose his wife," Wanda would say as we laughed.

Being saved and resisting my urge to sin wasn't easy, but I was determined to stay grounded this time around!

My mom, my dad and me (my first year
of college) in a family portrait.

*I*t was time for cheerleading practice. I grabbed my bag and raced over to the dance studio on campus. I had practiced the routine over and over, all week, until I got it. I even added extra moves with my arms to jazz up the routine. I couldn't wait to show off my progress!

When I entered the dance studio, Trina was already there. I quickly dropped my bag and got on the dance floor.

"Okay, ladies, this is your last shot. Let me see what you got!" Trina said as she played the up-tempo R&B music.

"Five, six, five, six, seven, eight," Trina shouted loudly and I got crumped! I pictured myself being in a music video and millions of people watching me worldwide. I got into character, and I killed the routine. I could tell by Trina's face she was amazed by my significant improvement. As I saw that I had gained her attention, I stepped up my confidence and put all my energy into the routine.

"Okay, Miss New York! I see you. Work it, girl," Trina shouted as I danced away.

Trina picked five of us out of the fifty girls that tried out. I was so happy to be a part of the pick. I couldn't wait to become a Saint Augustine's cheerleader!

* * *

Finally, my life was back on track. I was in the church. I was active at school. My grades were good, and I was on my way to becoming a cheerleader. Life was grand, and I was actually enjoying it!

One day I went to Wanda's shop, and this brown-skinned girl with a nice, short haircut walked through the doors.

"Hey, Wanda, girl. I need you so bad, girl. Look at my hair! It's a mess. I'm going to this big party tonight, and I can't look like this. Please, Wanda, *you* got to save me!" the girl pleaded in her thick Southern accent.

"Now, Jackie, you know my book is filled. I have too many customers. I can't take you today," Wanda replied as she continued

Chapter Forty-Nine

to fix her client's hair.

"Look, Wanda, you don't understand! Everybody is gonna be at the party. I'll do whatever you want me to do. What you need, me to clean the shop? I'll clean your house, wash your car, or whatever else you need, girl! Please, don't let me go to the party looking like this. Little Vicious is performing at Kamikaze's with Doug E. Fresh, and I'm up in there," Jackie said in her thick country accent as everybody in the shop laughed.

"Girl, you always wait to the last minute to get your hair done," Wanda shouted.

"I know, girl. I'm sorry! It won't happen again, I promise!" Jackie pleaded.

"Oh, all right," Wanda said as she gave in to Jackie's request.

Jackie sat down on the chair next to me as I checked her out. She was fly, especially for a country girl!

"Oh, Jackie, this is Jamie. She's from New York, and she goes to Saint Augustine's too," Wanda said as she introduced me to Jackie.

"Okay, you a New Yorker. My dudes are from New York. Do you know 9 Fingers and 2.5? They from New York," Jackie asked me.

"Naw, what borough are they from?" I asked.

"Oh, I think they said they from Mount Vernon," Jackie responded.

"Oh, no. I'm from Queens. I don't know them."

"Oh, girl, they're mad New York dudes down here, and they got mad money. I ain't never seen you at Saint Augustine's before. I go there too."

"Oh, for real? I'm around. I live in Baker Hall."

"Do you drive?"

"Yeah, I have a burgundy Audi."

"Oh, so you're the chick I heard them talk about. Okay, you're the little fly girl from New York," Jackie said as I smiled.

"So do you be going out?" Jackie asked.

"Not really. I chill on campus for the most part."

"Oh, man, girl, you got to come hang out with us. Girl, we be having a ball. Matter fact, why don't you come to the club with us tonight? It's gonna be the joint. Everybody from everywhere is coming!" Jackie said as I thought about the opportunity to have fun.

"Well, I don't know," I said reluctantly.

"Girl, live a little. Plus, I want to introduce you to my friends from New York," Jackie said convincingly.

"Well, I guess a little fun won't hurt," I answered.

"Okay, cool. Me and my home girl Theresa will meet you at Baker Hall at 10 o'clock, and then you can follow us down to the club," Jackie said as she got into Wanda's chair to get her hair done.

"Look, Jackie, Jamie is only seventeen years old, and she's a good girl. Don't be having her get into anything crazy," Wanda said as she put the hair cape around Jackie's neck.

"Oh my goodness, she is a baby. That's so cute. You know I ain't going to get her into nothing crazy, Wanda," Jackie replied.

"Jamie, you be careful. Jackie, how old are you?" Wanda asked.

"I just turned twenty-five," Jackie replied.

"Okay, Jamie, Jackie is a senior. Be careful. You can't do all the things she does!" Wanda warned me in front of Jackie.

"I'm my own person, Wanda. I'll be okay," I said as I watched her start on Jackie's hair.

Something about Jackie fascinated me. She definitely wasn't your typical country girl. She rocked all name brand clothes, and she had a sort of New York swagger. Jackie represented freedom and fun to me. I couldn't wait to go to the club with her!

* * *

I went home and changed into my Tommy Hilfiger shirt, my Girbaud Jeans, and I put on my brand-new Jordan's. I was dressed and ready to go to the club. Jackie was on time like she said. She called me down from my dorm room at exactly 10 o'clock.

I walked out of Baker Hall and approached the silver Mitsubishi Mirage she was in.

"Hey, Jamila, this is Theresa. Theresa, this is Jamila," Jackie said as she introduced me to the girl that was driving the car. Theresa was a dark chocolate, slim girl with short hair.

Jackie began to stare at me hard.

"What's the matter?" I asked.

"Girl, you can't go to the club looking like that!" she exclaimed.

"What do you mean? My clothes are name brand!" I said defensively.

"Now it's not even about that. Ain't nobody wearing baggy jeans to the club! You don't have a pair of tight jeans and a fitted shirt?" Jackie asked.

"No," I said. I was confused and sort of embarrassed.

"Girl, you are hard as hell, huh? A little gangsta chick. We got to soften you up. Get in the car," Jackie instructed, and I climbed in.

Jackie took me to her apartment, which she shared with Theresa and another girl named Jamila. Theresa and I were the same size, so she had me put on one of Theresa's tight outfits. I felt awkward in the tight clothes, because that wasn't the style in

New York. Baggy clothes were in at the time, so I dressed just like a dude.

I squeezed into the tight jeans and Jackie and Theresa gassed me up. "Oh, look at you. You look so cute! You even got a nice little shape," they both said as I stared at myself in the mirror.

"Hurry up! We gonna be late for the club," Jackie said as they raced me out of the house.

We pulled up to Kamikaze's and drove in to the nightclub parking lot in Raleigh, and it looked like a car show! There were all types of Lexuses, BMWs, Benzes and Jeeps with out of state tags in the lot.

"Girl, I told you it was gonna be hot tonight. I can't wait to see how many numbers I'm going to pick up tonight!" Jackie screamed as we stared at the cars.

We quickly fixed ourselves up and walked into the jam-packed club. Jackie and Theresa were both extremely popular. All types of guys kept coming up to them all night long! It bugged me out how much attention they got because dark-skinned girls in New York typically got little attention! It was clear country dudes were different. Brown-skinned girls were in, and I loved it!

I was so attentive and excited. I could tell these dudes had money. Everyone had Moët bottles in their hands, and they were just throwing money around!

"Jamila, you want a drink?" Jackie asked.

"Well, no, I don't really drink," I answered.

"Girl, I'm gonna get you a strawberry daiquiri. It taste good. It won't hurt you," Jackie said as Little Vicious came out on the stage. Little Vicious was a young Jamaican artist who sang the song "Freak." I loved his song and couldn't wait to see him perform!

Jackie passed me the drink, and I sipped away as I watched Little Vicious perform. The music came on, and I felt like I was back in New York. The daiquiri had me feeling right, and I began to dance like never before. The guys and girls surrounded me, which made me go extra hard. I was doing all the latest dances, and everybody crowded around to see me. Jackie and Theresa were amazed. They also liked the attention that I brought to us. Some girls stood next to us and acted like they wanted to battle me, and I lost it!

I jumped on top of the pool table and started dancing, and the club went wild! Everybody was cheering me on, even Little Vicious! All types of guys were trying to dance with me and talk to me all night. I had such a ball!

* * *

After that night at the club, Jackie and Theresa loved hanging out with me. They would pick me up every day and have me come to their apartment. They even introduced me to the parts of Raleigh I never even knew existed. I finally got to see the hood, which brought me back to my element. There's something about the ghetto that just made my blood boil. I felt like I was at home!

Jackie and Theresa were both from Lake City, South Carolina. They were super seniors who seemed like they would never graduate. Life for the two girls was all about dudes and partying.

I became very close to Jackie. She called me her little sister. She had a Coca-Cola-bottle shaped body. She was known for her huge butt. Her shape was incredible, and she had all the "get-money" boys on her.

Jackie and Theresa introduced me to all types of hustlers from everywhere. The drug trade in Raleigh in the mid-'90s was off the chain! Drug dealers made five times more down South than they did in New York. You could tell how much a dude made by the car he drove. All the dough boys drove Lexuses, BMWs, and Benzes.

Jackie introduced me to a crew of boys from Mount Vernon, New York. They migrated down South and were making huge money! Jackie's apartment was the hangout spot. All the dough boys came through to chill. Everybody that was anybody knew Jackie and Theresa. The New York boys made the girls' apartment their second home. And, the girls received the perk of the boys sharing their wealth with them.

The first day I hung out with Jackie and Theresa after the club, they had their guy friends take me shopping. Jackie helped me switch up my whole dressing style. She picked out fly designer tight clothes for me to wear.

I never saw anybody shop more than me, but Jackie and Theresa did. Every day they had different boys taking them to different malls. We would even ride out of town to go to different stores. Jackie put me on to Coogi Sweaters and DKNY way before they became popular. She was a label queen for real, and she specialized in getting guys to buy her stuff.

I was in absolute awe of Jackie and Theresa! They had it going on for real. It was typical to come to their house and see gambling matches go down in the living room. Jackie had a skill of connecting together different boys from different hoods. She would invite them all over to gamble. Each guy would have his own ego, trying to show how much money he made. So, they would gamble away large amounts of money, and Jackie was sure to get her cut!

I witnessed c-lo dice matches where the boys were gambling ten thousand dollars a roll! My eyes bulged out of my head when I saw stacks and stacks of money tossed on the floor. There had to be at least over a hundred thousand dollars on the living-room floor. Jackie would hold out a 9 mm gun to guarantee nobody got robbed in her house, and no one ever did! Jackie's house was the hot spot, and I loved every bit of the action!

Jackie and Theresa had different guy friends, but they had two main dudes. Theresa's boyfriend was Ellison, and Jackie's boyfriend was PooJay. They were best friends and local "get-money" boys from Raleigh. Ellison and PooJay were extremely popular. Ellison was more laid-back, and PooJay was trigger-happy. PooJay's gunplay made the whole town respect both of the boys.

Ellison was a light brown-skinned boy who wore a short blow out. PooJay was a dark chocolate boy, who wore long braids, cornrowed to the back. Jackie was head over heels about PooJay. She was well known for having relations with a lot of boys, but PooJay locked Jackie down!

I was the new young girl on the team with Jackie and Theresa. I quickly got noticed and got attention from the boys, because I was a part of their crew.

Jackie tried to hook me up with several sets of dough boys, but I was trying my best not to revert back to my old ways. As time went by, I could no longer help myself!

* * *

Partying became a regular ritual. We went to the club every Tuesday, Thursday, and Saturday night. Going to the club became business for us. We would scout out all the new hustlers on the scene, and it was one of our jobs to bag them!

During the week, we shopped for outfits to wear to the club. We never wanted to be seen twice in the same outfit. Jackie and Theresa didn't believe in hustling. Jackie taught me, "We use what we got, baby, to get what we want!" That became our policy, and I joined in on the pursuit.

We were on a mission! From the club, to the Waffle House, to the hotel, to the mall! That became our normal routine. If he had money, one of us was on it! Jackie taught me how to get whatever I wanted from whomever! She became my new instructor, and I followed Jackie's lead. I was no longer going into a relationship seeking emotional fulfillment; I was strictly there for one purpose only: getting the money.

If I was with one guy and the next came along with more money, the first had to go! We would all go out and compete to see who would come home with the most numbers. I was very competitive, so whatever I did, I had to take it to the top!

Soon, I had all types of hustlers in my back pocket. I wanted to show Jackie she wasn't the only one that could work the system. Look out, country girls, there's a new chick on the scene!

* * *

Overnight, I became a different person. Some mornings I couldn't even stand to look at myself in the mirror because of the bad acts I engaged in the night before. I no longer had time to go to cheerleading practice, so I quit. I didn't have time to go to church either. All I was concerned about was dudes, money, shopping, and the club! I really didn't even want to go to school either.

I practically lived at Jackie and Theresa's house and got all entangled in their world! Jackie's house was also the stash house and the cook-up spot. Ellison and PooJay would bring keys of cocaine and break them down, cook up, and bag up. I felt right at home. I even showed the boys some tricks Trini taught me on how to stretch the coke.

The boys loved me, and I became their little sister too. Whatever Jackie and Theresa got from them, I got it too!

Shopping in Raleigh and Durham became common to us. It got played out to see all the girls at the club rocking the same clothes. We decided we wanted to look different so I started taking Jackie and Theresa to New York to go shopping. It became an every-other-week thing. We were back and forth from North Carolina to New York. We spruced up our wardrobe with all the latest fashions from New York, and everyone in the town seemed to admire us even more!

I became very close to Jackie, causing Theresa to become envious of our relationship. Jackie and I could relate more, so we enjoyed each other. I idolized her. I wanted to be just like her. She showed me a lot of attention. I spent many hours with her. Jackie's roommate, Jamila, didn't like the relationship I had with Jackie either. She felt like I was interfering in Jackie and Theresa's relationship, so she always gave me the cold shoulder. I didn't care. As long as I had Jackie, I was good!

* * *

One day when I was coming back from shopping with Jackie, Ellison, and PooJay, there was a big red notice on the door from the health department.

Ellison ran to grab the notice that was stuck on the door. It read: "This is a certified notice to make you aware that you tested positive for the following diseases: Chlamydia, Trichomoniasis, and Gonorrhea. Please report to the health department immediately for vaccination." Ellison read the letter aloud and started laughing and pointing at me.

"Boy, my last name is Davis. That's the other Jamila, not me!" I responded. We all laughed and joked. I couldn't believe the health department in North Carolina came out to your house if you had a venereal disease! To make it worse, they gave her a ten-day notice. If she didn't go get treated within ten days, they would put a warrant out for her arrest.

Jamila became the laughingstock of the boys. Every time she would come in the house, the boys would laugh and joke. "She's on fire tonight," Ellison would scream, and boy, did I make a mistake when I laughed.

"Oh, so you find something funny?" Jamila said in a furious tone. She caught me by surprise 'cause we hardly ever spoke. Before I could get any words out of my mouth, this larger, thick, brown-skinned girl, Jamila, snuffed me. *Boom!* Right in front of everyone! I wasted no time and began to fight her back. She was way bigger than I, so I knew I had no wins with wrestling. I quickly grabbed her hair by the roots and gained control over the fight. I started punching her in her face, but she was able to push me off of her.

Boom! Jamila hit me again, and we rumbled. I knew if I lost this fight in front of the boys I would never hear the end. The surprising part is no one jumped in to break up the fight. I guess they wanted to see if I had skills or not.

Jamila got me down to the floor, and I bit her and got her off of me. I grabbed her hair again, and we went back at it. We fought for a good ten minutes. I didn't care if we fought all night. I wasn't giving up!

Finally, Jamila yelled, "Get her the hell off me," and Jackie broke up the fight. I didn't win, but I sure didn't lose. I maintained my respect.

After the fight I began to question my new friendships. Were these really my friends or were they my foes? I became very confused. Theresa thought Ellison and I had something going on. She also didn't like the fact I had more of Jackie's attention than she did. I had my own car, and so did Theresa. Jackie didn't have a car so she used me and Theresa as her cabs to take her wherever she had to go. As time went by, I no longer felt good about all that I was doing. I felt convicted. I wanted out, but I felt like I was already in too deep!

* * *

The semester was coming to an end, and I met this boy named Lou-Lou going to the store. Lou-Lou had walnut-colored skin and was a wild-looking country boy with long, thick coarse hair. He was a dough boy, but he didn't make money like Ellison and PooJay; yet, I liked him. I enjoyed spending time with him and hanging out in his hood. For some reason I felt comfortable with him, and Quarry Street became my escape from Theresa and Jackie.

Quarry Street was a drug-infested block. The block had little row houses lined up next to each other. It reminded me a lot of Kinston. Most of the people who hung out on the block were poor.

Lou-Lou was getting the most money on the block, so he was the king of his little area, and when I came around Lou-Lou treated me like a queen.

Jackie hated Lou-Lou. She used to call him the dirty ugly boy.

"I don't understand. Out of all these boys that like you, why would you choose the brokest, ugliest one of them all?" she would say. Ellison and PooJay didn't like him either. They made more money than Lou-Lou, but Lou-Lou was a firecracker. He was also known to be gun-happy. When he suspected Ellison and PooJay to be talking about him, Lou-Lou threatened to shoot up their block.

I had to keep Lou-Lou away from Jackie and the boys, so we always met up on his block. As time went by, I really grew to like Lou-Lou a lot, so I was ready to settle down and chill with him. That didn't sit well with Jackie at all!

It seemed like constant confusion and problems were occurring between us. The tension grew so crazy that I stopped going by her house.

I finished the semester and aced my classes, and I held my mother to her promise of getting me my own apartment.

I was determined to get the flyest apartment I could find and style on everybody. I'd show them just what kind of girl I really was!

Randy "Stretch" Walker, Kim's brother.
R.I.P. Stretch.

*D*uring winter recess, I packed all my things and took them to my grandmother's house in Kinston. Then I got on the road and headed to New York.

I missed New York, and I missed my parents. I couldn't wait to chill out and spend the holiday with them. My parents were happy to see me. It felt just like old times, experiencing their joy.

After a couple of days I got bored. I was so used to constant excitement at school. I called Trini to see what was up with him. It turned out that Trini had moved down to Wildwood, New Jersey, right outside of Atlantic City, and he was hustling hard out there.

"Baby, what's up?" Trini said to me over the phone.

"Hi, Trini. I'm in New York. I'm down from school on vacation. I want to see what's up with you," I said.

"Oh, why don't you come visit me down in Atlantic City? Let me treat you to a good time."

I ended up taking Trini up on his offer and drove down to South Jersey to meet him. Trini looked super good! It was obvious he was making a ton of money in South Jersey. He had the swagger of a Don. He wined and dined me the whole weekend I spent with him in Atlantic City. I enjoyed his company. It felt just like old times.

As I lounged in the hotel room with Trini, his cell phone kept ringing. "Yo, who's that?" I asked.

"It's nobody," he replied.

Trini rolled over, and I slipped his phone into the bathroom. I was curious to see what he had been up to. I looked at the missed call, and I immediately recognized the number. It was the twins, Renée and Michelle's number that had been calling him. I was sick to my stomach. I couldn't believe the twins would cross me like that!

I called back the number and a voice answered. "Trini?" but it wasn't Renée or Michelle's voice.

"Ah yo, who is this?" I yelled into the phone.

"Who's this?" the girl answered back.

Michelle grabbed the phone.

"Ah, yo, who's this?" Michelle said in a nasty tone.

Chapter Fifty

"This is Jamila, and why the hell are you calling Trini?" I demanded.

"Oh, oh, I, um, Jamila, what's up?" Michelle said nervously.

"Oh, so you hooking chicks up with Trini?" I asked.

"Oh, no, um, I ain't got nothing to do with that. Stacey and him linked up on their own," Michelle said back as she stuttered.

"You know how many opportunities I had to hook Lenroy up with chicks and I never disrespected you," I yelled.

"No, well, um, you and Trini aren't together, so I thought—" Michelle said as I interrupted her.

"First off, we are together, and I see how y'all trifling chicks get down. Why would you want my leftovers?" I shouted. Michelle continued to try to explain, but I hung up.

Trini was in the bed sleeping, and I woke him up.

"So you want to mess with my friends now? What kind of mess are you on?" I said rudely waking him up.

"Yo, Milla, I ain't thinking about them girls. You see who I'm here with," he replied.

I was mad as hell at Trini, but I sure wasn't getting ready to let Stacey have him. I made Trini call her in front of me and tell her he was with me and he didn't want her. It felt good to see I still had my status with Trini. I made Trini feel guilty all weekend long. As a result, I got a makeup gift. Trini bought me a banging set of rims for my Audi.

He and I decided to try to rekindle our old relationship. We both still clearly had love for each other. I loved Trini, but I didn't trust him. I knew things could never be the same, but I sure wasn't getting ready to let Stacey have him. Trini stayed in touch with me my whole time in school. I often drove up to see him, and he would take me and Jackie shopping, just like he did with my friends in high school. Trini knew just how to keep a smile on my face, and I loved it!

* * *

I went back to Raleigh before the semester started to go apartment shopping. I checked out all the affordable apartments in town. After an extensive search, I finally found the apartment I wanted.

It was a beautiful two-bedroom garden-style apartment with a loft upstairs, on a small cul-de-sac block in the cut. The apartment had top-of-the-line amenities and a wonderful view of the city. It was available for rent, and I had to have it!

I convinced my mom to come down and see the apartment. She liked it too and cosigned for me to get it.

Jackie ended up moving out of Jamila and Theresa's apartment, and she moved in with me. I took the room upstairs with the loft, and Jackie had the bedroom on the first floor that led out to the patio.

You couldn't tell me and Jackie anything! We knew our apartment was fly. In our minds, we had it going on! We wasted no time showing off our new apartment to everybody.

School started back, and I got back up with Lou-Lou. He began coming to my apartment to spend time with me.

One day Lou-Lou came to the house to see me and Ellison and PooJay were there. I quickly ushered Lou-Lou upstairs, knowing they all didn't get along. Lou-Lou overheard them laughing and joking about how dirty and ugly he was, and he lost it!

"Ah, yo, y'all dudes, want it with me?" Lou-Lou said as he went to swing on PooJay.

"Yo, Lou-Lou, chill," I pleaded. "I just got this apartment. You gonna get me kicked out!" I shouted.

"Yo, what?" PooJay said as he lifted up his shirt and showed Lou-Lou his gun. In a matter of minutes, things had gotten real serious!

Jackie jumped in front of PooJay, and I jumped in front of Lou-Lou. The look in both of their eyes let us know they weren't playing. I managed to get Lou-Lou out the door. I walked him to his car and convinced him to get in.

"Yo, you messing with Ellison?" Lou-Lou questioned as he grabbed me by my collar.

"No, that's like my brother," I responded nervously.

"I don't want to hear that shit. You be acting like you on their side. If I'm your man, why *I* got to go? It's *your* apartment," Lou-Lou said.

"Listen, it ain't all about that."

"Yes, it is! You letting them lame dudes disrespect me," Lou-Lou shouted.

"How am I letting them do anything? Whatever y'all got going on happened way before you even met me."

"Yeah, all right. They are gonna see what it is," Lou-Lou said as he pulled off.

I took a deep breath and went back in the house. What a close call! Ellison and PooJay laughed, reenacting how Lou-Lou looked when PooJay showed him his gun.

"That punk don't want it with me," Ellison bragged.

"Ah, yo, what was that?" I asked as I saw a shadow pass the door.

"I don't see nothin'," Jackie said as the boys kept joking. Suddenly, there was a knock on the door. I opened it. My mouth flew open. There stood Lou-Lou who had on a ski mask covering his nose and his mouth. He was with two of his friends I recognized.

"Get the fuck down," Lou-Lou said to Ellison and PooJay as he ran up in the house with his friends, who had their guns out. I was frightened to death.

"Oh, so I'm a punk," Lou-Lou said as he hit PooJay with a big gun.

"Give me all the money and your gun," Lou-Lou shouted as he held the gun pointed at PooJay's head. I was scared to death! Jackie and I stood frozen.

Lou-Lou's friends patted Ellison and PooJay down, took all their money and Poo-Jay's gun. Jackie and I were staring in disbelief. We couldn't believe what was happening. As Lou-Lou and the boys got up to leave and turned their backs, Ellison pulled out his gun and started running after them and shooting. Lou-Lou started running and shot back. Lou-Lou's bullet shattered my whole front window! I felt like I was experiencing a bad nightmare.

Ellison didn't catch Lou-Lou that night, but they were determined to get him back. After Lou-Lou shot up the crib, I didn't want anything to do with him. I was caught all up in the beef, and I knew sooner or later it was going down!

* * *

I continued my regular party routine. Every Tuesday night it was popping off at the Vibe Club downtown Raleigh, and every Thursday and Saturday it was on at Kamikaze's. I became a regular club head. I enjoyed the party scene until Dino decided to move down to Raleigh!

It was a Thursday night, and I was dressed to impress. Jackie and I jumped in the car and headed to Kamikaze's. We were regulars and had our own little section in VIP.

Everybody in the town knew who we were, and they respected and admired us.

I loved to dance, so I was always showing off my skills on the floor. I was dancing on the dance floor with this boy when I got pushed out of nowhere.

"Ah, yo, what you doing?" Dino said as he yoked me up.

"Ah, yo, money, chill," the boy I was dancing with said to Dino.

"Oh, you want it?" Dino said as he snuffed the boy and caused a whole brawl on the dance floor. I was so embarrassed!

Dino came to Raleigh trying to make a name for himself. He told everybody I was his wife and started fighting random people about me! Dino almost ruined my entire social life. Thank God, Wanda told Billy that Dino couldn't stay with them anymore, so he had to go. Dino completely turned me off. He was a zero compared to the new dudes I was dealing with in Raleigh. Dino was very aggressive and abusive.

I wanted desperately to avoid him. He felt as though he possessed me and I was his property. Dino had me under pressure. Whenever he came anywhere near me, I began to run. I had a real psychopath on my hands!

* * *

PooJay and Jackie were still going hard with each other. With Lou-Lou out of the picture, PooJay was at our house all the time.

One day PooJay brought his friend, Little Gerald, by our house, who had just come home from federal prison. He was dark chocolate boy who wore long braids. Gerald and Poojay began to hang out together frequently. Little Gerald was always at our house.

As time went on, Ellison and PooJay's relationship began to get shaky. It was clear Little Gerald wanted PooJay to himself. Gerald came on the scene and blew up. All the girls in Raleigh were talking about him, and PooJay ended up cutting Gerald into the drug business.

Ellison didn't care for Gerald, but he accepted him because of PooJay. Little Gerald became the third wheel in PooJay's and Ellison's major drug operation.

* * *

One Saturday night, I met this boy named Busy at the club. He had on a cream and black Avirex coat and some black Gore-Tex boots. I could tell by his style he was a "get-money" dude. I cased Busy out and began dancing by him all night until he finally approached me. We exchanged numbers, and he introduced me to his partner, Eric, who was from Harlem.

"Yo, why don't you come to New York with us?" Busy suggested as he sipped his Moët straight out of the bottle.

"Yeah, we can do that some time," I replied.

"Look, I got the white stretch limo outside. My boy and I got to handle some business in New York tomorrow. Come with me and we can go shopping together in New York," Busy said. I contemplated his offer and went over to Jackie to gain her approval.

"Yo, Jackie, I told you them dudes got paper. That's them with the white stretch limo outside. Ole boy wants me to come to New York with him tonight," I whispered to her as the music played in the club.

"Yo, girl, you don't even know them! You can't go to New York with them," Jackie protested.

"Girl, please? What they gonna do to me, kill me? Girl, I'm going; please come with me," I pleaded.

"Girl, PooJay would kill me! I ain't going," Jackie said.

"All right, here's my car keys. I'll call you when I come back in town," I said boldly and I walked toward Busy.

"Girl, you crazy," Jackie yelled.

"Maybe, but I got a good feeling about this one."

Busy, Eric, Busy's brother, and I got into the stretch limo, and the driver drove to New York, and we passed out in the back of the limo.

I woke up and opened my eyes. I couldn't believe I left the club with total strangers. Busy had his arms around my shoulders as he snored away.

By the time everyone got up, we were almost in New York. We talked for hours, and I actually vibed with Busy. He wasn't your typical dough boy. He was actually very intelligent.

It was about 11 o'clock in the morning when we arrived in New York. We went straight to Eric's building in Harlem. He lived right around the corner from Qiana's house. We stopped at Sylvia's Soul Food Restaurant in Harlem to eat breakfast. It was Sunday morning, and Sylvia's was having their Sunday Gospel brunch.

I listened to the Gospel music as I sat at the table with total strangers. I knew my irrational behavior was getting out of hand, but it seemed as if I was no longer in control.

"Yo, are you all right?" Busy asked as we ate our food.

"Yes, I'm okay," I replied.

"So why do you look like you're about to cry?" he asked.

"Oh, the music just reminds me of home and my mother," I answered.

"Where is your mother?"

"She lives in Queens."

"How far is Queens from here?"

"Um, about thirty minutes away."

"Oh, okay, that settles it. We're going to see your mother. I want to meet her anyway," Busy said aggressively.

We finished eating our food and got back in the limousine to go see my mother. I was nervous about what she would think about me being with Busy, but it was the weekend, and I would be back to Raleigh in time for school tomorrow.

"Listen, if my mother asks, tell her you are in the entertainment business," I instructed him.

We headed over the Triborough Bridge and entered into Queens. I rang my doorbell, and my father answered.

"Jamie, what are you doing in New York, baby?"

"Oh, Dad, I'm just here with some of my friends for the weekend. They're in the music business, and they had a show. I came to see you and Mommy real quick before we leave."

"Oh, that's nice you thought of us, but your mother is at church. It's Sunday, baby," my father said as I stood inside the living room.

I quickly used the bathroom and headed down the street to my old church,

Maranatha Baptist Church. "Y'all want to come in?" I asked Busy and his friends, as we approached the church.

"Oh, no, God might strike us down," they said as they laughed.

I went into the church service and sat in the last pew. I got there just in time to hear the end of the sermon.

"God is looking for people who will be faithful to Him. He's tired of the stubborn people who only serve Him for their own purposes. You got a choice today, people. Either you're hot or you're cold. Either you're in this thing or you're out! The Bible says if you're lukewarm, He'll spit you right out!

"God has a good plan today, church. He wants to bless His people. What you're looking for in man, you can only find in God. It's time today, church, to get rid of your idols. Who are you serving? Is it a job? Is it a car? Is it a house or a man?

"I don't know what it is, church, but anything you put before God, He will take it away. You see my God is a jealous God. He sits up high, but He looks down low. He knows the heart of His people.

"Judgment day is coming, church. Somebody that is sitting in this building won't get another chance. You continue to keep coming to church, but your heart isn't in this thing. Some foolish idol has stolen your heart from God.

"God has given you many chances, and you keep making the same mistakes. Are you not tired yet of going around in circles, chasing your tail? God loves you. He's got a plan for your life. He didn't bring you this far to leave you here.

"Church, let's get this thing together. Let's stop playing and get right with God. Can I get a witness? Do I have any real Christians who want to serve the Lord wholeheartedly? Judgment day is coming. Will you make it? Turn to your neighbor and ask them, will you make it? Come on, church, let's get this thing right this morning! Do I have anybody who wants to give their life back to Jesus today?" Reverend Mixon preached passionately.

After his sermon, the choir stood up and sang "Come to Jesus," and the church altar was open for people to come rededicate their lives to the Lord.

All I could think about was all my broken promises to God. Every word Reverend Mixon said was like a knife cutting through me. I felt like such a failure. Tears streamed down my eyes as my life flashed before me, from the time I was a little girl singing in the church choir to now. Boy, what a difference!

I stood up as the pastor made his invitation to come to the Lord, but I froze, filled with conviction. I couldn't keep making false promises that I knew I couldn't keep. Instead of going forth, I stood still and I cried. As tears flowed from my eyes, my mother turned around and spotted me. She quickly made her way to the back of the church.

"Jamie, what are you doing here?" Mama asked as she wrapped her arms around me tightly.

"I just wanted my mommy. I miss you so much!" I held tightly on to her as I cried.

"I miss my baby, too!" my mother said back as we both cried in each other's arms.

I didn't tell my mother what I was going through, but it's as if she felt my pain. Her hug felt like a million pounds of love; I was comforted by her that day. I missed the relationship I once had as a child with my mother. As she hugged me in the back of the church, I felt as though I had gained that relationship back.

After church I brought my mother outside to meet Busy who was inside the new white stretch limousine. The two of them spoke for a while. As we left, my mother kissed me and looked into Busy's eyes. "Please, sir, take care of my daughter. She's a good girl," my mother pleaded.

"Yes, ma'am, I certainly will," Busy replied back in such a respectful manner. He honored his promise to my mother. He treated me like a queen. He showed me more love and affection than any of my previous boyfriends.

Busy was a big-time hustler who had just been discharged from the navy. He hooked up with Eric from New York, and the two of them took it to the top. Their coke was official, and they began to take over the drug trade in Raleigh. Busy had more money than Ellison and PooJay and all the other hustlers in Raleigh put together!

As time went by, Busy made me his girl, and that didn't sit too well with Jackie, PooJay or Ellison. They couldn't make fun of me or put me down about Busy like they did Lou-Lou. Busy was in a class all by himself.

No matter who was around, Busy treated me like a queen. Anything I wanted, I got it. He made it known to the world that I was his girl and that he was in love with me.

Busy encouraged me to stay in school and get good grades. He couldn't stand Jackie and Theresa. He wanted me to give up my apartment and live with him. I was feeling Busy, so I was willing to take his advice. I was finally ready to settle down and just be with him.

Chapter Fifty-One

One day I was sitting on the couch watching television when PooJay, Gerald, and Ellison came in the house.

"What's up, funny style?" PooJay said as he walked in the house.

"Funny style? I ain't no funny style," I said back, feistylike.

"Yeah, you done got with that rich boy, and now you done switched up. You forgot where you came from," Ellison interjected.

"That's not true. Why y'all always be tripping?" I asked as Ellison sat on the couch next to me.

"Oh, so you still got love for us?" Ellison questioned.

"I sure do," I replied.

"Okay, good. I need you to do me a favor. I need you to drive with me, Theresa, and Little Gerald to New York. We got some important business to go handle."

"Ellison, I just came back from New York. I don't feel like taking that long drive."

"C'mon, Jamila. I'll take you shopping or whatever. Theresa can't drive the whole way by herself," Ellison pleaded.

"Oh, man, Ellison, when you trying to go?" I asked.

"This weekend."

"Oh, okay, I'll see," I replied.

I really didn't want to go to New York, but I didn't want to let the boys down either. Busy and I were supposed to go down to Atlanta together. I couldn't imagine what I would say to him to make up an excuse of why I couldn't go.

I contemplated the situation all weeklong. I didn't want to stand Busy up, and I didn't want to be considered funny style by the boys either. I was caught between both sides, and I didn't know what to do.

I finally broke down and told Busy I was going to New York with the boys, and he was absolutely furious!

"I can't believe you gonna choose them snakes over me," he shouted through the phone.

"But, Boo, I promised them I was gonna go. Everybody thinks I'm acting funny since I got with you," I said.

"Why do you care what they think? You with me now. You don't need them. Jamila, I'm telling you they ain't your friends," Busy snapped and hung up the phone on me.

I felt so crazy, but my word was my bond. I told Ellison I would go, so I felt I had to be a woman of my word.

* * *

The weekend came and Theresa came over to our house. She was packed and ready to go on the trip. My relationship with Theresa was shaky. We spoke but we were very distant. I knew she didn't like my relationship with Jackie, and I also knew she thought me and Ellison had something going on.

The whole ride down we made small talk as I thought about Busy. I loved going to New York, but this time, I didn't. Something just didn't feel right about this trip. We rode straight into New York, and the boys got out to meet their drug connect in Harlem.

Ellison and Little Gerald snapped on each other the whole way down. It was clear the boys were only friends because of PooJay. They finished their business, and Theresa drove them to 125th Street, where we all went shopping.

The rapper Keith Murray was having a concert at the club Kamikaze's on Tuesday night, so Theresa and I went shopping for outfits we could wear to the club. The boys did the same. We shopped for the rest of the afternoon, then Ellison asked us to drop the boys at the airport. They had to get back to Raleigh to handle some other important business for PooJay.

We dropped the boys off at the airport, and then we headed over to my friend Shalon's house to spend the night. I couldn't go to my house because I knew my parents would flip out about us being in New York.

Shalon and I had fun reminiscing about old times. Theresa was bored and kept nagging me about us getting back on the road. I wasn't ready to leave New York. I was tired and wanted to chill.

Theresa and I began to argue about me not wanting to leave. We were in her car, and she threatened to leave me. Something in my spirit didn't feel right. Everything inside of me told me to stay in New York for at least another day. Theresa had the upper advantage because she drove her car. She packed her things and left the house. I had no choice but to run behind her.

"Okay, Theresa. I'm coming. Hold up!" I yelled as I hugged Shalon tightly, got my things, and left.

The whole ride back to North Carolina was shaky. We ran into snow in Maryland. We could hardly see on the road as we continued to drive. "Come on, Theresa, let's pull over and get some rest," I suggested.

We pulled over for a couple of hours until the snow cleared up. While I was driving, a deer crossed the road and I almost crashed! One thing after another happened as my heart began to pace.

"Theresa, we should have stayed in New York another day," I shouted.

"We couldn't, Jamila. I told Ellison we were coming right back," she rebutted.

Our whole trip back was absolutely miserable. Theresa and I argued all the back to Raleigh. I refused to drive any more so Theresa drove us back into town.

As soon as we entered Raleigh onto Capital Boulevard, police cars surrounded us.

"Jamila, Jamila, get up. There's mad police officers pulling us over," Theresa shouted.

"Okay, then, pull over," I said, half-awake.

"Jamila, you know I got a bunch of coke in the trunk."

I could hear the panic in Theresa's voice. "Oh my goodness," I said as I just dropped my head.

"Let me see your license and registration," the police officer said in a strong country voice, as he approached the driver's window.

"Yes, Officer. Can you please tell me why we are being pulled over? I wasn't speeding, sir," Theresa said.

"No, you weren't," the officer said, "but we got a tip that a gray Mitsubishi Mirage with South Carolina tags was coming into Raleigh and that you have drugs in the car. Ladies, I need you to step out of the vehicle and put your hands on the car," the white officer said in a strong Southern drawl.

At least fifteen cops surrounded us with their guns out. I knew at that moment it was all over. The K-9 dog came, and the police quickly located the key of cocaine that was stashed in the trunk of the car.

"You ladies are under arrest," the officer said as he handcuffed us and put us in the back of the police car.

Theresa began to cry frantically. I couldn't even cry. All I thought about was Busy telling me not to go to New York!

We got down to the police station, and they put Theresa and me into two separate interrogating rooms. I sat in the cold dark room for about an hour while the detectives were questioning Theresa.

After they finished, they came into the room to question me.

"Young lady, my name is Detective Keenan, and I'm the head detective covering this case. You ladies are in a bunch of trouble. We apprehended at least a key of cocaine out of the vehicle. Your friend already told us what we need to know. Now you got a choice. Either help yourself or rot in jail," he said in his strong country accent.

"Sir, I don't know anything about no drugs. I was coming up to New York to go shopping," I quickly said.

"I ain't no fool, girl. You better tell me the truth, or I'ma make sure you spend the rest of your life in prison," Detective Keenan said sharply as he banged on the table in the interrogation room.

"Listen, sir, you're scaring me. I would like a lawyer, please," I said, which made Detective Keenan even more furious.

"Oh, so you think you're a big city slicker. I got something for you, gal," he said as the officers walked out of the room and ended the interview.

They sent Theresa in the room to talk to me.

"Girl, what's going on?" I asked her.

"I'm getting ready to put on a wire and deliver these drugs to Ellison," Theresa said in a tearful voice.

"Oh, wow. You're bugging," I said.

"Girl, I ain't got no choice. They said I can get twenty-five years for this. These ain't my drugs," she shouted.

"But a wire? That's crazy." I shook my head. I was still in handcuffs, and they had put shackles on my feet when I refused to talk. Theresa was free to move about as I sat shackled down in the chair.

"Jamila, will you come with me?"

"Hell no, girl. I ain't got nothing to do with all that. Yo, let these people know I just came with you to go shopping."

Theresa left the room and went with the detectives to set up Ellison. I stayed back in the dark interrogating room shackled down.

Several hours later, the police brought both PooJay and Ellison into the police station handcuffed. Ellison shook his head as he looked into my eyes.

"I ain't got nothing to do with this!" I said as Ellison passed me.

"I know, Jamila. The dude Little Gerald set us up. He's an informant," Ellison said.

"I told you, PooJay, I never liked that dude. We all locked up, and he ain't nowhere around. You know he did this!" Ellison said to PooJay.

"Man, I don't believe Little Gerald did this," PooJay insisted.

"When are you gonna wake up? Everything was fine with us till your snitch-ass friend came home," Ellison yelled.

We all stood shackled together before the magistrate. The old white magistrate seemed happy to give each of us a two million dollar cash bail. At that moment it sank in. I was really in trouble! It was like I was living a nightmare. I couldn't believe I was actually about to go to the county jail. I was in a state of shock!

Theresa shook frantically as we were driven to the Wake County Jail in the police car. We went through booking, and they took our fingerprints and pictures. I felt like a real hardened criminal. They gave us an orange jumpsuit, a blanket, and two sheets, and then sent us upstairs to population.

"Oh my God, what if the girls up there do something to us?" Theresa said as she cried.

"Listen, hurry up and wipe your face. If these chicks see any punk in us, they are gonna try us. Try your best to look hard and don't smile," I instructed.

To our surprise, everybody was locked in already, so we just went into our assigned individual cells and we were locked in. Tears poured down my eyes as the bars of my cell shut behind me. All of my aspirations and dreams flew out the window. In a split moment, all my bad decisions had caught up to me. In the end, one poor choice had ruined my destiny!

A family portrait of my brother Kee, my
mother, my father and me (as a toddler).

*A*fter I prayed for help the answer came in a way I least expected. Captured behind bars, I no longer had the free will to do what I pleased. I was trapped off and isolated. This time it wasn't my own desires that kept me hindered. It was God's plan to preserve me.

In an orange prison jumpsuit, with a tiny Ziploc bag of toiletries and a small folded mattress in my arms, firsthand, I experienced the repercussions of my actions. My past finally caught up to me. I had had many chances and many warnings, yet I ignored all of them. I was determined to have as much fun as I could, my own way. I was convinced I could beat the odds; now, the odds stood firmly against me. My quick-money scheme backfired, and I was left to reap the consequences.

Locked in a tiny cell, I cried out passionately to God, "Lord, please save me!" I was so frightened and deeply broken within. At that very moment, I wanted to close my eyes and die. I was only seventeen years old, and I was locked up, held under a two million dollar bond. There was no one I knew in the entire world who could rescue me, not even my parents! It would take nothing less than a miracle to save me from the wrath that I faced—a mandatory minimum of fifteen years in prison. Hopeless and distraught, I only wished I could turn back the hands of time. But I couldn't.

Did life really have to turn out this way for me? No, it didn't. My own choices forged my destiny. Every negative choice we make in life comes with a consequence. Sometimes the costs we are forced to pay are severe! Today, I seriously regret my actions. Through intensive tears, hurt, and pain, I learned never to do things I would ultimately regret.

My message to you is: Think about the consequences for your actions before you act. Can you bear the consequences of the lifestyle that you live? Are you ready for what comes next? Don't just think about the moment or achieving instant gratification. Weigh your options! Living life in the fast lane has only one ultimate result—grief. Take it from me and avoid unnecessary pain. Do the right thing! If not, it will cost you!

Reflection

My brother Kee and me on a recent visit, in 2015, at the Danbury
Federal Prison Camp in Danbury, Connecticut.

*L*ocked in a tiny, single-bed cell, alone, my heart began to race as I thought of the events that led to my downfall. I couldn't even sleep. I just kept replaying all the events in my mind. I couldn't believe Little Gerald had set us up. As reality hit me, I began to cry. I thought about my grandmother and how she always told me no matter what problems you may have or how bad you may think they are, just call on Jesus and let Him fix them for you.

I fell down on my knees, and I began to cry out to the Lord.

"God, I know You are disappointed in me, and I'm disappointed in myself. I've gotten myself into a world of trouble, and, God, I don't know what to do. I know what I've been doing is wrong, and, God, I desperately wanted to serve You and do the right thing. I got all confused and caught up that I made so many bad decisions.

"God, I need You. I don't want to stay in jail for the rest of my life. I have a two million dollar bail, and I know when my parents find out, they are going to kill me. Will You help me, Lord? Will You deliver me from this self-destruction that I know I created?

"And, Lord, if You are still listening, will You please forgive me? I'm sorry, Lord. I'm so, so very sorry." I prayed passionately and fell down on the floor and began to cry.

In time, I sat on the floor in my cell and sang every Gospel song I could think of until I regained my inner strength. Then, I fell asleep on the small blue mattress in my 5½-by-9 jail cell.

I woke up the next morning and stared at the white cinder-block jail cell walls that surrounded me. All I could think was, *How did I get myself in this bad situation?* I had no clue what my destiny would become.

The electronic door of my cell began to automatically open. I instantly spotted the glaring eyes of the other female inmates looking in at me.

"Yeah, that's the girl right there. She's the one we saw in the newspaper who set up Ellison," a mean-looking masculine female with a low haircut shouted in a deep accent.

All eyes were glued on me as I exited my cell and entered the

Epilogue

crowded dayroom area of the Wake County Jail for breakfast. My heart began to race as evil eyes glared at me. I couldn't believe the girls thought I set up Ellison.

I had to think quick as I saw the masculine girl approaching me. She was too big for me to take on. Inside I wanted to die. The recent chain of events was too much for me to handle. All I could think was—how in the world did I get caught up here?

*J*amila T. Davis, born and raised in Jamaica Queens, New York, is a motivational speaker and the creator of the Voices of Consequences Enrichment Series for incarcerated women. Through her powerful delivery, Davis illustrates the real-life lessons and consequences that result from poor choices. She also provides the techniques and strategies that she personally has utilized to dethrone negative

thinking patterns, achieve emotional healing, and restoration and growth.

Davis is no stranger to triumphs and defeats. By the age of 25, she utilized her business savvy and street smarts to rise to the top of her field, becoming a lead go-to-person in the Hip-Hop Music Industry and a self-made millionaire through real estate investments. Davis lived a care-free lavish lifestyle, surrounded by rap stars, professional sports figures and other well known celebrities.

All seemed well until the thorn of materialism clouded Davis' judgments and her business shortcuts backfired, causing her self-made empire to crumble. Davis was convicted of bank fraud, for her role in a multi-million dollar bank fraud scheme, and sentenced to 12 1/2 years in federal prison.

Davis' life was in a great shambles as she faced the obstacle of imprisonment. While living in a prison cell, stripped of all her worldly possessions, and abandoned by most of her peers, she was forced to deal with the root of her dilemmas- her own inner self.

Davis searched passionately for answers and strategies to heal and regain her self-confidence, and to discover her life's purpose. She utilized her formal training from Lincoln University, in Philadelphia, Pennsylvania, along with her real-life post-incarceration experiences and documented her discoveries. Revealing the tools, techniques and strategies she used to heal, Davis composed a series of books geared to empower women. Davis' goal is to utilize her life experiences to uplift, inspire and empower her audience to achieve spiritual and emotional wholeness and become their very best, despite their dilemmas and past obstacles.

Voices International Publications Presents

Voices of
CONSEQUENCES
ENRICHMENT SERIES
CREATED BY: JAMILA T. DAVIS

Unlocking the Prison Doors: 12 Points to Inner Healing and Restoration

ISBN: 978-09855807-4-2 Textbook
ISBN: 978-09855807-5-9 Workbook/Journal
ISBN: 978-09855807-6-6 Curriculum Guide

Unlocking the Prison Doors is a nondenominational, faith-based instructional manual created to help incarcerated women gain inner healing and restoration. In a comforting voice that readers can recognize and understand, this book provides the tools women need to get past the stage of denial and honestly assess their past behavioral patterns, their criminal conduct and its impact on their lives and others. It provides a platform for women to begin a journey of self-discovery, allowing them to assess the root of their problems and dilemmas and learn how to overcome them.

This book reveals real-life examples and concrete strategies that inspire women to release anger, fear, shame and guilt and embrace a new world of opportunities.

After reading *Unlocking the Prison Doors,* readers will be empowered to release the inner shackles and chains that have been holding them bound and begin to soar in life!

VOICES
INTERNATIONAL PUBLICATIONS
"Changing Lives One Page At A Time."
www.vocseries.com

Voices International Publications Presents

$\mathcal{V}oices_{of}$
CONSEQUENCES
ENRICHMENT SERIES
CREATED BY: JAMILA T. DAVIS

Permission to Dream:
12 Points to Discovering Your Life's Purpose and Recapturing Your Dreams

ISBN: 978-09855807-4-2 Textbook
ISBN: 978-09855807-5-9 Workbook/Journal
ISBN: 978-09855807-6-6 Curriculum Guide

Permission to Dream is a nondenominational, faith-based, instruction manual created to inspire incarcerated women to discover their purpose in life and recapture their dreams. In a way readers can identify with and understand, this book provides strategies they can use to overcome the stigma and barriers of being an ex-felon.

This book reveals universal laws and proven self-help techniques that successful people apply in their everyday lives. It helps readers identify and destroy bad habits and criminal thinking patterns, enabling them to erase the defilement of their past.

Step-by-step this book empowers readers to recognize their talents and special skill sets, propelling them to tap into the power of "self" and discover their true potential, and recapture their dreams.

After reading *Permission To Dream*, readers will be equipped with courage and tenacity to take hold of their dreams and become their very best!

INTERNATIONAL PUBLICATIONS
"Changing Lives One Page At A Time."
www.vocseries.com

Voices International Publications Presents

$\mathcal{V}oices_{of}$
CONSEQUENCES
ENRICHMENT SERIES
CREATED BY: JAMILA T. DAVIS

Pursuit to A Greater "Self:" 12 Points to Developing Good Character and HealthyRelationships

ISBN: 978-09855807-7-3 Textbook
ISBN: 978-09855807-8-0 Workbook/Journal
ISBN: 978-09855807-9-7 Curriculum Guide

Pursuit to A Greater "Self" is a non-denominational, faith-based, instruction manual created to help incarcerated women develop good character traits and cultivate healthy relationships.

This book is filled with real-life examples that illustrate how good character traits have helped many people live a more prosperous life, and how deficient character has caused others to fail. These striking examples, along with self-help strategies revealed in this book, are sure to inspire women to dethrone bad character traits and develop inner love, joy, peace, patience, kindness, generosity, faithfulness, gentleness and self-control. This book also instructs women how to utilize these positive character traits to cultivate healthy relationships.

After reading *Pursuit to A Greater "Self,"* readers will be inspired to let their light shine for the world to see that true reformation is attainable, even after imprisonment!

"Changing Lives One Page At A Time."
www.vocseries.com

NOW AVAILABLE FROM

VOICES
INTERNATIONAL PUBLICATIONS

"To-date, I have served 16 years of the 30 year sentence that was handed down to me. I feel like I was left here to die, sort of like being buried alive!"
— Michelle Miles

In 1982, during a period when illegal drug use was on the decline, President Ronald Reagan officially announced the War on Drugs. In support of his effort, Congress passed bills to tremendously increase the sentences imposed on drug dealers, including lengthy mandatory minimum sentences. With drug sentences accounting for the majority of the increase, in less than 30 years, the U.S. prison population exploded from 300,000 to more than a million! The statistics are well known, but the true faces of those imprisoned and the effects of their incarceration is less publicized.

The High Price I Had To Pay 2, is a captivating real-life story about the life of Michele Miles, a 21 year old, African American woman, who grew up in Marcy Housing Projects in Brooklyn, New York. Miles lured in by her boyfriend Stanley Burrell, tried her hand in the drug game, as a way to escape poverty. Through what she believed to be a promising opportunity, Miles became partners in the notorious "Burrell Organization," which became a thriving enterprise. Overnight, Miles went from "rags-to-riches." In her mind, she was living the life of her dreams.

All was well until the FEDS got wind of the operation. With the help of informants, the Burrell empire swiftly crumbled and the key players were arrested, including Miles. In the end, her role in the drug conspiracy led Miles to receive a thirty year sentence in federal prison.

Miles' story gives readers an inside view of the life of women serving hefty sentences for drug crimes, and the effects of their incarceration. This story will leave you shocked about the rules of prosecution for drug offenders in the U.S. judicial system and make you think, Should a first time, non-violent offender, receive a thirty year sentence?

Visit www.smashwords.com/books/view/377047
to download your FREE e-book today!
ISBN: 978-09911041-0-9
www.voicesbooks.com

"Step-by-step, through each commandment, I will teach you how to take adversity and turn it into the launching pad for your success!"
— Sunshine Smith-Williams

Some foolishly believe life is a matter of choice, based on the cards they are dealt. Yet, a Boss Chick knows she can reign as captain of her own ship, regardless of how steep the tides may come! Because life in fact is a matter of choice, a Boss Chick chooses to strategically call the shots and she plays to win! Although she may face challenges at sea, a Boss Chick never travels without her navigation. As a result, when others around her falter, she always seem to have the answers to get ahead, turn around her situations and come out on top!

The key to a Boss Chick's success resonates by the standards she sets and rules she lives by, which keep her rooted and grounded, and give her wisdom to turn adversity into triumph. Everything she needs to know to become a virtuous woman, discover her purpose, find a mate, keep him, gain notoriety and wealth are now outlined in *Sunny 101: The 10 Commandments Of A Boss Chick*, a must-have empowerment guide for today's striving women!

This self-help companion is a road-map designed to empower women to avoid the common pitfalls that often derail many from achieving their dreams. Author Sunshine Smith-Williams enlightens readers how to overcome life obstacles and utilize challenges as fuel for success. Not only does she instruct readers on what to do, through captivating, real-life examples she teaches her readers how to strengthen their endurance, sharpen their insight and reign as an ultimate Boss Chick!

Step-by-step through each poignant Commandment, Smith-Williams equips her readers to overcome fear, increase their self-esteem, build powerful relationships and rise as a shinning star amongst the pack. By implementing a lifestyle, based on morals, values and principles, and setting practical goals, readers are challenged to step up their game, raise the bar on their expectations, and finally live the life of their dreams!

Some believe no woman can have it all, but Smith-Williams enlightens her readers how to beat the odds! No matter what obstacles they may face in life, regardless of background, color or creed, girded with *Sunny 101: The 10 Commandments Of A Boss Chick*, any woman can position herself to come out on top!

Through her candid voice of reason, broken down into easy-to-read revelations, practical analysis and jewel drops, which are sure to stir the soul and stimulate the mind, let Sunshine Smith-Williams teach you the ropes, and you too can become a Boss Chick!

MARCH 2015

ISBN: 978-0-9911041-6-1
www.voicesbooks.com

COMING SOON!

The Trade Off

THE SEQUEL TO SHE'S ALL CAUGHT UP!

A MEMOIR

JAMILA T. DAVIS

ORDER FORM

Mail to: 196-03 Linden Blvd.
St. Albans, NY 11412
or visit us on the web @
www.vocseries.com

QTY	Title	Price
	Unlocking the Prison Doors	14.95
	Permission to Dream	14.95
	Pursuit to A Greater "Self"	14.95
	The High Price I Had To Pay 1	7.99
	The High Price I Had To Pay 2	7.99
	The High Price I Had To Pay 3	9.99
	She's All Caught Up- 15.00	15.00
	How To Navigate Through Federal Prison	39.95
	Sunny 101: The 10 Commandments Of A Boss Chick	14.95
	Total For Books	
	20% Inmate Discount -	
	Shipping/Handling +	
	Total Cost	

* Shipping/Handling 1-3 books 4.95
4-9 books 8.95
* Incarcerated individuals receive a 20% discount on each book purchase.
* Forms of Accepted Payments: Certified Checks, Institutional Checks and Money Orders.
* Bulk rates are available upon requests for orders of 10 books or more.
* Curriculum Guides are available for group sessions.
* All mail-in orders take 5-7 business days to be delivered. For prison orders, please
allow up to (3) three weeks for delivery.

SHIP TO:

Name: _____

Address: _____

_____

_____

City: _____

State: _____ Zip: _____

Made in the USA
San Bernardino, CA
22 December 2019